When the foundation.
what can the

Psalm :

Jimmy and Carol Owens with Clifford Hill

Scripture quotations are from the following versions:

AB   The Amplified Bible, ©1954, 1958, 1962, 1964 by Zondervan Publishing House

KJV   King James Version

NEB The New English Bible, ©1961, 1970 by the Delegates of the Oxford University Press and the Syndics of the Cambridge University Press

NIV   New International Version, ©1973, 1978, 1984 by International Bible Society

NKJV New King James Version, ©1979, 1980, 1982, Thomas Nelson, Inc., Publishers

NLT   New Living Translation, ©1996 by Tyndale House Publishers

PH   New Testament in Modern English, ©1958, 1960, 1972 by J.B. Phillips, The Macmillan Co.

TLB   The Living Bible, ©1971 by Tyndale House Publishers

Heal Our Land: Strategies For Prayer & Action
By Jimmy and Carol Owens with Clifford Hill

First published as "Restoring a Nation's Foundations" in 2007 by Four Square Media in the US.

This version is produced by Centre for Contemporary Ministry, Moggerhanger Park, Bedford MK44 3RW United Kingdom to be available to Heal Our Land Uk and distributed by C and M Ministries Trust of the same address.

Final UK Editing by Monica Hill for the Centre for Contemporary Ministry.

British Library Cataloguing in Publication Data:
A catalogue record for this publication is available from the British Library.

International Standard Book Number: 978-0-9533429-7-6

First Edition

Printed in Great Britain by the MPG Books Group, Bodmin and King's Lynn, for the Centre for Contemporary Ministry.

Please visit **www.healourlanduk.com** for event information

CONTENTS

FOREWORD

Jimmy and Carol Owens became my friends when we were college-aged kids just beginning to learn the grace of God's power in our lives and the purpose of his call upon us. Since those days that we remember with such holy joy and happiness, we have often been partners in witnessing mighty workings of our almighty Father. What they write about here holds the keys to God's *mightiest* of workings: how he can, wants to, and will change entire nations... if we accept our role.

For that condition to be met – *"If my people... will humble themselves and pray"* – most of us need new eyes to see and a hope that will overthrow obstacles to our vision. We have all been fed on futility by the tenor of our times, and it breeds a paralysis of hope. But the truth is that the Church was born to answer such hopeless moments. These can be our finest hours; if we're nourished by the truth that shatters the futility that passivity has bred.

The liberating power of God's revealed truth in his Word, and the rejoicing power of his re-echoed truth through Spirit-filled music, have been united through Jimmy and Carol's mission. By means of these dual tools – their music and their writing – many are coming to believe that each of our nations can be healed!

I believe it is an apostolic order of this book you have in your hand – one meant to create vision. It is apparent that this is what the Apostle Paul had in mind when he wrote, *"I ceaselessly pray for you... that the Father would give you the spirit of wisdom and revelation, that, knowing him, your heart's eyes might see and understand the high hopes of his call to you!"*. Ephesians 1:15 -18

He prays three things:

1. *for an enlightenment through the Father's gift of spiritual help -* **"wisdom and revelation"**

2. *for an increased* **"knowing"** *of the Lord himself – that, "knowing him" (that is, more of his own heart and nature, his love and purpose for us) and*

3. *for eyes that see* **"hope"** *– a hope that is energized by a captivating vision of the resurrection power of Christ and his power potential waiting to be expressed through his Church!* Ephesians 1:19 -23

The Holy Spirit who ignited those truths in the Holy Scriptures is igniting their firepower to hosts of God's people today. In nation after nation, futility and passivity are being shattered as faith and passion for intercessory prayer are now being awakened. The Spirit of hope is still seeking to show us all there is still time left to heal!

For too long, too many have been lulled to sleep by the notion that the Bible only predicts gloom and doom for "the last days." It is true, this old world has had its problems and worse ones are coming.

But that isn't the whole story in God's Word, because for these dark times there is also a simultaneous promise of two grand and glorious possibilities:

- an overflowing harvest of spiritual fruitfulness, attended by unlimited restoration through national and individual recovery.

- an overflowing harvest of spiritual fruitfulness, attended by unlimited restoration through national and individual recovery. note especially Joel 2:24-25

This book is about those possibilities, and how they can be realised and released through us who will let our eyes be touched by the Spirit, that we may see the hope; that in this winter of our world's discontent, we may see the springtime of God's promise, *"Ask the Lord for rain in the time of latter rain, and [He] will make flashing clouds, and give them showers of rain... ".* Zechariah 10:1

Jack W Hayford

Former President, The Foursquare Church International
Chancellor, The King's College and Seminary

"When the foundations are being destroyed, what can the righteous do?"
Psalm 11:3 NIV

That's what this book is about – what the righteous can *do* – what *you* can do – at a time like this, when the spiritual foundations of our Christian nations are being threatened by a neo-pagan worldview. For the sake of our freedoms, our children, the gospel, and the Kingdom of God, we must not let it happen without a struggle.

"Who are the righteous?" you may be thinking, "Does this Scripture have anything to do with me?" Hold that thought. There's a marvellous answer to that question, and we'll get to it in a few pages.

The Word of God says, *"When the enemy comes in like a flood, the Spirit of the Lord will lift up a standard against him"* Isaiah 59:19b NKJV. A standard is a pennant or banner carried into battle to rally the troops. Today, the enemy *is* coming in like a flood, and the Holy Spirit is lifting up a standard to summon an army of prayer warriors to the spiritual battle.

This warfare isn't against flesh and blood but against spiritual wickedness see Ephesians 6:12, and our weapons aren't made by man but are mighty through God to pull down strongholds see 2 Corinthians 10:4. Our part is to show up and volunteer.

Yes, there are things we *can do*: One is to learn and practise God's principles of intercessory prayer and spiritual warfare for nations. Others have to do with mercy and justice, and still others with our role as salt, light, and leaven to our society. We will consider God's crucial requirements for answered prayer and the healing of a land. We will suggest specifics – things we can do as ambassadors of the Kingdom of God and as citizens of our country – *to help secure God's blessing on our land.*

The dictionary gives one definition of intercession as "prayer to God on behalf of another or others." The Latin prefix *inter* means "between." In intercessory prayer we stand between others and God, asking for favour or forgiveness for them. Or we stand between others and Satan, pleading for God's protection and deliverance.

True intercession, however, involves more than prayer; it involves our lives. *"Life intercession"* is what we do in addition to praying, by standing between others and despair – by ministering to the lost, the hungry, the homeless and the hopeless – and by doing our part to maintain righteousness and justice in our society. It is the outworking of God's prescription for national healing given in Isaiah 58:6-12. *Through* prayer, God does mighty things we can't do, and *in prayer*, he shows us what we *must do* and then empowers us to do it.

Yes, *you* are needed. One dedicated intercessor can make a difference in our society. Two are even better. But most effective of all is a church – or a coalition of churches – led by informed, determined, visionary clergy.

These are the key people, the God-appointed leaders who are bringing their churches into a world-shaping ministry. We want to help. We hope this book will encourage all intercessors, from beginners to veterans, but we've included a special section, **Appendix B** "A Word to Pastors and Leaders." Here we've taken the liberty of sharing some ideas that we've seen work wonderfully in churches across our nation the USA and in others, in the hope that these ideas will help them fan the flame.

This book is well suited for your personal study, or it can become an exciting group Bible study/prayer laboratory. Either way, we suggest that as you finish reading each chapter, you follow through the list of things to think over and pray about.

Almost anyone can lead a group study; you don't have to be a teacher. See **Appendix A** for directions on how to do it.

As you experiment and make discoveries in this laboratory, alone or with partners, it will take you one step at a time from the foundations of personal preparation to the courage and clamour of the spiritual battlefield. Each step can be a transforming experience that will help equip you for the work of nation-changing intercession.

If my people, who are called by my name, will humble themselves, and pray and seek my face, and turn from their wicked ways, then I will hear from heaven, and will forgive their sin and heal their land 2 Chronicles 7:14 NKJV.

In this verse God prescribes four remedies for the healing of a land: humility, prayer, worship, and repentance. The Holy Spirit has burned the words of this promise, spoken by God to King Solomon in ancient Israel, into the hearts of God's people in many nations. Particularly since the early 1970s this has become the theme verse for the intercession movement in many nations all over the world.[1] But how do you apply these words to your nation today? In a sense, you don't – not to your nation as a whole. "If *my* people..." God said. He doesn't expect the ungodly to pray; he holds *his* people responsible for that.

Who are the people of God? The people of God today are those who publicly acknowledge God as their Heavenly Father and believe the gospel. They are a nation within nations, salting (preserving and flavouring) and lighting the culture. They're a nation's hope for wellbeing and survival. They are the true Church – a praying, moving force that can affect the destiny of a nation and of the world see Acts 15:14, Galatians 3:26. This book is addressed to those believers.

To call yourself saved, or a child of God, or righteous, is not arrogant or boastful. We're acutely aware that we aren't saved through any goodness of our own, but entirely by the grace of God, through faith in the suffering, death and resurrection of his Son, Jesus Christ. Salvation is a free gift, available to "whosoever" will believe in him see John 3:16.

Even the faith is the gift of God to those willing to receive it. The Bible tells us that through this great miraculous interchange we are *made righteous* in God's sight. Jesus took our sin on himself and carried it away. *"Behold! The Lamb of God who takes away the sin of the world!"* John 1:29 NKJV.

Because of Jesus' sacrifice, his righteousness is *imputed*, or attributed to us who believe and confess him as our Saviour. So when God, the Just Judge, looks at us, he sees us as righteous.

If you have any doubt as to your salvation, be assured that God wants you to know for sure, not to hope or guess that you're saved, or to wait until it's too late to find out. The Bible says in 1 John 5:13 NKJV, *"These things I have written to you who believe in the name of the Son of God, that you may **know** that you have eternal life, and that you may continue to believe in the name of the Son of God."* If you're not sure, it's too important to put off. We suggest you put a bookmark here and go to **Appendix C** Making Sure of Your Salvation, and take care of that before anything else. You can settle it right now. Once you're standing on that solid spiritual ground, *you have become one of God's people who can make a difference in our world.*

US President John F Kennedy shook some sense into the "What's-in-it-for-me generation" of the Sixties when he said, "Ask not what your country can do for you, ask what you can do for your country." It's still a good question.

In our day and age, when so many books are about how you can "find yourself" and be blessed, happy, fulfilled and prosperous or have warm fuzzy feelings, American Pastor Rick Warren wrote *The Purpose Driven Life*, in which the opening words are "It's not about you." To everyone's astonishment, it became the number one hardback non-fiction book in history[2], at the last count surpassing 30 million copies. That should tell us something about the spiritual hunger of people today, and give us tremendous hope for our world.

The fact that you're reading this book should tell us something about you, as well. It tells us that you're interested not just in *getting* something, but also in *doing* something – for your country, for other people, and for the Kingdom of God.

We don't want to be seen as prophets of doom and gloom, with wild eyes and white robes and sandals and 'Repent! The End is Nigh!' sandwich boards. Some preachers go to such extremes to avoid that image that they concentrate only on good times and blessings and happy attitudes. We want to bring hope, and certainly there is no greater hope than the hope of the gospel, but to be realistic, we must acknowledge that there is good news and bad news. We see the bad news on our TV screens every day. The good news is that there are things we can do about it! And that's what this book is about.

Three final notes before we begin:

1. This is not primarily a political book. We realise that believers hold various political opinions, and we want this book to unite a righteous army not divide it. The few political issues we'll touch on are really moral and spiritual issues, which are the Church's assignment.
2. We are neither lawyers nor judges. Where we comment briefly on legal issues, no legal advice is intended.
3. This book was written originally with America in mind, and published under the title, Restoring a Nation's Foundations. However, the biblical principles we talk about here are applicable anywhere (although Christians in some nations may not

have the freedom of expression that we in free countries have) because God deals even-handedly with the peoples of the world, depending on their response to his rulership see Jeremiah 18:7-9. Still, we pretty much left readers in other nations to wend their own way through the Americanisms to find the core of the book. Then along came Clifford Hill.

Clifford has a vision for the United Kingdom – to say nothing of the rest of the world – to turn to God and turn the world around again. Not only is he a visionary, but he is a fine writer as well. He offered to help us to make the book more accessible throughout the rest of the English-speaking world. We have indented the pieces he has specifically written particularly in **Part 1** Chapters 2 and 3 which are wholly his, and has made invaluable suggestions, additions, and improvements in our original book.

We owe him many heartfelt thanks.

Jimmy & Carol Owens
Authors

---

[1] Some have argued that the Hebrew word used here for "land", 'erets, means the ground, and this is true, but Strong's concordance shows that it is also translated as the earth, country, or nations.

[2] Publishers Weekly.

The year is 1973. From the air, Northern Ireland looks green and peaceful as our little group flies into Belfast after a white-knuckle trip from London. But on the ground things look grey and grim. The airport runway has been freshly cratered. The streets are lined with bomb-blasted buildings, graffiti defaces the walls, and rolls of barbed wire seal off alleyways.

A bloody seven-year resurgence of "The Troubles" between the Catholic Irish Republican Army (IRA) and the Protestant Ulster Defence League (UDL) is in progress. British soldiers, originally welcomed by Republicans as peace keepers, are now seen as a provocative presence patrolling the city and are beset by IRA terrorists at every turn. We are in a virtual war zone.

Nevertheless our troupe, including American singer/actor Pat Boone, Jean Darnall, a few other Americans and twenty or more English singers and band, presses on. Joined by a Belfast mass choir organised for the event, we've come to present *Come Together,* our musical calling for spiritual unity among Christians in this place where they seem more inclined to shoot at one another than to unite.

At our auditorium a shattered window marks the spot where a British soldier died the day before. The IRA terrorists obviously are not in the mood for unity. Nor is the internationally known UDL pastor who advises us to leave town. We decide to stay anyway.

Before leaving home we had asked God for a specific Scripture to guide us and were convinced that he gave us Psalm 20:1-2: *"May the Lord answer you in the day of trouble; May the name of the God of Jacob defend you; May he send you help from the sanctuary, and strengthen you out of Zion"* NKJV. With that assurance we push on.

On the day of the event, the city is tense. Apprehensive but excited and determined, 1,700 Protestants and Catholics line up at the doors and around the block. Outside, they are subjected to a body search. Inside, sharp-eyed, armed soldiers stand guard. It's the first public interfaith meeting of any kind in the seven years since the current Troubles began and the government is taking every precaution.

The music starts. The audience responds tentatively at first. Then they begin earnestly to praise and worship. As they do, something stirs in the atmosphere. Many weep. Some go to their knees. The Holy Spirit moves and the love of God falls like a sweet rain.

A priest comes forward and begs forgiveness from his protestant brothers and sisters who love Jesus as he does. He asks God to forgive them all for their animosities and to shed his Spirit among them. Protestant pastors rush to pray with him and to repent of their own hatred. The meeting breaks wide open. As pastors, priests, laymen and soldiers join hands and mingle their tears and prayers and renounce ancient hatreds, one of the sponsors quietly draws Jimmy's attention to two men who are embracing and praying together. One is a radical IRA leader and the other is an English major in full battle dress. The police later tell us that, during our stay there, for the first time since the seven-year Troubles began, there was not a single reported act of political violence in the city.

Why? Because during this time, not only Belfast Christians but also our home church, The Church On The Way in Van Nuys, California, pastored by Jack Hayford, and another small but spiritually aware California church, were fasting and praying for Belfast as they had promised to do. They were *"sending help from the sanctuary."* When we returned home, we received a letter from a small group of zealous young Christian intercessors in Israel who had heard about our upcoming ministry in Belfast. The letter read, in part, "We were fasting and praying for you every day here in Zion." They were *"strengthening us from Zion..."*

Because of our experience of God's intervention in Northern Ireland, we became convinced that he would move on behalf of any nation in response to determined prayer and fasting. From that conviction came our musicals on national intercession and a lifetime concern for the spiritual welfare of our nation and of our world.

In the years since then we've heard of other such interventions in answer to united prayer. Here are two examples:

2006, Washington, DC

From July 1st to the 13th there were 14 murders committed in Washington, D.C., prompting a "Crime Emergency" by city officials. The Christian Defence Coalition sponsored a six-day, around-the-clock prayer vigil, in a large tent on the National Mall. During that time there were <u>no murders</u> committed in the District [3]. And by March 2007, when most major cities were reeling under a "skyrocketing" of violent crime (Orlando's was up 188 percent over two years ago [4]), Washington DC's homicide rate was substantially down.

1984, Los Angeles

Thousands of Christians from all over the world, including several thousand from Youth With a Mission, converged on the city for a massive outreach during the summer Olympics. Local churches were mobilised for prayer well in advance. Christians prayed, prophesied, warred in the Spirit, prayer walked and witnessed everywhere. John Dawson reports in his book, Taking Our Cities for God that later a friend of his was conversing with a Los Angeles coroner. The coroner said that normally they receive 78 bodies a day, including many that are victims of murder. "But during the two weeks of the Olympic Games there were no murders." If God will do this in America, he will do it anywhere. Intercession works!

We believe that as Christians continue to pray for their nations with understanding and persistence, meeting God's conditions as laid out in the Scriptures, he will respond with national healing! He's only waiting to hear from people who care.

He's waiting to hear from you...

---

[3] Breaking Christian News, July 28, 2006.

[4] CNN, 3/9/0.7

TO SAVE OUR SOUL

We sit by and watch the Barbarian, we tolerate him; in the long stretches of peace we are not afraid. We are tickled by his irreverence; his comic inversion of our old certitudes and our fixed creeds refreshes us; we laugh.

But as we laugh we are watched by large and awful faces from beyond; and on these faces there is no smile.

Hilaire Belloc

Chapter 1 - The Soul of a Nation

Do nations have souls? Well, that depends on what you mean by soul. If we accept the dictionary definition of *soul* as "the moral and emotional nature – the vital principle which moves and animates all life," the answer is yes. Every city and country has a unique emotional and moral character, or ethos, that shapes its politics, its art and its trade. So how does God respond to this animating moral character of a nation? It's a straight-forward proposition: God protects and blesses a God-honouring nation and withholds his blessing from, or curses, a sinful one see Jeremiah 18:7-10; Deuteronomy 28.

Rebellious Nations?

The ultimate punishment of a rebellious nation doesn't happen overnight. As we look back at the rise and fall of nations, we see the pattern over and over again. God lets the rebelliousness go on, with increasing warning signs, until it reaches a point of no return, then acts swiftly to stop it. He promised Abram (Abraham) that he was going to give his descendants the land occupied by the Amorites, but the time was not yet. He said "The sin of the Amorites has not reached its full measure" Genesis 15:16 NKJV. We don't know what God considers the "full measure" of any nation's sin, or how high our nation's sin gauge has risen in his eyes. But there comes a time when the gauge reads FULL, and God sorrowfully says "Enough!" and gives the nod to an avenging angel or summons a fierce foreign power to carry out the sentence. The question for any nation is: is our tank filling or emptying, and what must we do about it?

Now punishment, when it comes, doesn't always mean direct fire and brimstone from heaven. Sometimes God may simply remove his protective covering from a nation that he once shielded but which has become rebellious see Isaiah 22:8 and let sin flourish unrestrained until the culture degenerates to the point of self-destruction.

A close inspection of some of the passages regarding God's dealings with ancient Israel shows that his judgment may come in various ways:

1. **The lifting of his protection.** "Then God removed the protective covering of Judah" Isaiah 22:8 AB. "The Lord has withdrawn his protection as the enemy attacks" Lamentations 2:3b NLT.

2. **Direct punitive action** – hardships of increasing severity – including drought, war and epidemics – but always with the opportunity of repentance and restoration see 2 Chronicles 7:13-14.

3. **Finally, subjugation and destruction.** "Your land will be laid waste, and your cities will be in ruins" Leviticus 26:33b. See also Deuteronomy 28:49-52.

These are not threats to be taken lightly. Both the Scriptures and history record this process in chilling detail. One of the most tragic passages in Israel's history is found in Isaiah 63:9-10: *"In all their affliction he (God) was afflicted, and he personally saved them. In his love and pity he redeemed them and lifted them up and carried them through all the years. But they rebelled against him and grieved his Holy Spirit. That is why he became their enemy and personally fought against them"* TLB.

1 Corinthians 10:11 says that the things that happened to our spiritual forefathers are illustrations of the way God works and are written down as examples for us. If our nation continues in rebellion, will we not suffer for it, too?

If we are undergoing the process of judgment, what stage have we reached? Certainly not the final stages, but could we be in the warning stage? Is God trying to deal with the souls of our nations? It does seem he's trying to get our attention:

As *governments* progressively legalise sin by saying, "Yes, we shall," where God has said, "Thou shalt not," they find themselves in ever deeper trouble.

As *leaders* seek solutions to momentous military and economic problems and at the same time legislate God out of the national life, they find to their consternation that things aren't working out very well.

As *citizens* flagrantly parade in the streets, flaunting their mutiny against God, they are spitting into the wind and targeting their nation for punishment.

But know that whenever punishment comes, God does not take pleasure in it. Even in the beginning, when Adam and Eve sinned and had to be turned out of the garden, God did it "while covering their nakedness and promising them redemption, a redemption involving great sacrificial love on his part – the incarnation and death of his Son".[5]

One reason judgment is so long in coming is that God hates so much to have to bring it. He is "a gracious God, merciful, slow to anger and full of kindness" Jonah 4:2 TLB. Judgment Day has not come yet because "he is waiting, for the good reason that he is not willing that any should perish, and he is giving more time for sinners to repent" 2 Peter 3:9 TLB. "He is giving us more time to get this message of salvation out to others" verse 15.

Jesus cried out in sorrow: "O Jerusalem, Jerusalem... how often I wanted to gather your children together, just as a hen gathers her brood under her wings, and you would not have it!" see Luke 13:34-35. And he wept as he foretold the city's destruction by their enemies because his people rejected him see Luke 19:41-44.

However, multi-thousands of dedicated Christians have received the Lord with open hearts. Many of these are intercessors who have witnessed and bombarded heaven with prayer and, for years, have secured God's mercy on the nation. Intercession works! But as a country becomes increasingly secularized and more spiritually polarized, it needs a vastly larger, stronger, intercessory army to jump into the fray.

Be assured that God will answer gladly as we intercede for the restoration of our country's godly foundations.

God's heart of compassion cries out with mercy and grace, "Return to me and I will return to you!" Malachi 3:7b NKJV.

Turn to the Lord, oh turn to Him,

Turn to the Lord again,

Don't make the Lord your enemy,

Still he wants to be your friend

'Turn to the Lord' from Heal Our Land,
© Fairhill Music Jimmy and Carol Owens

The Search for Intercessors

Through the prophet Ezekiel, God poured out his grievances against Israel, his chosen people. Then he said this, "'I looked for someone who might rebuild the wall of righteousness that guards the land. I searched for someone to stand in the gap in the wall so I wouldn't have to destroy the land, but I found no one. So now I will pour out my fury on them, consuming them in the fire of my anger. I will heap on them the full penalty for all their sins,' says the Sovereign Lord" Ezekiel 22:30-31 NLT. The NIV translates that last line this way: "'I will consume them with my fiery anger, bringing down on their own heads all they have done,' declares the Sovereign Lord."

God says that righteousness is a wall that guards the land. When that wall is broken down, the inhabitants are left at the mercy of their enemies and the judgment of God. God is saying that unless intercessors intervene, society will simply reap the fruit of its own sin. When intercessors fail, judgment falls. God is still looking for intercessors to "stand in the gap" and hold off his judgment so that a great revival can sweep the world and multitudes can find salvation before the final curtain drops.

With determination intercessors can help pray down protection against the weapons of our nation's enemies.

With determination we can help build spiritual buffer zones around our cities and nations to restrain evil in our governments, immorality in our society, crime in our streets, and the encroachment of false religions and the occult in our communities.

With determination we can help bring about revival in our churches and nation-changing spiritual renewal.

If all the Christians who care about the state of their nation will only learn what to do and how to do it, we can change things radically. We hold the key to our nation's survival. This isn't merely about preserving a political agenda or an economic system. The soul of a nation needs to be saved. Only changed hearts can really change a society. For people to be godly, they must first know God.

For people to know God, they must first hear the gospel. The goal of intercession for the nation is not to appease an outraged God so that people may safely continue in sin. Rather it's to bring about and maintain conditions in our society that aid the spread of the gospel until God's redemptive work is done.

The Real Enemy

It seems that much of what goes on in our world today creates strong barriers to these redemptive purposes of God. But instead of blaming God or other people for every bad thing that happens, we need to recognise who our real enemy is – where he came from, what he does, how he does it, and what we can do to stop him.

We'll discuss this enemy in more detail later. Suffice it now to say that he hates everything God created and pronounced good. His sole purpose in existence is chaos. Jesus said, "The thief's purpose is to steal, kill and destroy. My purpose is to give life in all its fullness" John 10:10 TLB. Jesus came to destroy the works of the devil see 1 John 3:8, and now he continues that work through the Church, his Body. We're at war whether we want to be or not. Our defence is in worship, putting ourselves under God's covering, and learning the biblical methods of counteracting this enemy in our world. Satan brings destruction; the Church brings healing. Satan brings despair; the Church brings hope.

Fighting Your Own Battles?

If you feel you're having a hard time with problems of your own and can't possibly take on the problems of the nation, that's like saying you don't have time to fight the fire in the kitchen because you need to clean the garage. But amazingly, meeting God's conditions for effective intercession often brings solutions to those personal problems while preparing you to bless the nation.

It takes diligence. Praying even a few minutes a day can make a difference in our nation's future Be aware, though, that no matter how powerful and persistent our intercession, we won't always see immediate results. Sometimes it's a matter of two steps forward, one step back, or of standing with our fingers in the dyke to keep evil from breaking through and flooding us all. But never think our prayers aren't making an impact. Our influence has never been more crucial. If we stay with it, we'll win.

The great Nineteenth Century evangelist Charles Haddon Spurgeon encourages us all: "There is nothing that intercessory prayer cannot do... Believer, you have a mighty engine in your hand – use it well, use it constantly, use it now."

---

5 *Dutch Sheets*, A Biblical Response to the Terrorist Attacks on America, September 14, 2001

Talk About This:

1. What characteristics do you see as the "soul" of your city? How do you think God views this? p14

2. What positions and actions do you think we have taken nationally that might get us into trouble with Him? What are we doing right? p14

3. Can you think of some instances where God may have "lifted his protective hand from our country?" p14

4. Name a key ingredient we need in order to "rebuild the wall of righteousness" or establish "buffer zones" that guard the land. Will you ask God to give you that essential quality? p16

5. Do you think God will still respond to intercessors on behalf of the nation? Why? p17

6. What do you see as the ultimate goal of intercession that asks God to withhold judgment? p17

7. Who is our real enemy in our struggle for the nation's soul? What is our best defence against that enemy? p17

Pray About This:

a. Pray for the whole Church to become a powerful intercessory force!

b. Pray for God to pour out grace and withhold judgment so that multitudes may yet find the Lord before the final curtain falls.

c. Pray for those who determine our politics, arts and trade. Pray for these leaders and "motivators" by name, if possible. You can find the names of television executives, for instance, by going to the network web sites.

Chapter 2 - Shaking the Nations

Clifford writes...

Here's the amazing thing about the Almighty: He cares about us and he wants to be involved in the life of the nations of our planet. He waits for us to ask for his advice and listen to his warnings and instructions. When we do, the results can be stunning:

In the early 1980s when the Cold War stand-off between East and West was still at its height and the threat of nuclear warfare hung over the world, God began to alert those who were listening to him to the significant new developments on the world scene that were about to happen.

Seeking God in Israel

The great prophets of Israel whose mission was to act as watchmen to the nation were the inspiration behind an international gathering of 153 men and women with established ministries recognised in their own nations at Mount Carmel in northern Israel in the spring of 1986. They came from different regions across the five continents to seek what God was saying to his church and through the church to the nations. I was one of the small leadership team. The Carmel gathering was linked to a larger gathering of 5,000 Christians from around the world who came together at the 'Bin Yineh Ha' Oomah' (Israeli National Conference Centre) to celebrate Easter in Jerusalem in a year that coincided with Passover.

The Carmel gathering was at the 'Ya'arot Ha'Carmel', a rehabilitation and medical centre for the survivors of the Holocaust, set up as part of the German Government's reparations after WWII. By 1986 the number of survivors using the facilities was quite low and the centre was looking to diversify its role. We were the first conference and the first Gentiles to use the centre. Our worship had a strong Hebraic content, which was attractive to the elderly residents, many of whom shyly came in to the conference room and sat at the back enjoying the music and imbibing the atmosphere of worship. During the week, two of the residents had what they described as a 'visitation of Jesus' during the night and asked for help in understanding what had happened to them. Several of the conference participants were Israelis, including Lance Lambert, Benjamin and Reuven Berger, who had had similar personal experiences and were able to minister to them.

A Fast of Words

It was not an easy conference with participants from different cultural and church traditions - some with limited English language. We spent the first two days hearing from each other what was happening in our different nations and what God was saying in those circumstances. We then sought to listen to God for a collective understanding of the worldwide scene.

We tried to have as little formal organisation as possible so that God could be the main speaker. But with many strong leaders, all eager to participate, the difficulties mounted and it became clear by the middle of the week that we had not heard anything that was a clear word from God.

At that time we received a message from a young Messianic believer in Jerusalem saying that she believed God was 'calling for a fast of words'. She could not have known what was going on at Carmel but this clearly spoke into our situation. We immediately called for 24 hours of silence and it was during this time that we received many words from the Lord. As they were shared the following day, excitement mounted as we saw a clear pattern of agreement emerging. In most of the words reported there was a reference to 'shaking the nations'.

Hearing from God

Numerous biblical passages were quoted such as Isaiah 2. 12-22, "The Lord Almighty has a day in store for all the proud and lofty, for all that is exalted and they will be humbled....when he rises to shake the earth." But the key Scripture was in Haggai 2.6-7, "This is what the Lord Almighty says: 'In a little while I will once more shake the heavens and the sea and the dry land. I will shake all nations, and the desired of all nations will come, and I will fill this house with glory,' says the Lord Almighty."

That prophecy was given in 516 BC, the year when the rebuilding of the temple began following its destruction by Nebuchadnezzar 70 years earlier. The whole Middle Eastern world had just been shaken due to the overthrow of the Babylonian Empire by the Persians. Now God was promising that at some future date he would shake not only the nations but also the whole natural order of creation. We noted that Haggai's prophecy of a cataclysmic shaking was repeated in Hebrews 12.26 which was written near the end of the first century AD, so that meant the prophecy was referring to a future date beyond the apostolic era. It says:

"At that time his voice shook the earth, but now he has promised, 'Once more I will shake not only the earth but also the heavens. The words "once more" indicate the removing of what can be shaken – that is, created things – so that what cannot be shaken may remain. Therefore, since we are receiving a Kingdom that cannot be shaken, let us be thankful, and so worship God acceptably with reverence and awe, for our "God is a consuming fire"."

Shaking the Foundations

The significance of the reference in Hebrews 12 is that the shaking of the nations is linked with the coming of the Kingdom of God. That does not mean that it is speaking of the final consummation of the Kingdom at the end of the world; but it is speaking of a time coming when God will shake all the institutions of our human civilisation upon which people build their trust. The prophecy is referring to a time when "created things", the foundations of our materialistic world, will crumble dramatically; and that this will be a time when people will be forced to review their lifestyles as well as personal and corporate values.

Of course, prophecies can have more than one fulfilment because human beings rarely learn anything significant from history and the same mistakes are made generation after generation, but there can be no doubt that the collapse of the world banking system that began in September 2008 is the kind of event referred to in these Scriptures. God is never taken by surprise and he alerts his listening people to the significance of events – particularly to those events that are milestones in the fulfilment of his purposes so that his church can be prepared to meet fresh challenges.

As Amos said, "Surely the Sovereign Lord does nothing without revealing his plan to his servants the prophets" 3.7

The USSR First

At the Carmel gathering in April 1986 we received a startling prophecy that a great shaking of the nations was about to begin with the shaking of the Soviet Union. This was was reported to the larger Jerusalem conference. At that time the USSR appeared to be at the height of its power. But three weeks later the Chernobyl power station exploded showering much of Europe with radioactive dust that even contaminated grass eaten by sheep on the mountains of Wales thousands of miles away. But its greatest pollution was in the Ukraine, the bread basket of the USSR.

This forced the Soviet Government to import grain from the USA for which they required dollars. These were granted in return for promises of a new era of openness which led to what they termed 'glasnost' and 'perestroika'. The new openness and reform led directly to the downfall of the Communist empire in Eastern Europe, the fall of the Berlin Wall and the breakup of the USSR.

The Western Nations Next

A further prophecy given at that time warned that not only Russia would be shaken but also the Western nations with their materialistic greedy empires of mammon. In Luke's Gospel, Jesus foretold a time coming when the greed and corruption of the nations would be exposed when he said, "For there is nothing hidden that will not be disclosed, and nothing concealed that will not be brought out into the open. Therefore consider carefully how you listen" Luke 8.17, 18a.

The Financial Crisis

These words were recalled on 11 December 2008 at a meeting in the House of Lords in Westminster, London. Christians from both Houses of Parliament and leaders in the church and business met to review the financial crisis and to seek God about the matter. Despite the diversity among the Christian leaders present there was remarkable unity which was seen as evidence of the presence of God.

This led to unanimous agreement that the financial crisis was not primarily due to a failure of economic policy but to moral and spiritual corruption.

These men and women recognised - any nation - and that Christians could not call upon the nation to repent without first repenting themselves.

They felt they has a clear word from God calling for a season of repentance and prayer in the church.

Exposing Greed and Corruption

The following months of 2009 exploded with evidence of corruption in the banking and financial systems of the Western world. It's extent and depth shocked the nations and further undermined confidence in the banks and financial institutions which precipitated further falls on the stock market. It also provoked deep public anger in the Western nations, particularly in the USA, Britain and Europe where enormous sums of public money were used to bail out corporations and stave off their collapse. Taxpayers were angry that their money was used, not simply to counter widespread unemployment, but to allow banks and insurance corporations to pay million-dollar and million-pound bonuses to executives and directors whose failed policies, driven by avarice and acquisitive gain, had provoked crisis.

At the same time, large-scale financial scams and the misdemeanours of politicians and others in public life were 'brought into the open'. Personal and social values were being examined and public debate was beginning to focus upon lifestyles. As unemployment was rapidly spreading across the world, people were forced to re-examine their spending patterns and distinguish between the essential and the unnecessary.

Demonstrating Kingdom Values

This focus away from self-indulgence and material acquisition was exactly in line with the prophecy of Hebrews 12, but more importantly it would give Christians the opportunity to speak about Kingdom values – the things that really last as distinct from the material values that for generations have driven Western society. But was the church ready? Is it ready now for such a world-transformational task of demonstrating Kingdom values to a secular world obsessed with material wealth and pleasure? The church itself is not immune from these secular values and many individual Christians enjoy affluent lifestyles far in excess of their needs which must surely grieve God in an age when half the world's population goes to bed hungry each night.

What's Gone Wrong?

The financial crisis caused many Christians in the Western nations to ask searching questions about how it had all gone wrong. This was in part an outcome of the call for repentance in recognition of the church's responsibility for the state of the nation. This recognition was given a sharper edge because of mounting evidence in the West that our centuries-old Christian heritage was rapidly being eroded through the advance of secular-humanism and Islam. But none of the opponents of the Gospel would have had power or influence to damage the nations if the church had not lost confidence in its message and lost sight of its mission.

When Christians know through personal experience the truth of the promise that "He that is in us is greater than he that is in the world" they are fearless in the face of all opposition.

But once the church loses confidence in the Word of God, as happened in the 20th century with the impact of liberal scholarship gaining ascendancy in many Protestant denominations, its credibility among unbelievers is lost and is impossible to regain without a paradigm shift in mindset and mission. Many believe that the shaking of the nations is providing the opportunity for just such a shift.

A Sea Change in History

The 1960s brought a sea change in the history of Western Civilisation: that decade saw the rise of a pop culture that aimed to change the values of the modern world; but it was a period that also saw the beginnings of a fresh move of the Holy Spirit that brought new life and

spiritual energy to churches of all branches. It saw the birth of the Jesus Movement, the Charismatic Movement and the House Church Movement, but also the infusion of new life into long-dormant traditional churches. Interest in missions soared, and movements such as Youth with a Mission and Operation Mobilisation sprang up to take the gospel to the world.

In the 1970s Jimmy and Carol's worship and intercession musicals, *Come Together* and *If My People*, were presented hundreds of times throughout Britain, and America and other countries. Many of the largest cathedrals and halls in the UK were filled with praise and prayer. The Worldwide Marches for Jesus drew millions around the globe. There was a new spirit of cooperation among churches and a renewed emphasis on intercession. Even underground youth movements behind the Iron Curtain were experiencing a fresh visitation. This was a genuine movement of the Spirit of God perfectly timed to deal with the changing social situation and its challenge to faith. God was rearming his church for battle. He was equipping the body of Christ to withstand the onslaught of secularism.

Of course there were excesses in some places (there always are), at which some "staid guardians of sterile orthodoxy," as A W Tozer called them, quickly condemned the whole move of God. Messy and painful as revivals sometimes may be, they surely beat apathy! But all revivals seem to have a shelf life. That's why they're called re-vivals. And this one was no exception.

A Second Chance

In retrospect it can be acknowledged that the charismatic renewal movement in Britain largely turned in upon itself and failed to achieve its purpose of transforming the nation.

Unfortunately at the same time many influential mainline churches were increasingly driven by liberal interpretations of the Bible. The outcome of this struggle for truth was that from the 1970s to the end of the century the world invaded the church instead of the church invading the world. But the good news is that in the 21st century God is giving us a second chance. The shaking of the nations through the great financial crisis is making people think about their lifestyles and personal values.

This is opening people up to the truth in a new way. At the same time there is a greater move to prayer among Christians who recognise the plight of the Western nations and know that a new move of God is the only hope to secure the future. In Britain, increasing numbers of believers are crying out to God to heal their land.

Talk About This:

1. In reading the prophetic scriptures from Isaiah 2 and Haggai 2, given to the intercessory group in Israel, do you feel a "shaking of the nations" is happening now? In what ways? p20

2. How do you see moral and spiritual corruption affecting the well-being of a nation? What biblical basis could you find for this? p21

3. What responsibility do you think the church bears for the state of the nation? p22

4. Do you feel the Church is ready to demonstrate a focus away from self-indulgence and materialism and onto the Kingdom values that bless a nation with compassion and purity? How can we do this?

5. What difference does faith in the written Word of God make in the personal lives of Christians, and in our calling to impact society? p23

6. What are areas of influence where you believe "the world has invaded the Church, rather than the Church invading the world?"

Pray About This:

a. Ask God for direction from the Holy Spirit as you pray for the nation. He knows the problems and their underlying causes; He will help you pray.

b. Pray for a move of God to bring revival to the churches and a great spiritual ingathering in the nation. Lift up the name of Jesus over Great Britain. And please include other nations in your prayers as you feel led.

c. Pray for direction throughout the church, so that our life-styles will demonstrate the love of God, bless our society and give credibility to our witness.

d. Pray for a new hunger for the Word of God, and a greater understanding of his character and ways.

Chapter 3 - The Social Revolution

Clifford continues...

A social revolution of immense significance has taken place over the past 40 years throughout the Western world. The factors driving these changes are complex but this is not the place to undertake a sociological analysis. We need, however, to note that some of these changes have greatly benefited humanity such as the vast technological and medical advances leading to increased life expectancy, better health care, the growing economic and social independence of women, and the great strides that have been taken towards breaking down racial barriers.

Despite this increased racial harmony the gap between rich and poor nations remains stubbornly wide. It is a modern obscenity that people in many Western nations are suffering from obesity while in the poorest nations multitudes die of starvation.

Social Problems

Other changes over the past 40 years have led to difficult social situations. They include the separation of sexual activity from procreation through contraception and abortion, the changing of societal attitudes and values in regard to sexual relationships and marriage, the breaking down of sexual taboos which has led to a high rate of teenage pregnancies in most Western nations and to sexually transmitted infections among young people reaching epidemic levels in Britain.

These social problems among young people in the West are usually compounded by lifestyles that include addictions to alcohol and drugs which often lead to high rates of crime. Research shows that most of these social problems are linked with family breakdown.

Family Breakdown

It is family breakdown that has had the most alarmingly negative effect upon the health of society and the well-being of children. Many of the social ills presently affecting society throughout the western world stem from marriage and relationship breakdown.

In Britain even the shortage of housing is affected because every family that splits needs another house and where women are left with small children they are often dependent upon the state for support which affects the national economy.

When the family disintegrates, the foundations of society begin to crumble because it is the family that is responsible for teaching children the norms of personal and social behaviour and an acceptable moral code. This is certainly not a blanket indictment of single-parent families. Some find themselves in this situation through no fault of their own, and many of these succeed in raising fine children despite their hardships. Nevertheless, all the research studies in Britain, America and other nations show that marriage provides the ideal environment for raising children and that the level of family breakdown often acts as a monitor of the social and moral health of the nation.

Social Values

When personal and corporate values break down the stability of society is affected. In fact most of the social ills of Western Civilisation are linked to the collapse of moral standards in a vast number of families.

All the evidence shows the links between the breakdown of values and a vast range of social problems such as homelessness among young people, crime, poverty, illiteracy, sexual vice, pornography, underage sexual activity, abortion, drug abuse, alcoholism, violence, child abuse, suicide, and more. Many of these have been with us for a long time, but they have soared to new heights (or sunk to new depths) in once-Christian nations where we can trace their rise to a turning away from God and a consequent dissolution of family life.

Back to Jimmy and Carol...

"It's Not My Fault!"

Of course you will probably say "I'm not the one doing all those things. I'm living a good life, minding my own business, going to church, giving to the poor. It's all those nonbelievers that are bringing judgment on us. It's not my fault."

But, to a degree, it is our fault, isn't it? God put us here with an assignment: to shape the moral and spiritual condition of our society.

We say "But Christians are a minority; we don't have that much power."

Actually we are not the minority we've been led to believe we are. There are more than enough of us to change the course of nations if we pull together. That's why we, the people of God, need to identify with and confess the sins of our nation, spread the gospel and do all we can to reverse the situation. The Bible reminds us that we reap what we sow "and those who sow trouble reap it" Job 4.8.

Could Britain or America disappear into the depths of history, even as the 'unsinkable' Titanic sank into the cold North Atlantic? One strategically placed weapon of mass destruction could at least make us into quite different nations than we have known. And even now a host of fanatics and the demons that drive them are trying hard to make that happen. We need to turn again to the Rock of our salvation.

We are not predicting imminent and total destruction, but we must ask ourselves whether our nation is setting itself up for punishment. Do we really think God is not watching?

What calamities must he allow, to bring us again to that foundational place of dependency on him?

Clifford continues...

Now the Good News!

The good news is that God is still at work. In the UK, for instance, from the beginning of the new millennium the decline in church attendance has slowed and most of the liberal theological colleges have closed.

A new breed of evangelicals is emerging who are fully committed to applying biblical principles to social action.

At the same time there is a growing commitment to prayer, with small home-based Bible study and prayer-groups forming throughout the land. Many of these groups include believers from different church traditions, thus contributing to the breaking down of denominational barriers and creating a new Christian unity.

This emphasis upon prayer is growing out of an increasing awareness of the desperate plight of the nation and of the whole of Western civilisation. It is paving the way for the church to respond positively to the shaking of the nations. Historically, spiritual revivals grow out of the foundations laid by prayer and it is prayer which is encouraging many Christians in Britain in the expectation of a fresh move of God to change the nation.

A Growing Army of Prayer

In the USA, shortly before the turn of the 21st century over one million men gathered for a solemn prayer assembly on the Mall at Washington, DC, and fifty thousand prayer events were held on the National Day of Prayer in 2007. In 2009 "The Call" is gathering thousands, including some national leaders, to enormous gatherings for repentance and prayer. Other encouraging signs in America are the boldness in the witnessing of many young believers, the emphasis on marketplace evangelism, the rise of before-work prayer groups in the workplace and the growth in the numbers of people who appear to be born again. And around the world, millions of students gather annually at "See You at the Pole" prayer rallies.

Some of the largest prayer meetings in the world are to be found in West Africa. In Nigeria at Easter each year millions gather for prayer, the largest being at a place called Prayer City on the road between Lagos and Ibadan where between 10 million and 12 million come together for an outdoor prayer meeting.

If this great army of intercessors in each nation can be marshalled to speak, pray, and work together, the potential for nation-changing renewal is high. As they rally to the battle for revival and spiritual awakening, they are rebuilding the moral and spiritual foundations and spearheading a spiritual force – the praying Church – that moves God on behalf of nations.

These leaders are encouraging people to respond to God's 'ifs' – his crucial requirements for answered prayer. These 'ifs' have to do with personal purity, attitudes and actions – and especially with relationships – to God and to other people.

Elementary as these conditions sound, this is where powerful prayer ministry begins. Before we consider these 'ifs' further, remember, you don't have to be an expert before you begin.

Right now you can turn to the suggestions and prayer list at the end of the book, roll up your sleeves and tackle this thing. If you are born again, walking in the light, not tolerating any known sin, you are as eligible for answers to your prayers as the most mature saint. James said *"You do not have, because you do not ask God"* James 4.2 and Jesus says:

"The Father will give you whatever you ask in my name" – which means praying in line with the will of God John 15.16.

Talk About This:

1. Discuss some of the factors that have brought about a social revolution in the Western world over the past 40 years, What have been their effects in your own nation? In your local community? p25

2. What role do you feel the Church has played, or failed to play, in these social conditions? Can we still kneel down, and stand up, and help transform our society?

3. What crucial role does family play in influencing a nation? p25

4. Discuss the "Good News!" that is happening in the church in both Britain and the United States. How can you encourage these things in your own church? p26

Pray About This:

a. Pray that all of us in the church will have the courage and wisdom to address ungodly social issues — through both intercessory prayer and civil action.

b. Pray for courage and wisdom on behalf of all political and spiritual leaders. Lift them up by name before the Lord.

c. Pray for the strengthening and protection of families across the nation. Plead for wisdom for parents everywhere, and mutual love and support between spouses. Pray for family relationships to be based on the Word of God.

d. Pray for revival, ingathering and a renewal of biblically based understanding and faith in the churches.

MEETING GOD'S IFS

If my people will... **then** *I will...*

2 Chronicles 7:14

Chapter 4 - If My People...

You are all children of God through faith in Christ Jesus.
Galatians 3:26 NLT

We are heirs of the Father,
We are joint heirs with the Son.
We are children of the Kingdom,
We are family, we are one!

"We Are Family"   Jimmy and Carol Owens

The People of God – a Family

The Church is the family of God – brothers and sisters, drawn from every race and nation, adopted into one family, children of one Father, indwelt by one Holy Spirit, joint heirs with Christ, united by blood: the blood of Christ. The Apostle Paul wrote, *"I bow my knees to the Father of our Lord Jesus Christ, from whom the whole family in heaven and earth is named"* Ephesians 3:14-15 NKJV.

Profound truths about how this spiritual family should operate are simple enough for children to understand and practise. And since Jesus advised us to become as little children, allow us to take some examples from our Grammy-nominated children's musical, *Ants'hillvania.*[6] Our hero, Antony, is the Prodigal Ant. He's tired of working with the rest of the ants and living by the Wisdom From Above. He wants to be independent from his family. He is now an Independ-ant!

The Church is the family of God working together, all of us. Unfortunately, we often don't practise it enough or do it very well. Take our *Ants'hillvania* character, Miss Millicent Millipede, as an example of non-cooperation. Onstage, her voluminous skirts and petticoats cover several dancers who make up the parts of her segmented body and many legs. When life is smooth and undemanding, she glides along beautifully. But at the least challenge from an enemy, each pair of feet takes off in a different direction. She's left on the ground, dishevelled and defeated, in a tangle of legs and white pantaloons. Churches have the same problem. When we compete instead of coordinate, we become a divided and ineffective force in the battle for our nation's soul.

It is easy to ignore our own failure for the conditions in our society and fix the blame on "them": crooked politicians, greedy industrialists, grubby militants and social misfits. "Lord," we pray piously, "straighten these people out so we can have some peace and quiet in our society."

Amazingly, the Lord doesn't seem to be as concerned with straightening "them" out as he is with straightening out his own family. Only when God gets us into proper relationship with himself and with our fellow believers will we be unified and fit for him to use to turn the nation around.

So, before he can heal the land, he must start the healing work in us: *"If **my** people who are called by my name... "*

Love and unity in the Church begins with individual relationships, and our attitude toward these relationships depends on how we view other people. Some people are harder to love than others, especially those folks who seem afflicted with the malady called OPD (Offensive Personality Disorder). But with God's help, loving is do-able.

"All right," you may say, "I'll try. But how do I make myself love and accept people who hurt me and make my life miserable? If love just isn't there, there's nothing I can do about it, right?" Yes, there is. The key word is *"do"*. Do love. We can do the thing that is most Christ-like, no matter how we feel. We can turn inward to the Holy Spirit for his reservoir of quiet answers and acts of blessing rather than dealing out our own snappy retorts. Often, however, nothing will heal a damaged relationship until we deal with the crucial issue of forgiveness.

Setting Yourself Free

Nothing maintains peace in any family or relationship as well as two heartfelt little words: "I'm sorry." Unless it's two heartfelt little words: "You're forgiven." With those words, we not only set others free from our unforgiveness, but we set ourselves free from our own anger and bitterness.

A depressed young woman came to us for prayer. After some gentle probing, we found the problem: she was enraged at people who were making her life miserable, and she couldn't seem to change her attitude.

We asked her if she'd ever confessed her resentment as sin. No, she said; she'd never thought of it that way. Jimmy suggested she give all that hatred to Jesus and let him get rid of it for her. She immediately began to confess. She named them all: her husband's boss and co-workers, relatives, neighbours. Her list sounded like the telephone directory. We listened in amazement, wondering how she had ever functioned under such an emotional load.

When she finally finished, Jimmy led her in a child-like but profound prayer: "Lord, I bring this sin to you and ask your forgiveness. I'm releasing all these people from my resentment. I'm putting this rubbish into a big bag and giving it to you to carry out of my life forever. I know this is your will, and I'm trusting you to do it for me."

Then Jimmy prayed that for every person she had named, God would carry away her bitterness, bring love in its place and give her peace. When he finished praying, Jimmy cautioned her that if her old thought patterns came back, she might have to think back to that night and reaffirm what she had done. Some things take time, he said. But when we saw her weeks later, she was still glowing. "You told me it might take time," she said, "but it didn't! I was free that night and I've been free ever since." "Oh, me of little faith," Jimmy muttered as we watched her walk away, smiling and holding her head high.

Through unforgiveness our friend had put herself in a place of torment, and through forgiveness she had set herself free. Jesus told the story of a servant who was forgiven a great debt by his king, but who had a fellow servant thrown in jail for his failure to pay him a tiny amount. When the king heard about it he was outraged. *"Wicked servant!"* he cried, *"Why couldn't you have had mercy on him just as I had on you?"*

The king then gave him over to the torturers until he paid all he owed see Matthew 18:21-35 NIV.

That's scary. And here's the scarier part. Jesus said, *"This is how my heavenly Father will treat each of you unless you forgive your brother from your heart"* v 35 NIV.

How many Christians live in depression and spiritual defeat, not recognising that they're tortured by a torment of their own making? If you feel angry, depressed and distanced from God, it could be torment caused by unforgiveness. But you don't have to live this way. If you've brought the bondage on yourself, you can set yourself free by an act of your own will:

- Lay your unforgiveness all out before the Lord.
- Confess it as sin, mentally stuff it in a big rubbish bag, and ask him to carry it away.
- Receive your forgiveness by faith.
- Be free!

Be humble enough to ask for help if you can't get victory by yourself. If you have uncontrollable anger or mood swings, get counselling. You'll find you're not alone, and that people will be caring and supportive rather than shocked and condemning.

Willingness to forgive is absolutely critical for the intercessor: Jesus tells us not to bother coming to the altar (the place to meet with God) if we're at odds with someone. Leave your offering, he said, and go and make peace. Then come back to the altar See Matthew 5:23-24. *"Your heavenly Father will forgive you if you forgive those who sin against you; but if you refuse to forgive them, he will not forgive you"* Matthew 6:14-15 TLB. So, sin blockades our prayers, and unforgiveness is sin. Our prayer offerings sit on the altar, waiting for us to forgive.

"But what happens if I apologise to someone, or forgive them for old wounds and try to make peace, but they don't want any part of it?" Well, first, make sure your apology or forgiveness is genuine. People can tell. Don't go with the attitude, "I used to hate you *(you rotter)* but the Lord convicted me."

But if you can express contrition or forgiveness with an unclouded face and they still won't receive you, then you've done your part. The Bible says, *"Do your part to live in peace with everyone, as much as possible"* Romans 12:18 NLT. Your forgiveness is unconditional, but it takes two to make peace, and if the other person doesn't want it, you might pray for them, but you're under no further obligation to try to make it happen. (Although nothing hinders you from keeping on trying if you want to.)

Building Intercessors: Starting Young

No relationships are more crucial to our spiritual power than those in our own homes, because when we're out of harmony at home, we feel out of harmony with God. Then our prayer lives suffer and often our relationships with our spiritual family suffer too. Nothing seems right. So how do we get things back on track?

Intercession can be a means of family restoration as we practise God's 'ifs'. It also gives us a place of agreement and common focus, and this includes the children. Children can become serious intercessors if we start them out on things that matter to them. It can even work with independent teenagers.

We "adopted" our children's teenage friends, many of them from dysfunctional homes. Without pinpointing their character flaws, we listened to their hearts, taught them to forgive, and helped them pray about their concerns. Soon they began to pray for one another. As they saw God answer, their faith soared, their prayer horizons expanded, and their lives were radically changed.

Many children of Youth With A Mission (YWAM) families are veteran intercessors. Their talented King's Kids International group ranges in age from six to sixteen. One Easter, they were invited to perform on the Don Ho show in Honolulu. As they waited backstage to go on, they broke into small groups to pray. They asked God to have mercy on the unsaved adult performers and melt their hearts.

After the show, the performers surrounded them. The kids told them about Jesus. Showgirls, wrapped in their dressing gowns, began to cry. One of them reached out to the children saying, "Oh, you're so clean and I'm so filthy. What should I do?" It was an evangelist's dream come true – and the children knew what to say and how to pray. They aren't little parrots, these kids. They pray with faith born of experience.

Once, while they were singing on the streets in one of the rougher districts of the city (under the watchful eyes of YWAM leadership), a crowd of prostitutes, addicts and other such citizens gathered to listen. A transvestite approached Joshua, the six-year-old son of one of the leaders and said mockingly, "Wouldn't you like to pray for *me*?" Little Joshua asked his father if it was okay, then took the man's hand and prayed that Jesus would forgive his sins and save him. The man began to shake and scream, then sank to his knees on the sidewalk, crying out to God. Later, he wrote a letter to the YWAM base, saying that he had indeed given his life to Christ on the street that night. He had cleaned up his life-style and was making a fresh start. A little boy's simple faith and prayer power had changed everything for him.

Kids will often pray with amazing faith and persistence. But they must be taught – no, they must be shown. And they have no better example than their parents. Give your kids a chance. Teach them the principles for effective intercession and then live them out yourself. It takes time and dedication, but it may be one of the most important commitments you'll ever make.

As you do this, both you and your children can become powerful ambassadors for the Kingdom of God in your daily lives.

The People of God – A Kingdom

In addition to being family, God's people are ambassadors of his kingdom, *"For he [the Father] has rescued us out of... Satan's kingdom and brought us into the kingdom of his dear Son"* Colossians 1:13-14 TLB. *"Now then we are ambassadors for Christ"* 2 Corinthians 5:20 KJV.

As ambassadors, we are meant to be bearers of the authority of Jesus' name. Understanding this is crucial to our spiritual strength and our power in intercession. *"Go in my name... and I am with you always."* Matthew 28:19-20.

What does it all mean? How does it work? Try to picture a little girl we know. She's only six but she is nobody's fool. She learned early how to use her father's name with authority – and with results. She keeps the local juvenile roughnecks in line by announcing, "Remember, my daddy is Frank Williams and he's a policeman!" Standing there with flushed cheeks and blazing eyes, small dimpled fists planted on her hips, she is confident and impressive. At least she impresses the troublemakers, who clear the area immediately. They've had dealings with her daddy. They understand the authority he represents and that he is both willing and able to deal with anybody who pesters his little girl. The fact that she stands small and alone against several 'roguish' little boys doesn't faze her; she has complete confidence in the results she can achieve through her father's name. She never fails.

Jesus came to frustrate the devil's plans and he has commissioned the Church to do the same. see John 3:8, John 14:12. Invoking Jesus' name, when it's done with faith, wisdom and understanding, imposes his presence and power over Satan's kingdom.

However, Jesus' name is not just something we habitually paste on at the end of a prayer, or a magic word that works automatically to give us what we want – like putting a coin in a sweet machine. It's meant to be used by mature and obedient people prepared to accomplish the will of God.

The Church on earth is the functional outpost of God's Kingdom. The good news is twofold:

1. Those who are bound by sin and Satan can be released.
2. A more powerful kingdom than his has come, offering asylum and eliverance through us, Christ's ambassadors.

To do our job properly, we have to learn

- *the extent of our authority and responsibility*
- *the will of God as expressed in his Word*
- *how to receive instructions through the disciplines of prayer.*

And we must stay plugged in to our source of power. The Holy Spirit was Jesus' guide and power source, and he must be ours. He's the one who reveals the things of God to us, enables us, appoints us, and anoints us. So whatever your understanding may be of how and when you received the Holy Spirit, be sure you're filled with him now.

Get Back In the Pool

Every so often television will show an old film titled *Cocoon*. It takes place in a retirement home where the residents are finishing out their years in weakness and boredom. On their morning walk, three of the old gentlemen decide to investigate a mysterious deserted mansion next door. There they discover an indoor swimming pool. They get their swim trunks and towels and plan a break-in.

The men don't know that the pool contains large "cocoons," which hold dormant alien survivors of a space ship crash. They're waiting for an interplanetary rescue team, and they exude an incredible amount of transferable energy.

When the old men slip arthritically into the pool, they discover the cocoons. They find them impossible to open, so they decide to ignore them and go on with their swim. Within a few minutes they're cavorting in the water like dolphins. Later the other retirees watch in amazement as their rejuvenated friends go out on the town for a night of break dancing. Soon their secret is out and everybody is in the pool.

Then – disaster. The house is boarded up. The pool is unavailable. Within a few days the old folks' energy fades and their joy disappears. The dancing feet begin to plod, the hands grow feeble and the knees weak. They are tired, discouraged and powerless. They need to get back in the pool.

We're like that. Sometimes our spiritual lives, once so joyful and energetic, become mundane. Our dancing feet plod, our hands grow feeble and our knees weak. We need to plug into our power source. We need to get back in the pool.

The Bible says to *"ever be filled (or ever be being filled) and stimulated with the Holy Spirit"* Ephesians 5:18 AB. It says the disciples were filled and then refilled with the Spirit. Acts 2:4; Acts 4:31. It says they were *"continually filled throughout their souls with joy and the Holy Spirit"* Acts 13:52 AB.

"No matter what level of spiritual maturity we are on, we need renewed appearances, fresh manifestations, new visitations from on high... We need the windows of heaven to be opened again and again over our heads. We need the Holy Spirit to be given again as at Pentecost" (Charles Spurgeon).

The Holy Spirit is God's great gift to the intercessor; he intercedes for us and helps us in our intercession see Romans 8:26-27. He shows us what to pray for and how to pray for it. Our job is to search the Scriptures, wait, and listen for his voice in our hearts. This takes time and patience, but it is the key to the heart of God and to making the kind of intercession he is eager to honour .

If you've never turned over control of your life to the Holy Spirit, you can do it now. Open yourself up to God and ask him to keep you filled with himself. He has promised to do it:

If a son asks for bread from any father among you, will he give him a stone? Or if he asks for a fish, will he give him a serpent instead of a fish? Or if he asks for an egg, will he

give him a scorpion? If you then, being evil, know how to give good gifts to your children, how much more will your heavenly father give the Holy Spirit to those who ask him?
Luke 11:11-13 NKJV.

Here's a short, simple prayer you can pray for a fresh infilling of the Holy Spirit. If you pray it and mean it, God will honour it:

Heavenly Father, I yield myself to you. Fill me anew with the Holy Spirit. I invite you to take control of my very being. Teach me and use me for Jesus' sake. Help me by faith to receive more and more of your life within me. I thank you for the precious gift of your living presence.

Amen.

---

[6] written with Cherry Boone O'Neill, Sparrow Records.

Talk About This:

1. Why is spiritual cooperation among churches so important? p28
2. Why is forgiveness critical for the intercessor? p32
3. If you have difficulty in forgiving, are you willing to try something as simple as Jimmy's method? Are you willing to ask for help? p31
4. How could you adjust your family's schedule to make time for regular intercession together? Think of ways to involve your children?
5. What does it mean to be an ambassador of Christ? p34
6. What do you have to know in order to do the job? p34
7. Think of the Holy Spirit's role in intercession. Are you willing to ask God for more of his Spirit? How do you really think he will respond?

Pray About This:

a. Pray, silently if you like, and ask God to bless *all who have wounded you!*
   You can then receive your own freedom from bitterness. If in a group be free to ask for help from the group or from your leader.
b. Pray for a fresh infilling of the Holy Spirit.
c. Pray for unity in your church and among the leaders in the church community.
d. Ask for wisdom and persistence to involve the whole family in intercessory prayer.
e. Pray for the Prime Minister's Cabinet and other counsellors.
f. Pray for individual requests.

Chapter 5 - If *My* People *Will Humble Themselves*

"God sets himself against the proud and haughty but gives grace continually to the lowly."
James 4:6 AB

"Humble yourselves in the sight of the Lord and he will lift you up."
James 4:10 NKJV

"Humble themselves and pray" – there's a reason why they come in that order. Before we can pray acceptably, we need to prepare ourselves by cultivating the quality of humility.

Why is it so important? How does pride mess up our lives? As a case in point, let's go back to our hero, Antony. He is full of arrog-ants and overconfid-ants, as he leaves home to seek his fortune, singing as he goes:

> *I'm gonna be rich, I'm gonna be famous,*
>
> *I'm gonna be dashing, I'm gonna be free!*
>
> *I'm gonna be wise, I'm gonna be noble,*
>
> *I'm gonna have power,*
>
> *I'm gonna be wonderful, beautiful, marvellous meee!*

Right from the start, everything goes wrong for Antony. After many hard knocks and close shaves, he returns home to his father – broke, bedraggled and humbled – and with a new perspective on life. He has become a Repent-ant. His "Independ-ant's Song" not only shows us Antony's character but may reveal our own as it addresses some ramifications of God's first big *'if'* for the preparation of an intercessor and the healing of a nation: humility.

"I'm Gonna Be Rich!"

Sounds great at first, doesn't it? But love of money corrodes our values, warps our perspective and messes up our spirits. Even Christians may be prone to use money as a gauge of personal value and a source of pride – an ungodly and destructive standard. Money is a power tool. In the hands of the righteous, it's a constructive marvel. In the hands of the immature and self-indulgent, it is disastrous.

The Bible says, *"Beware that in your plenty you don't forget the Lord your God... for when you have become full and prosperous... that is the time to watch out that you don't become proud..."* Deuteronomy 8:11-14 TLB.

Heart Check:

- Have material goals become the focus of my life?
- Have the fruits of success dulled my appetite for the things of God?
- Where is my heart? Jesus said, *"Where your treasure is, there will your heart be also"* Matthew 6:21 NKJV. If what I treasure most is material, my heart will be earthbound.

- Am I spending more money on grown-up toys and status symbols than I am on feeding the hungry and spreading the gospel? Jesus said, *"A man's life does not consist in the abundance of his possessions"* Luke 12:15b NIV. If God has prospered you, ask him why? Prosperous Christians are meant to enable those who minister and help the needy. To miss God's purpose for prosperity is to lose it all.

"I'm Gonna Be Wise!"

If we really want the heart and mind of God as intercessors, we'll have to lay down our own wisdom and intellectualism and humble ourselves like the simplest children.

Jesus said, "I thank you, O Father, Lord of heaven and earth, that you have hidden these things from the wise and prudent and revealed them to babes" Luke 10:21 NKJV. In another place he said, "I tell you, whoever does not accept the Kingdom of God like a child will never enter it" Mark 10:15 TLB.

This is a difficult *"if"* for the proud intellectual who has worked hard for his degrees, and to whom Scripture seems hard to accept. But the Bible says God has chosen *"the foolish things of the world to confound the wise, and... things which are not, to bring to nought things that are; that no flesh should glory in his presence"* 1 Corinthians 1:27-29. Or, in Harald Bredesen's version: "God has chosen the nincompoops to confound the compoops." It may require the scholar to bow in humility and teachableness before the one who is Wisdom.

Humility is sometimes hard for spiritual leaders in the church, too. No matter how big and successful our ministries have become, we're still children to God. If we want God's fellowship, we do well to remember that he reveals his heart to the meek and the humble and resists the proud. As one astute preacher, a Scotsman, observed, "Hae ye not noticed that God has the most disconcerrrting way of blessing the wrrrong people?"

And now, a big one:

"Beautiful Me!"

Black is beautiful. So are brown and white and red and yellow. God created us all as we are, and we're right to feel good about it. However, when racial pride becomes racial arrogance, we're headed for serious trouble.

The multicultural, multiracial Church of Jesus Christ holds our greatest hope for peace. All Christians have one Father and all are related – not only by the blood of Adam, but by the blood of Jesus. Our relationship calls for acceptance and honour, respect and courtesy, justice and equality between all God's people.

Some good starts have been made in this direction:

- The Lutherans publicly apologised for Martin Luther's malignant anti-Semitism, which had provided a spiritual justification for the Nazi atrocities of Hitler's Germany. Their action drew great appreciation from the Jewish community.

- The Southern Baptist Convention voted officially a few years ago to label their years of slavery and discrimination as sin. They formally begged the pardon of the black community in America. The Church of England recently did the same in the United Kingdom.
- African Enterprise, led by Michael Cassidy, worked tirelessly to bring reconciliation in South Africa when apartheid gave way to democracy and was a major factor in creating a peaceful transition rather than the bloodbath many had predicted.
- In 2007, the 200th anniversary of the abolition of the slave trade was commemorated by the Centre for Contemporary Ministry by sailing a replica 18th-century slave ship up the River Thames into London, mooring it at Tower Pier and opening it to the public, seeking reconciliation with Africans and Caribbeans. A high point was the washing of one another's feet on the slave ship deck on Maundy Thursday. Wilberforce would have loved it.
- The International Reconciliation Coalition John Dawson, President has ministered to the wounds of Native Americans and African-Americans, as well as in major events of reconciliation throughout the world.

These are major acts of fence-mending that help bring us into unity. They fulfil a vital act of reconciliation: repentance for past and present wrongs. But those who have been wounded by bigotry may find that God requires them to forgive their enemies before they receive apologies or restitution. "While we were yet sinners, Christ died for us" Romans 5:8 KJV. God asks us to operate in the ways of his Spirit rather than in hatred and revenge. It's called grace.

Prayer of Reconciliation

Heavenly Father, we come humbly on behalf of our forefathers, the Church, and ourselves, to confess our sins of racial arrogance and hatred. We apologise to you, Lord, and to one another. We have grieved your heart, wounded your people and divided our churches and our society. In Jesus' name, forgive us.

Those of us who have been wounded ask for supernatural grace to truly love and pray for those who have persecuted us; to forgive those who have despitefully used us, to show that we are the children of our Father in heaven see Matthew 5:44-48.

Give us open hearts and hands, to help the disadvantaged. Help us bind up lingering spiritual wounds and societal wrongs of the past. Father, we pledge to treat all people with justice, dignity, respect and kindness, so the world may see your people loving one another and loving the lost world that Jesus loves and died to save.

Amen.

Humbling ourselves in confession and prayer is a great start towards reconciliation. But it's only a part of the process. It requires more than an apology and a few tears. There is life intercession to be done. It requires that we take a stand for righteousness. Clifford gives us a powerful example:

Before the passing of the Race Relations Act 1994 it was common in England, in areas where immigrants from the British Commonwealth were settling, to see advertisements saying, "No blacks". In fact, some went farther, saying, "No Blacks, no Irish, no children, no dogs!" How exclusive can you be! But such a spirit of xenophobia was quite common in Britain in the 1960s.

Clifford says...

> Monica and I pastored a church in Tottenham North London at that time. We had a large mixed congregation with many Africans and Caribbeans. We attracted the unwelcome attention of the National Front – a far right xenophobic political group who picketed our church on Sundays. Then one night they attacked our house, throwing white paint over the front door and painting on the pavement in front of the house in huge letters the words NIGGER LOVER.

> Of course, this achieved some publicity and we lost a few members of our congregation. But God brought good out of evil. The incident shocked many fair-minded people and caused them to re-think their attitudes, while others came offering to re-paint the front of the house free of charge. It was a testing time, but with the help of God we stood absolutely firm and weathered the storm. It taught us a great deal about relying totally on the Lord. It showed us we could do nothing in our own strength, but when we humbled ourselves and put our trust in our Loving Father he would bring us through even the most difficult times.

"Marvellous Me!"

Then there's spiritual pride. What a lot of difficulty spiritual elitism can cause! "Our group has the true doctrine, you know," even if it is only implied, immediately builds barriers to *spiritual unity*. Presumptuous leaders who believe they have a special connection to the voice of God; arrogant shepherds who overstep their authority; well-meaning intercessors with calluses on their knees who challenge others to Olympian feats of prayer that only discourage them – these are examples of spiritual pride.

We are meant to *lead and encourage* one another, never to intimidate. I Peter 5;1-6 Nowhere is Jesus' model of humility more important than in the leadership of his church. Derek Prince said it well: "The Bible never says that God will make us humble. The Bible always tells us to humble ourselves. It is not something God will do for us. It's something we have to do for ourselves."

When we've humbled ourselves and made sure there's nothing between us and God, we're ready to pray, for our own needs and those of others.

Talk About This:

1. Why are issues of pride and humility so important to God and to our spiritual authority? p37

2. Did you do the personal "Heart Check on p31 Might any of this require a change of attitude or lifestyle for you?

3. Discuss some of the great reconciliation efforts on p38 & 39

4. What more might Christians do to "mend fences" and help heal wounds among the divisions in society, locally, nationally and internationally

5. How far do we go with the godly principles of love and acceptance without abandoning foundational ideals, either politically or spiritually?

Pray About This:

a. Pray for clear vision to see areas of pride or overindulgence that might hinder your effectiveness in healing your society.

b. Pray for opportunities to help "mend fences" that have been broken down through arrogance or bigotry. Ask God to show your group existing efforts for reconciliation where you might help.

c. Pray the Prayer of Reconciliation. p39

d. Ask God to open opportunities for you personally, or for your group, to help heal racial or cultural wounds.

Chapter 6 - If My People Will Pray

The Privilege of Prayer – Priceless

Prayer is conversing with God. Understanding this has helped many Christians transition from the rote recitation of formal memorized prayers to the warm conversational experience of intimate fellowship with the Lord. Brother Lawrence, the seventeenth century monk who wrote *The Practice of the Presence of God,* learned to be aware of God in every moment of his life, whether in worship services or in mundane chores such as washing the dishes and he taught others to do the same.

First Thessalonians 5:17 says *"Pray without ceasing."* Is that possible? Most of us could never reach that lofty ideal, but we can aspire to it. Brother Lawrence's word "practice" is the key. Practice makes, if not perfect, at least a lot better. If God is never far from our consciousness we'll find ourselves conversing with him throughout the day: "Thank you, Lord, that was beautiful!... What do you want me to do about this, Father?... Lord, help me figure this out... I love you, Lord... I'm sorry, Lord; I didn't mean to do that..." That's "praying without ceasing."

Brother Lawrence said that when he failed in his duty he told the Lord, "If I'm left to myself I will always do that," and then went cheerfully about his business without his peace being ruffled. He said we might get so used to God's presence and be continually filled with joys so great that we may have to "use means to moderate them and to hinder their outward appearance." What a way to live!

We can call on God anywhere. *"Call to me,"* God says, *"and I will answer you, and show you great and mighty things which you do not know"* Jeremiah 33:3 NKJV. Prayer brings heaven to bear on our situation. It brings us help, solutions and revelation.

John Wesley went so far as to say, "God does nothing except through prayer." God looks for those who will partner with him in his Kingdom business by inviting his presence and power into their circumstance. Our part is simply to believe him, obey him, and use this marvellous means to bring about his will.

In the Sermon on the Mount Matthew chapters 5-7, Jesus tells us how to pray and how not to pray. He says that if we pray ostentatiously in public places in order to be seen by others, public admiration is the only reward we'll get. He tells us instead to pray in private to our Father and he will reward us openly. He says, *"Don't babble on and on as people of other religions do. They think their prayers are answered only by repeating their words again and again. Don't be like them, because your Father knows exactly what you need even before you ask him"* Matthew 6:7-8 NLT.

Then he gives us an example of how to pray. This has come to be called "The Lord's Prayer" verses 9-13. He didn't mean necessarily for us to repeat this prayer as a formula without saying anything else, although it sums up in broad terms just about everything we might need to pray for. It's a vital pattern for intercessors to follow.

Throughout the gospels Jesus gives us precious promises to hang our faith on. Here are some of them:

"Ask and it will be given to you; seek and you will find; knock and the door will be opened to you." Matthew 7:7 NIV

"Whatever you ask for in prayer, believe that you have received it, and it will be yours." Mark 11:24 NIV

"Yes, ask anything, using my name, and I will do it." John 14:14 NLT

"If you remain in me and my words remain in you, ask whatever you wish and it will be given you." John 15:7 NIV

These, together with other Bible promises, are our foundation for praying in faith.

But there's a condition: *"He will listen to us whenever we ask him for anything in line with his will"* I John 5:14 TLB.

Here's how these dependent promises link together: *"You have not because you ask not. You ask and do not receive, because you ask amiss"* James 4:3a NKJV.

We "ask amiss" when we want something that is clearly opposed to the laws or will of God. Then we're in for a spiritual blockade. It can happen even to experienced intercessors. Therefore we need to find the will of God so we can ask in faith. Then we will see results.

Praying the Scriptures

The Bible shows you the will of God. It is your best prayer partner, the secret to a powerful prayer life. In your daily Scripture reading, see what that portion has to say about how you should live. For instance, recently we started together re-reading the Psalms. Here's how the first one begins:

"Blessed is the man who walks not in the counsel of the ungodly, nor stands in the path of sinners, nor sits in the seat of the scornful. But his delight is in the law of the Lord and in his law he meditates day and night" NKJV.

Well, that gives us plenty to pray about: "Lord, help me never to follow ungodly people, or to be fooled by them, or to take pleasure in the company of those who mock you. Put a fresh love for your words in my heart so that I won't sin against you. Forgive me if I've failed in these basic things, and renew me in my spirit."

Then we might pray Luke 21 where Jesus is teaching about judgment in the last days. In itself, this is not a happy thought. But wait. Here is our excited, positive hope: *"Keep awake then, and pray that you may be found worthy to escape all these things that will take place, and to stand in the presence of the Son of Man."* verse 36, AB.

Well, how do we find that wonderful escape route? Can we ever be worthy to stand in the Presence? Yes. And we pray those Scriptures that tell us how; that we have been made, and are being made, worthy in Christ. We make declarations of the Scriptures:

"I have been crucified with Christ, nevertheless I live; yet not I, but Christ lives in me..." Galatians 2:20: KJV.

You, Lord, "by the glory of your grace, have made me accepted in the Beloved."
Ephesians 1:6: KJV.

"It is Christ in me, the hope of the glory." Colossians 1:27: (Author's paraphrase)

Here are some other examples of how to use Scripture in prayer:

- Christians who are being falsely accused or persecuted may pray Psalm 54 with faith: *"Save me, O God, by your name, and vindicate me by your strength. Hear my prayer, O God... for strangers have risen up against me, and oppressors have sought after me... Behold, God is my helper... He has delivered me out of all my troubles."* NKJV. Psalms 35 and 56 are also good ones to pray in similar situations.

- People facing danger, such as soldiers going into battle – or loved ones praying for them – take comfort in praying Psalm 91, inserting their names in the applicable spots.

- Our friend Jean Darnall, when asked to pray for someone who is sick, sometimes gives them a list of printed-out healing Scriptures with the prescription, *"Read aloud three times a day, first to the Lord, second to yourself, and third to the devil."* This is a wonderful faith-strengthening exercise.

- An elderly gentleman we know prays Jude 24 every time he starts to hoist himself up out of the bathtub: *"Unto him who is able to keep you from falling..."* (He knows that's not exactly the kind of falling the Scripture meant, but it works for him.)

When we take the Word of God and turn it into prayer, we can pray with confidence. Remember I John 5:14, 15: *"Now this is the confidence we have in him that if we ask anything according to his will, he hears us. And if we know he hears us, whatever we ask, we know that we have the petitions that we have asked of him"* NKJV. The Scripture shows us his will so we know how to pray expectantly, in faith.

This is a vital key to answered prayer.

What to Pray When You Don't Know What to Pray

Prayer based on claiming God's scriptural promises gives us something sure to hang our faith on. But sometimes we can't find Scriptures that seem to fit our situation and we just don't know how to pray.

Either we don't know enough about it to pray intelligently, or it may be such a tangled mess that we don't know where to begin. In these cases the most useful prayer may be the prayer that never fails: "Your will be done!" When we pray for the will of God we can trust in the intercession of the Holy Spirit.

Likewise the Spirit also helps in our weaknesses. For we do not know what we should pray for as we ought, but the Spirit himself makes intercession for us with groanings which cannot be uttered. Now he who searches the heart knows what the mind of the Spirit is, because he makes intercession for the saints according to the will of God. And we know that all things work together for good to those who love God, to those who are the called according to his purpose. Romans 8:26-28 NKJV.

Talk About This:

1. What attitudes can we carry that allow the gracious character of Christ to manifest through us even in the face of disagreements or outright attack?

2. If times become tighter economically, do you think God might require some changes in the lifestyle of more affluent Christians in order to help others? Would that affect you personally?

3. Within our communities, what holds our greatest hope for racial and cultural peace?

4. God promises to answer prayers that are prayed "in his will." How do we make sure our prayers are not contrary to the will of God?

5. Have you tried praying the scriptures? How has it influenced your prayer life?

Pray About This:

a. Pray for courage and determination to show up, speak up, and stand up for biblical truth, even in the face of oppression or threat of persecution.

b. Ask for a more generously giving heart in order to show practically the loving care of Jesus Christ.

c. Pray for any pressing national needs.

d. Pray for church leadership – particularly in your own church!

Chapter 7 - If My People Will Seek My Face And Turn From Their Wicked Ways

Blessed are they that keep his testimonies, and that seek him with the whole heart. They also do no iniquity: they walk in his ways.
Psalm 119:2-3 KJV

Thanksgiving and Praise – The Gateway to God's Presence

When a hurricane devastated parts of the southern United States, the television news showed people wandering around in despair. But one lady had a different attitude. As she shovelled debris out of the shell that once had been her home, she said, "It'll be all right. God will bring something good out of it yet." And she said it with a smile. This lady understood God's character and believed his promise: *"We know that all things work together for good to those who love God, to those who are called according to his purpose"* Romans 8:28. Her smile was a defeat for Satan, who would have used this disaster to make her bitter and unbelieving.

Thanksgiving and praise are choices – acts of the will in obedience and faith; proclamations that God is triumphant over all the works of the devil. This stands us in the place of victory and ushers us into the place of intercession. *"Enter into his gates with thanksgiving and into his courts with praise"* Psalm 100:4.

King David, the psalmist, wrote, *"When I consider your heavens, the work of your fingers, the moon and the stars, which you have ordained, what is man that you are mindful of him, and the son of man that you visit him?"* Psalm 8:3-4 NKJV. And David didn't know then what we know now about the vastness of God's universe.

Isaiah was a prophet with the difficult task of bringing enslaved and cynical Israel back to faith. They needed to trust God again in order to be delivered from Babylon and return to the Promised Land. Their God, Isaiah said, was the Creator of the universe and he held the nations in his hands "like a drop in a bucket." He asked:

> *"Who has measured the waters in the hollow of his hand, or with the breadth of his hand marked off the heavens? Who has held the dust of the earth in a basket, or weighed the mountains on the scales and the hills in the balance? Lift your eyes and look to the heavens: who created all these? He who brings out the starry host one by one, and calls them each by name. Because of his great power and mighty strength, not one of them is missing"* Isaiah 40.12 & 2.

Why would the One who created all this consider us worthy of notice? It's a manifestation of grace beyond imagination. Yet people treat God as a sort of heavenly butler who obediently fills their requests and who should be grateful for a smile or a nod. Great intercessors know better. They are invariably fervent thanks-givers who know that God manifests himself where he is praised see Psalm 22:3.

Thanksgiving and praise fix our focus on God. That's why the Patriarchs often began their prayers with a long litany of his miracles of creation and deliverance. By the time they got through with all that, their faith was red hot. Veteran intercessors have found a key to answered prayer: *"Delight yourself also in the Lord, and he will give you the desires of your heart"* Psalm 37:4 NIV. So, they abandon inhibitions and openly speak their love to God.

You may say, "I'm not used to openly expressing praise to God. I think I'd feel awkward, even in private." Let the Psalmist help you. Find a quiet place and read some praise Psalms aloud to God. Then continue to thank him in your own words. Sometimes it helps to sing simple choruses during your individual worship times when nobody can hear you but God.

We have a motley collection of old valentines; made by hand, crooked, paste-smeared, misspelled, and funny. We wouldn't trade them for anything because our kids made them. They were gifts of love which delighted us. We know the Father receives our stammering expressions of love in that same spirit of delight. He doesn't want it to be perfect; he just wants it to be from us.

But there's another kind of praise that honours the Lord. He is pleased when his people gather together, not only in formal church services, but even in small groups, and just talk about him. Have you ever looked back on an evening with your friends and thought, "We had this long conversation about the Lord and all the things he's done for us, but we never took time to praise him?" But that's exactly what you were doing; you were praising the Lord. To praise doesn't mean just to compliment him to his face, it also means to tell others about his goodness. The Bible says:

> *"Then those who feared and loved the Lord spoke often of him to each other. And he had a Book of Remembrance drawn up in which he recorded the names of those who feared him and loved to think about him. 'They shall be mine,' says the Lord of Hosts, 'in that day when I make up my jewels. And I will spare them as a man spares an obedient and dutiful son.'"* Malachi 3:16-17 TLB.

Our thanksgiving and praise are a logical and important progression in intercession. They help us *"come boldly to the very throne of God and stay there to receive his mercy and to find grace to help us in our times of need"* Hebrews 4:16 TLB. They give us space between the nitty-gritty of everyday life and the change of spiritual venue we need as we seek God's face in worship.

Worship – Seeking God's Face

Our Creator God is an awesome monarch who doesn't need our vote to retain his office or our approval to ratify his actions. The prophets and apostles fell before him like dead men. They weren't afraid of punishment; they were simply afraid of *him*. God is like a force of cosmic energy that we're unable to touch and still live. But in Jesus he's given us a "transformer" who makes him available and touchable to us.

In Old Testament times only the high priest could enter the Holy of Holies where that powerful Presence waited, and even then only once a year and after ritual cleansing. But at the moment Jesus died on the cross, the heavy curtain, or veil, which concealed the Holy of Holies, was torn in two from the *top down*, signifying that the way to God had been opened for all of us who would believe in him.

The New Testament says, *"Now we may walk right into the very Holy of Holies where God is, because of the blood of Jesus. This is the new, life-giving way which Christ has opened up for us by tearing the curtain – his human body – to let us into the holy presence of God... let us go right in, to God himself, with true hearts fully trusting him to receive us"* Hebrews 10: 19-20, 22 TLB.

- *Worship* – seeking God's face – is the place of **intimacy.** It's the place for expressing and receiving love, as a bride gives and receives love from her husband: "For your maker is your husband – the Lord Almighty is his name – the Holy One of Israel is your redeemer; he is called the God of all the earth" Isaiah 54:5 NIV.

- *Worship* is the place of **conception.** It's where fruit bearing begins. From this personal, intimate relationship with our Lord, his character and works begin to grow out of us as naturally as a child grows out of the mother's womb or as fruit grows from the tree that gives it life. see Romans 7:4.

- *Worship* is the place of **rest.** "He makes me to lie down in green pastures; he leads me beside the still waters" Psalm 23:2 NKJV.

- *Worship* is the place of **restoration.** In a personal one-to-one place with God, we receive comfort for our heartbreaks, strength for our spirits and discipline for maturity. "He restores my soul Psalm 23:3 NKJV. To grown-up trusted sons and daughters, the Father offers privileges and authority that perhaps we're only beginning to understand.

- *Worship* is the place of **revelation.** Here the Holy Spirit teaches us, brings things to our remembrance, enlightens our understanding, and gives us new vision and direction see John 14:26.

- *Worship* is the place of **transformation.** see Romans 12:2. In the Holy Place of God's presence we are changed, cleansed and prepared for ministry and intercession.

Much as we would like to have all this happen instantly, that isn't the way it works. It's a process that will go on until we get to heaven, and it involves an old-fashioned method – repentance. Repentance – turning from our wicked ways – is one of God's required *'ifs'*, and it opens the gateway to intercession, where we see the face of God and receive healing for ourselves.... and for our nation.

Repentance – Clearing the Way

True story: Imagine the reaction when one serene summer evening on the edge of a small country town, just as the birds are settling down and the cicadas are tuning up, the local gas works explodes. The spectacular blast sends families racing outside where they find the eastern sky blazing like the sun. As they stand gaping, wondering what on earth is happening, one four-year-old boy immediately figures it out. Wild with excitement, he begins shouting, "Jesus is coming! Jesus is coming!" and with shining eyes, outstretched arms and guiltless heart, he runs as fast as he can go straight toward the light. If we thought Jesus was coming *right now*, would our first impulse be to run toward the light or find a place to hide?

If our consciences do not accuse us, if they do not make us feel guilty and condemn us, we have confidence (complete assurance and boldness) before God. And we receive from him whatever we ask... 1 John 3:21-22 AB.

If you come home and find your dog sitting huddled in a corner, wearing sunglasses, with his eyes darting at you and away again, you can probably guess he's prepared some sort of surprise for you. We're like that; when our consciences condemn us, it's hard to look the Lord in the eye.

If I regard iniquity in my heart, the Lord will not hear me Psalm 66:18 KJV.

Repent: to reconsider; to think differently; to turn from a past course of action. We've talked about repentance for corporate sins such as bigotry and social arrogance, but there are more personal sins of the heart that have to be dealt with before we can come to God with a clean slate.

For instance, sitting in our living room is Dawn, a throwback to the hippie life-style, living in her own time warp – all love and peace. She knows nothing about Christian ethics or morals; she only knows that Jesus has just come into her life and with all her heart she wants to please Him. She has a question: "Is there anything wrong with my living with my boyfriend and having sex with him?" she asks with wide-eyed innocence. "I mean, like, does it bother God?"

As we try to frame a tactful but true answer, she goes on: "See, I don't know what the Bible says about it, but I've been feeling very uncomfortable about it myself and I wasn't sure what I should do."

"Oh," we say, "well... "

"So," she says earnestly, "I kicked him out. And it really took a load off."

The Holy Spirit has done his job without any help from us, thanks, because he's found what he's looking for – honesty and a heart hot for holiness.

On the other hand, there is the unsaved and unhappy acquaintance who is a fairly successful businessman. He cheats his clients – not a lot – just enough to keep the profit margin healthy. He knows that if he wants a relationship with God, he'll have to make a big change, but he just can't do it; the cost is too high.

So he goes on with a torn heart, unable to enjoy what he's working so hard for – and risking his soul in the process see Mark 8:36.

God is out to purify the Church, to make us holy – one of us at a time. He's after our characters.

He's after our relationships with families, friends, sweethearts and business associates. All he needs from us are willing hearts.

Buddy Owens writes:

> "Repentance is not a once in a lifetime commitment. It's not simply an apology with a promise to do better. Repentance is a whole new lifestyle."

"Repentance is a determination to change the way we live – to stop, turn around, and head in a new direction.

"Repentance is cooperating with God in the transformation of our character.

"Repentance is a heart posture that is reflected in the choices we make.

"Repentance is an act of worship"

The Way of a Worshipper, Purpose Driven Publishing.

Once we've come to Christ and had our sins forgiven, God has made provision for us to maintain our condition of cleansing. *"If we walk in the light as he is in the light, we have fellowship with one another, and the blood of Jesus Christ his son cleanses us from all sin"* 1 John 1:7 NKJV... *" If we confess our sins, he is faithful and just to forgive us our sins and to cleanse us from all unrighteousness"* verse 9.

In Jesus' day, because people wore open sandals on dusty roads, it was the custom to wash their feet before sharing a meal. At the Last Supper Jesus took a basin of water and a towel, wrapped himself like a servant, and began washing his disciples' feet.

Peter protested, "No, Lord! You'll never wash my feet!"

Jesus answered, "If I don't wash your feet, you won't belong to me."

To which the ever-impetuous Peter replied, "Then wash my hands and my head too, not just my feet!"

Jesus may have smiled as he patiently explained, "A person who has bathed all over doesn't need to wash, except for the feet, to be entirely clean" see John 13:1-10.

This is a picture to us of the cleansing we can receive as we daily confess and turn away from our sins. We don't need to get saved all over again. We have been bathed – washed in the blood of Jesus – which was shed for the remission of our sins. After we have experienced salvation by his mercy – *"the washing of regeneration and renewing of the Holy Spirit,"* Titus 3:5 we can come again and again and receive cleansing of the parts of our lives where the flesh meets the dusty road. If we keep short accounts with God through our repentance, it never becomes a heavy, onerous duty, but a marvellous privilege of Grace – a doorway to spiritual freedom and joy.

God isn't wanting to make us feel bad as we confess and turn from our sins, but to forgive, refresh and renew us. A friend explained how he trained his young dog. When she was disobedient he would roll up a newspaper and give her a swat. She quickly learned, when she heard the sound of the paper being rolled up, to roll over on her back, her front paws together in doggie-prayer, and her tail wagging. "Now how can you swat a dog like that?" he asked.

So it is with us: if we roll over as soon as we hear the Lord rolling up the paper, we'll spare ourselves a lot of disciplining by our Master. But thank God for his discipline! Hebrews 12 tells us not to ignore it or be discouraged when he corrects us:

The Lord disciplines those he loves and punishes those he accepts as his children. If God doesn't discipline you as he does all his children, it means that you are illegitimate and are not really his children after all... But God's discipline is always right and good for us because it means we will share in his holiness. No discipline is enjoyable while it is happening – it is painful! But afterward there will be a quiet harvest of right living for those who are trained in this way.
Hebrews 12: 6-11 NLT.

If we neglect the duty and privilege of repentance, we allow our sins and failures to smother peace in our consciences. Instead, we carry a growing weight of guilt as we fall under the domination of habits – entrenched attitudes and besetting sins that separate us from our awareness of God's holy presence. We become fruitless and lose faith for our prayers to be answered. If we finally drag ourselves back to the Father in real repentance, we'll find his open arms, but we can't make up the time that was lost or easily lose our regret for having lost it.

There's no time like now to take care of neglected housecleaning. Take a few quiet minutes to look inside. Ask the Holy Spirit to reveal what needs to be taken care of – then listen. Don't dig and root around for something, just be quiet and let him show you.

Soon things will come to mind: the unforsaken secret sins, that bad-news love relationship, those delightful but ungodly friends who are influencing your lifestyle, the unethical business practices. Those are the things that have to go. Sometimes they're hard to get rid of, but repentance, confession and the cross are still the answer.

You might pray like this...

Father in heaven, I am yours. I love and worship you. Knowing and pleasing you are my eternal concerns. All other concerns I give to you – my relationships, my fortunes and my future. I want my ambitions and my character to conform to your plan for me. Forgive my sins. [Take your time here and name them.] I bring them all to the cross to be paid for by Jesus' sacrifice there. Cleanse me now for Jesus' sake. Now, by faith in your promise, I receive your forgiveness and cleansing.

Amen

Once you've done this kind of praying from the heart, be at peace. Don't keep beating yourself by repeatedly confessing and repenting of sins already put under Jesus' blood, forgiven, and forsaken. This is like digging up bones from a grave. Worst of all, it trivializes and insults Christ's work on the cross.

What God forgives, God forgets: *"Their sins and their lawless deeds I will remember no more"* Hebrews 10:17 NKJV. But often we have a hard time forgiving ourselves and we mistake our remorse for guilt. God can remove crippling regret, too, if we will let him.

Believe that he can and will take the biggest mess you've ever made, and repented of, and ultimately redeem it. If you understand that, you can be at peace.

Of course, if you're having difficulty breaking sinful habits or walking through deep repentance, by all means, go to your pastor or spiritual counsellor. They will help you find forgiveness and freedom.

Finding the Jesus-Attitude

A few years ago, Carol attended a large conference at which some of the best-known Christian speakers in America railed against pornographers, abortionists and homosexual activists. The crowd – Carol included – cheered. Yes, they agreed, we must do something about this unrighteous bunch now! However, some things began to bother her. While most of the speakers carefully directed their anger at the sin and not the sinner, some were vitriolic; some were sarcastic and insulting. Carol wondered: how would I feel if I were a homosexual feeling disturbed about my lifestyle, or a pornography addict wondering if I could ever be set free, or a pro-choice advocate having doubts about my stand on abortion? Would I be reluctant to come to these people for help? Would I feel that Jesus Christ, whom they profess to represent, also looks on me with scorn and revulsion?

But, some would argue, these people are bad, aren't they? Yes, of course they are; we're all bad without the grace of God, *"All have sinned and come short of the glory of God"* Romans 3:23 KJV. *"There is none righteous, no, not one"* Romans 3:10 NKJV.

Paul wrote to the church at Corinth, listing every kind of sinner you can think of, and then added, *"And such were some of you. But you were washed, but you were sanctified, but you were justified in the name of the Lord Jesus and by the Spirit of God"* 1 Corinthians 6:9-11 NKJV.

People are not lost because they're bad; they're bad because they're lost. It doesn't mean they aren't redeemable. They don't have the Spirit of God living in them, helping them to conform to the image of Christ. So they try to find pleasure, success, security, acceptance and love the only way they know how. God forgive us who have come to know him, for not telling the lost about the One who can make them good and acceptable in God's sight. No one is saved just by being good, and no one is lost just by being bad. All of us are lost sinners until we receive God's free gift of salvation. God reveals himself to seekers and welcomes them into his Kingdom, but lets the defiant have their own way and stay in the kingdom of darkness see John 3:18.

Evangelism is a declaration of war on the devil, not on lost souls. So, while we mustn't compromise our condemnation of the sin and its devastating consequences, we must ask the Lord to help us exercise love and compassion for people who are gripped in a terrible bondage.

There is a caveat for us here: concentrating on other people's sins gives us a beautiful opportunity to ignore our own. Involving ourselves with the big, objective issues such as prayer for the sins of the nation can make us feel wonderfully righteous. But national revival and cleansing have to begin with us, the Church.

The Church's image is at an all-time low. Unchurched people watch the television news and see priests and ministers accused of child abuse and other sins. They think this is really Christianity. No wonder they scoff at Christians. The world may not want to be pure, but it respects purity. The tragedy is that it doesn't see it in us more often. We can change this situation. We can confess and repent of our personal sins – all those things we've swept under the carpet and tried to ignore. Then we can repent as part of the Church.

To help you identify some failures of the Church and make a thorough confession, look back at some of the facts in Chapter 2 about the state of the nation. You may cover all these issues in one session or concentrate on one at a time for intensive meditation and prayer. However you do it, don't rush through it; be prepared for some serious intercessory work.

Prayer of Repentance as Part of the Church

Father in heaven, as we grieve over the wickedness in our nation, we recognise that it's partly because of our failures as your Church that our society is as we see it now.

Because we have tolerated impurity in the Church, our witness has been crippled.

Because of our silence, the voices of sin and rebellion have grown clamorous in our nation.

Because of our apathy, we have injustice in our courts and crime in our streets.

Because of our divisions, we've been too spiritually weak to stop the inroads of the devil. Forgive us, Lord.

Because of doctrinal pettiness and squabbling we have presented an ugly, fragmented picture of Christ to a world longing for spiritual reality and love. Unite us so the world may see you in us and believe.

Where we have become powerless by trusting in our own programmes, resources and traditions instead of being led by your Spirit; where we have compartmentalised religion to a few hours a week instead of making you the tivating force of our lives; where we've become idolaters by putting other things before you, forgive us.

Forgive us for tolerating evil and becoming friends of the world, compromising our high and holy calling. Because of our fear of offending the world by our protests.

We have pornography available in our living rooms, heresy and perversion taught in our schoolrooms, and the slaughter of the unborn in our hospitals and clinics.

We know, Lord, you are righteous and that we are covered with shame, because of our sins.

We know, Lord, you are righteous and that we are covered with shame, because of our sins... We know it is time for judgement to begin in the house of God. But we also know that you are merciful towards those who repent and confess their sins. Hear our confession, Lord, and restore to us all that we have lost through our sin.

Make us hungry for your word and powerful in prayer. Help us to abandon everything that offends you.

Wake up all your people to the ministry of prayer and fasting for our nation, with authority and confidence and power.

Let us be salt and light in our corrupt and darkened world. Let righteousness and holiness preserve our churches, our nation and us.

Amen.

Talk About This:

1. How do thanksgiving and praise prepare us for intercession? p46
2. If openly expressing praise and worship is new to you, have you tried the method in this chapter? How has it affected your prayer life? Your relationship with God? p47
3. How do you feel about your exciting privilege of direct access to God through Jesus Christ? If you feel your response hasn't been what it should be, what changes do you think you need to make?
4. What six things do we find in the Holy Place as we worship. p48
5. Has the book changed your concept of "repentance"? How?
6. Why is corporate repentance by the Church so crucial to the future of our nation? p53

Pray About This:

a. **Thanksgiving:** Name your blessings and express your whole-hearted gratitude for them. It will bless you again as you remember.

b. **Praise:** Praise God for all his amazing works of creation and redemption! Sing to him. Read Psalms aloud to him.

c. **Worship:** Focus on his presence. Declare aloud his majesty, divinity and power. Acknowledge that he is Lord above all spiritual and physical authorities that exist.

d. **Using the prayer in this chapter,** confess the failures of the Church. You might use the written prayer to get you started on different issues, then move right forward on your own! p49

PART

3

SPIRIT-LED PRAYER AND ACTION

Righteousness exalts a nation, but sin is a reproach to any people

Proverbs 14:34 NKJV

All who are led by the Spirit of God are children of God

Romans 8:14 NLT

Prayer is God's invitation to enter his throne room so he can lay his agenda over our hearts.

Henry Blackaby

Chapter 8 - God Rules!

"The Lord is King! He rules all the nations!"
Psalm 22:28 NLT

The Lord rules in power and might. The Lord rules in glory and light
In majesty, honour, glory, power. The Lord rules
Forever!
And our God rules in the kingdom of men
And his is the power to raise up, to pull down
For he is the Lord of all nations!
"The Lord Rules", by Jimmy and Carol Owens © Fairhill Music

Nineteen eighty-six: It is a fateful day in the Philippines. In this predominantly Catholic nation the church has finally taken an official stand against the oppressive Marcos regime and things are happening fast: the people take to the streets, President Marcos calls out the troops, and the revolution is on.

Grim and menacing, tanks growl through the streets of Manila. They reach the human barricade, and pause. It's the perfect scenario for a Tiananmen Square-style slaughter. But miraculously, face-to-face with their fellow citizens, the soldiers are ordered not to fire. Soon, many climb down from their tanks and join the crowd. With that, it's all over. God sovereignly gives the people a bloodless victory.

The action in the streets isn't simply the result of long-seething anger on the part of secular citizenry. It's the fruit of long seasons of fervent prayer and fasting by laypeople and clergy and the courageous stand for righteousness by priests and pastors. When the time finally is right, God moves dramatically in response to their intercession.

Later, we see a videotape of a speech made by the newly elected President, Corazon Aquino, at a huge all-night prayer rally featuring our *If My People* musical. She exhorts the people to serve Christ for the good of the nation. Like an evangelist, she finishes by having the people shout with her the motto: "Jesus Christ is Lord of the Philippines and of all nations!"

She knows that God is sovereign and that nations carry within themselves the seeds of his blessing or judgment, and she urges her people to serve him and thus build a "wall of righteousness" to protect the destiny of the Philippines. Their response will determine their future.

A personal aside: We had been invited to conduct a large presentation of our musical *If My People* in that same venue in Manila some time before the revolution. Cardinal Sin, (he had a lot of fun with that name) had been preaching fervently to the nation on the 2 Chronicles 7:14 Scripture. The date for the *If My People* presentation was getting close and preparations were well under way, when suddenly the Marcos government cancelled it because of the fear of Muslim violence. It remained for a new regime to broadcast it to the nation.

We later met Cardinal Sin, and his secretary/priest asked us, "Did you know that your song, "If My People Will Pray" was the theme song of our revolution?" We were astonished. He told us that when the revolutionaries took over the government radio station, they played the song around the clock. Many people sang it together as they went, unarmed, to face the troops.

Who is in Control Here?

God is in control, and he blesses or chastises nations depending upon their acceptance or rejection of his rulership.

In Leviticus 26 God lays down his terms before the people of Israel: If they obey him he promises peace and plenty, protection from their enemies, and his continuing presence with them.

Then there follows a series of *If / thens:* "If you will not listen and obey, then I will do these things..." And the punishments are the most awful list of calamities you can imagine, beginning with the chilling promise, *"I will appoint terror over you"* v.16 NKJV and progressing through disease, drought, decimation and destruction by enemies, desolation of the land, and ultimately dispersion as slaves among the heathen nations.

But the chapter ends with a gracious promise – another *If / then* – *"If they confess their iniquity, and the iniquity of their fathers,... then... I will not cast them away nor... utterly destroy them and break my covenant with them; for I am the Lord their God"* Leviticus 26:40-44 NKJV.

Now some would say, "Yes, but that was Israel. God doesn't deal with other nations the same way as he deals with Israel." True. We realise that neither America nor any other nation has the same covenant relationship that Israel has with God. Nevertheless, there is an overarching principle that characterizes God's dealings with all nations – Gentile nations, as well as with Israel:

> *Whenever I announce that a certain nation or kingdom is to be destroyed, then if that nation renounces its evil ways, I will not destroy it as I had planned. And if I announce that I will make a certain nation strong and great, but then that nation changes its mind and turns to evil and refuses to obey me, then I too will change my mind and not bless that nation as I said I would.* Jeremiah 18:7-10 TLB.

Does God ever change his mind? Absolutely! Look again at the last phrase of that Scripture passage: God says, *"I too will change my mind..."* His character never changes; his will never changes. But he changes his mind toward a nation, depending on its obedience or disobedience to him. When a nation repents, God relents. When a nation by and large abandons its allegiance to God; when the people become self-willed and hedonistic; when they ignore, or don't care about, what is happening in their society, they break down the protective "wall of righteousness" around the nation.

Then the destroyer simply takes over, and God doesn't stop him. Think of any modern totalitarian, genocidal government and see if the description doesn't fit. Hitler's regime, for instance, was extremely occultic and the people were deceived and mesmerised by it and millions died because of it. Communism was, also, violently, murderously, atheistic.

Scan through the Book of Isaiah, chapters 13-23, and you'll find God's warning messages to many Gentile nations. see also Jeremiah, chapters 46-51. However, he leaves room for a national change of heart, as when he sent Jonah to cry doom to Nineveh, and then spared them when they repented.

God's Orchestration

God has often put his people in place to orchestrate the fate of nations, bring deliverance to captives, and fulfil his own plans.

- Imagine Joseph, sold into captivity by his jealous brothers and taken to Egypt, where he's falsely accused and imprisoned. His miraculous gifting brings him to the attention of Pharaoh, who makes him ruler over all of Egypt, second only to himself. Joseph saves Egypt from famine and brings his family there, where they ultimately grow into the nation of Israel Genesis chapters 37 to 50.

- Baby Moses bobs gently in his little basket among the reeds of the River Nile, seemingly abandoned to the whims of chance. The next thing you know, he's an Egyptian prince. Then he's a slave. Then he's a revolutionary waging a titanic power struggle with Pharaoh for the freedom of the enslaved Israelites. God has orchestrated this whole complex political chronicle for two reasons: to reveal his power and lordship to Egypt see Exodus14:18 and to bring the fear of the Lord and deliverance to Israel see Exodus14: 31.

- Esther is a captive in Persia, where, because of her beauty and grace, she is chosen by the king to be his queen. When a plot is hatched to destroy all the Jews in the kingdom, she risks her life to save her fellow Jews from annihilation.

- Daniel is a captive in Babylon, who because of his God-given ability to interpret dreams is elevated to high office. When the king plans to set him over the whole realm, Daniel's enemies plot to have him killed. God miraculously saves him, and the king proclaims that all in his kingdom must tremble before the God of Daniel.

All of these rise from slavery to rulership in idolatrous nations. There they become instruments through whom God delivers his chastised people.

Learning the Hard Way

The Bible says, *"All governments have been placed in power by God"* Romans 13:1b NLT. There is no government anywhere that God has not put in power. The megalomaniacal King Nebuchadnezzar learned this the hard way. As he strutted around on the flat roof of his royal palace, he boasted that he had built the great city of Babylon by his own power to demonstrate his royal glory.

While he was still speaking, he got the shock of his life: A voice from heaven boomed, *"O King Nebuchadnezzar, you are no longer ruler of this kingdom! You will be driven from human society and live in the fields like a wild animal, and you will eat grass like a cow until you learn that the Most High rules in the kingdoms of the world and gives them to anyone he chooses."* Within an hour the king was out of his mind and out in the fields. He lived this way until his hair was as long as eagle feathers and his nails were like birds' claws.

Seven years later the Lord graciously touched Nebuchadnezzar again. His sanity returned, and he fervently praised and worshipped God and acknowledged him as Lord over heaven and earth. Then God restored his honour and glory and kingdom. see Daniel 4:29-34 NLT.

An interesting counterpoint to this story is that Nebuchadnezzar's royal palace in Babylon stands not far from Baghdad in modern Iraq, and was rebuilt by Saddam Hussein, who fancied himself a successor to that same Nebuchadnezzar. How the mighty have fallen.

The Bible says, *"It is God who judges! He brings one down, he exalts another"* Psalm 75:7. The Scriptures are full of other stories of God's rulership in the kingdoms of men, as when he tears the kingdom of Israel away from King Saul for his disobedience and gives it to David see 1 Samuel 15. Or when God removes Shebna, the wicked steward of Judah, saying, "I will roll you up into a ball, hurl you away violently, and give your authority to someone I can trust" see Isaiah 22:17-21.

God can even raise up the ungodly to accomplish his will: *"For the Scripture says to Pharaoh: 'I raised you up for this very purpose, that I might display my power in you, and that my name might be proclaimed in all the earth'"* Romans 9:17 NIV.

Another case in point: Nebuchadnezzar's son Belshazzar hasn't learned his father's lesson; he flouts God and flaunts his own vain glory. Suddenly, in a vision so terrifying it literally makes his knees knock, King Belshazzar sees the disembodied fingers of a hand writing his fate on the wall of his banqueting chamber. He dies that very night as the Medes and Persians break into his palace and conquer his kingdom.

A Catastrophic Good

Now, fast forward a few years. The Hebrews have been in captivity in Babylon for nearly 70 years. Their temple back in Jerusalem has been razed to the ground and the city's walls still lie broken down. And now the Medo/Persian Empire has conquered Babylon. Who will deliver them from this disaster? Daniel, a Hebrew whom God has already raised to a high position in Babylon, is doing his daily Scripture reading one day when he realises that the 70 years of the desolations of Jerusalem prophesied by Jeremiah are almost up, so what does he do, jump up and shout? No, he puts on sackcloth, gets down on his face, fasts for three weeks, confesses the sins of his people, and prays for God to bring about their release.

God stirs up the spirit of Cyrus, king of Persia, whom he had prophetically called by name two centuries before his birth and some 130 years before the Hebrew captivity even began, to rebuild his temple in Jerusalem.

So Cyrus calls for Israelite volunteers and sends 50,000 people to do the job. Who could have dreamed that a Gentile king would become the means of Israel's deliverance? God seems to love doing things like that – deliverances so mighty and unexpected that there is no question that only God could have pulled them off, and he gets the glory.

This sort of thing is what JRR Tolkien called a "eucatastrophe", an event so good that it is catastrophically good. God is *"able to accomplish infinitely more than we would ever dare to ask or hope"* Ephesians 3:20 NKJV.

The Sting

Nowhere is God's orchestration more mind-blowing than in the working out of his plan for our salvation. See his hand at work in the crucifixion: Even Pilate, the heathen governor of Judea, is put in his place of authority by the will of God. Although he seems to be the deciding voice in Jesus' fate, Jesus informs him, *"You would not have any authority whatsoever over me if it were not given you from above"* John19:10-11 AB. Pilate's authority was given to him because Jesus' death was necessary and foreordained for our redemption.

In foretelling his own death Jesus said, *"My Father loves me, because I lay down my life that I may take it again. No one takes it from me, but I lay it down of myself. I have power to lay it down, and I have power to take it again"* John 10:17-18 NKJV.

Although he isn't aware of the implications, Caiaphas has it right when he prophesies to the worried members of the Sanhedrin: *Being the high priest that year, he prophesied that Jesus was to die for the nation. And not only for the nation, but also for the purpose of uniting into one body the children of God who have been scattered far and wide. So from that day on they plotted together how they might put him to death* John 11:49-53 AB.

Jesus' death is the centrepiece of God's great deliverance plan. So he doesn't interfere as Satan sets up Jesus' betrayal through Judas, or as the ruling Jews demand his crucifixion, or as Pilate sends him to his death. It's a hotbed of mixed motivations, fuelled by fear and ambition and fanned by Satan. And God has coordinated it all.

The apostles recognised exactly what had happened. They prayed, *"Indeed Herod and Pontius Pilate met together with the Gentiles and the people of Israel in this city to conspire against your holy servant Jesus, whom you anointed. They did what your power and will had decided beforehand should happen."* Acts 4:27-28 NIV.

It's a divine sting operation! The Scripture says that if the rulers of this world had understood God's plan, *"they would never have crucified the Lord of Glory"* 1 Corinthians 2:8 AB. God allowed Satan to manipulate these influential people and bring about Jesus' death – and so orchestrate his own doom. Satan envisioned only Jesus' death; the resurrection and ascension – and our redemption – never entered his mind.

God and Governments

God can and does use governments either to bless or to chastise the people – or both. The books of Kings and Chronicles are the annals of God's dealings with Judah and Israel, based on the actions of their rulers. In chapter after chapter we see king after king, either obeying the Lord or walking in rebellion and causing the people to sin, and by their actions, bringing blessing or judgment on their nation. The Bible says, *"When the righteous are in authority, the people rejoice; but when a wicked man rules, the people groan"*. Proverbs 29:2 NKJV.

For example, let's look at King Asa of Judah. As Asa rides home from battle, Azariah, the prophet, runs out to meet him. "Listen to me," Azariah shouts, *"The Lord will stay with you as long as you stay with him! Whenever you look for him, you will find him. But if you forsake Him, he will forsake you."* 2 Chronicles 15:2 TLB. He warns the king that if the nation rebels against God, then God will plague them with trouble. War will come and crime will flourish.

Asa believes the prophet. He takes crucial action that not only keeps Judah out of trouble, but also sets a significant example for us: he leads the people in fervent repentance and God's judgment is averted. see 2 Chronicles 15:1-15

A President's Plea

US President Abraham Lincoln understood that when nations forget God, they reap judgment. He also understood that repentance and intercession bring mercy. He saw the biblical precedent of national leadership setting the example and sounding the call. Three times he issued proclamations for "A National Day of Humiliation, Fasting and Prayer." The proclamation for April 30, 1863 (written at the request of a unanimous US Senate) read in part:

> *"We know that by his divine law, nations, like individuals, are subject to punishments in this world, may we not justly fear that the calamity of civil war, which desolates the land, may be but a punishment inflicted upon us for our presumptuous sins, to the needful end of our national reformation as a whole people? We have been the recipients of the choicest bounties of heaven... We have grown in numbers, wealth, and power as no other nation has ever grown.*

> *But we have forgotten God. We have forgotten the gracious hand which preserved us in peace, and multiplied, enriched and strengthened us; and we have vainly imagined... that all these blessings were produced by some superior wisdom and virtue of our own. Intoxicated with unbroken success, we have become too self-sufficient to feel the necessity of redeeming and preserving grace, too proud to pray to the God that made us!*

> *It behoves us, then, to humble ourselves before the offended Power, to confess our national sins, and to pray for clemency and forgiveness".*

Mr Lincoln called for a day "holy to the Lord," dedicated to fasting and intercession, as the people suspended their normal pursuits and gathered in their churches and homes to seek God. His speech went on:

"... in the hope authorized by the Divine teachings, that the united cry of the Nation will be heard on high and answered with blessings, pardon of our national sins, and restoration of our now divided and suffering country, to its former happy condition of unity and peace".

Whether or not a nation receives such a call to repentance and intercession from its leadership, the Church has already received that very call from the head of another kingdom. He is waiting for us to stand between a disobedient nation and his own wrath.

Standing in the Gap

Aaron the high priest ran into the midst of the rebellious congregation of Israel as God began to pour out the discipline of death: *"For there is wrath gone out from the Lord; the plague has begun!"* Numbers 16:46 AB. Holding a censer of fire and incense, a symbol of prayer, he made atonement for them: *"And he stood between the dead and the living; and the plague was stayed"* v. 48 AB. Intercession is a part of the Church's duty as "priests unto God," just as it was a part of Aaron's priestly duty. see Revelation 1:6; 5:10.

The problem is the same today as it has been for centuries: the nations need to repent but, with a few historical exceptions, they don't. So God, in his mercy and love, listens for intercessors. Through them, the fate of nations can be changed. Without them, judgment will fall.

Confessing National Failures

Think of Moses, trembling and alone, standing between his guilt-laden people and a furious and dangerous God. Or Nehemiah, weeping, mourning and fasting for days for the restoration of his decimated nation. Or Daniel, an ongoing one-man prayer meeting and a powerful pattern for intercession for a nation. Chapters 9 and 10 of Daniel are outstanding examples of the effectiveness of the intercession of one righteous man.

Daniel's prayers were effective because he came with determination and humility: *"So I turned to the Lord God and pleaded with him in prayer and fasting."* Daniel 9:3 NLT. And he prayed the right kind of prayers: Young's Bible Concordance defines the word used for pray in 2 Chronicles 7:14 in this way: "to judge self, to pray habitually."

In other words, "If my people... will humble themselves, judge themselves, and pray habitually".

Daniel prayed by these principles:

1. He judged himself first. He confessed his own sins, not claiming any personal goodness, but throwing himself on the goodness of God for deliverance.
2. Then, he prayed habitually. Daniel didn't wait for days of desperation to sharpen up his prayer life; he was a prayer warrior with a disciplined spirit. And he hung on until he heard from heaven.
3. He named the specific sins of his nation and of the national leadership, confessing and repenting of them as if they were his own: *"O Lord, we and our kings, princes, and ancestors are covered with shame because we have sinned against you"* Daniel 9:8 NLT.

Nehemiah also identified himself with the sins of his nation when he prayed: *"O Lord God!... Look down and see me praying night and day for your people Israel. I confess that we have sinned against you; yes, I and my people have committed the horrible sin of not obeying [your] commandments"* Nehemiah 1: 5-7 TLB.

Daniel and Nehemiah's kind of "identification" praying brings dramatic results. Jesus, of course, is the greatest possible example, as he identified himself with the sins of a lost world and "stood in the gap" between us and the judgment of God.

Our nation, too, desperately needs faithful intercessors who will name her sins and repent of them on behalf of the people. And, like Daniel, we need to pray fervently for our leaders. We'll do this most successfully when we know how God wants us to pray for them.

Praying for the People with the Power

I Timothy 2:1-2 NLT says, *"I urge you, first of all, to pray for all people. As you make your requests, plead for God's mercy on them and give thanks. Pray this way for kings and for all others who are in authority, so that we can live in peace and quietness, in godliness and dignity. This is good and pleases God our Saviour, for he wants everyone to be saved and to understand the truth."*

Derek Prince, in his powerful book *Shaping History through Prayer and Fasting*, outlines this same Scripture in a series of simple, logical steps and tells why they're so important:

1. The first ministry and outreach of believers meeting together in regular fellowship is prayer.
2. The first specific topic for prayer is government.
3. We are to pray for good government.
4. God wants all men to have the gospel preached to them.
5. Good government facilitates the preaching of the gospel while bad government hinders it.
6. Therefore, good government is the will of God.

Good government provides freedom of speech and assembly, maintains law and order and allows unrestricted communication and travel. All these are vital to the spread of the gospel. So, God tells us to pray earnestly for good government so that people might be saved.

Satan, on the other hand, wants to keep people from hearing or responding to the gospel. So the diabolical puppet master uses unrighteous lawmakers and judges to restrict the influence of Christianity and the Bible, while "liberating" society into depravity through permissive legislation. The sex-for-sale and crime on our streets, the corruption in our government, the godlessness in our classrooms, and the titillating filth in films and television touch us all. When we're exposed to a culture where decadence is accepted so casually, we gradually become hardened to it.

The Bible says, *"Beware then of your own hearts, dear brothers, lest you find that they, too, are evil and unbelieving and are leading you away from the Living God. Speak to each other... every day while there is still time, so that none of you will become hardened against God, being blinded by the glamour of sin"* Hebrews 3:12,13 TLB.

Like Lot, living in Sodom, who was *"a good man, sick of the terrible wickedness he saw around him day after day"* 2 Peter 2:8 TLB, shouldn't we be sickened to the heart by the vileness in our culture? If we're not, shouldn't we ask ourselves why we aren't offended by the things God hates? If Christians – especially intercessors – become hardened and uncaring, Satan has won and our society is lost.

Intercessors are the lifeline of the Church and the nation as they pray for those in authority, plead for God's mercy on them, and give thanks for what God is going to do for them. We can pray down God's salvation on them, rather than his judgment. These are prayers from the heart of God who wants everyone to come to repentance and to the knowledge of the truth.

Not only do we need to pray for those in authority, we need also to let them know we're out here and we're paying attention to what they do. They don't need hate letters and ugliness from us; they need strong but sensible and civil opinions. They need encouragement and correction from concerned citizens.

The Church has the responsibility to speak out and to pray that our legislators will stop legalizing sin, or to ask God for new lawmakers who will, before our national unrighteousness becomes our ruin see Ezekiel 18:30.

The Ball is in Our Court

Summing up what we've just discussed about praying for government, we know that:

- "There is no government anywhere that God has not put in power," either to bless or to chastise.
- "The Most High rules in the kingdoms of the world and gives them to anyone he chooses."
- Good government is his will because it serves the spread of the gospel.
- "He will listen to us whenever we ask him for anything in line with his will"
  1 John 5:14 NLT

This means that God is willing to move on behalf of the nation. And since he always moves in cooperation with his praying people, that puts the ball directly in our court.

But now that we've convinced you to intercede for the government, we have to hit you with these famous words: "But wait! There's more!" Government is only one area of influence that impacts our lives and demands our intercession. Loren Cunningham, founder of Youth With A Mission, (YWAM) has identified what he calls the seven mind-moulders of society:

The battle for the soul of a nation rages in all of these institutions. Our intercession – or our apathy – will determine which kingdom rules in our society.

- Family
- Government
- Media
- Education·
- Business
- Religion
- Arts and Entertainment

Here's our prayer on behalf of the above seven institutions in our nation:

Prayer of Intercession for the Nation

Father, on behalf of our nation, we confess that we have offended you disgracefully with our ungodliness. We as a nation have become thankless, rebellious and unclean. We've ignored your guidance and spurned your presence. We've become a hedonistic, violent, greedy people. Our foolishness has led us to the brink of destruction. O God, forgive us and deliver us! We pray earnestly, desperately and expectantly for a massive spiritual awakening and transformation in our nation.

Father, bless and move upon all the leaders of our nation. Stir and transform their minds and make them righteous and wise. Pull down from power those with inflexible hearts who set their faces against you. Replace them with those who will be led by your Spirit and your principles. Give these new leaders wisdom, courage and grace. Protect them and their families from every ungodly influence and attack. Bless and prosper them, and bring their righteous plans to fruition.

Establish truth in our educational systems and give us godly teachers and educators who will be righteous role models for our children. Remove those who bring immorality, heresy or occultism into our classrooms.

Give us integrity, fairness and truth in our news media.

Bring righteous judgment in our courts, with equal justice for everyone in our society. Particularly in our High Courts and in Parliament bring your influence to bear.

Bring righteous laws onto the Statute Book of this nation because your Word tells us that righteousness exalts a nation.

Move sovereignly in the media and arts and entertainment industries. Pull down the ungodly and raise up men and women of your choice in this arena of unprecedented influence. Redeem it for your own; let it encourage righteousness and be a tool for spiritual growth.

Heal our homes and cement our family relationships with your love. Fill our homes with wisdom, fairness, compassion, affection, and fun.

Restore our blighted inner cities to places of safety. Send the Holy Spirit through your churches to save the lost, help the poor, heal the sick, deliver the addicted: to bind up the broken-hearted, and to give hope to those in despair.

Deliver the children who are subjected to abuse and fear and who are led into sin by those who should be their defenders. Protect them with your angels, Father, and heal their wounded hearts.

Help us, with wisdom, power and love, to regain the liberties the church has lost to those who neither know nor respect you.

Protect and encourage the Christian heroes of our nation; those who face threats of persecution as they confront the viciousness of entrenched depravity in their given arenas of influence. Heal the soul of our nation. May it truly be a righteous nation, filled with your glory.

Amen.

Talk About This:

1. What would make God change his mind about blessing - or not blessing - a nation? p55
2. How do you feel about the scriptural principle that God controls governments?
3. Do you believe that God pays attention to what is going on in a nation and deals with it accordingly? By what standard?
4. Is Daniel and Nehemiah's practice of identifying with the sins of the nation a valid one for the church? p61 What sins might you confess on behalf of your country?
5. Why is good government important for evangelisation? p56
6. How should we pray for all who are in authority? What should our prayer attitude be? p55

Pray About This:

a. If you are in a group you can divide up the Prayer of Intercession for the Nation on p63. Or you can pray it alone, a few sections at a time and let it be a springboard for your own concerns about the country. It touches on many issues and will help you cover them all.
b. Ask for wisdom and righteousness for your local officials.
c. Pray for the Prime Minister and his advisers.

Chapter 9 - Life Intercession

"Righteousness and justice are the foundation of your throne;
Mercy and truth go before your face." Psalm 89:14 NKJV

Life intercession involves Spirit-led action. It is what we do, other than prayer, to extend the boundaries of the Kingdom of God within our sphere of influence. It is involvement at a practical and loving level that will change our society gradually yet profoundly. Along with our fasting and prayer, it's what real intercession is all about. It will help keep our cities from exploding and give our witness credibility. It is right and righteous and we need to get involved quickly.

Although we need to act individually whether or not others respond, these things are done most successfully as a cooperative outreach by the Church. This won't happen without pastoral leadership. There is something vital here that many preachers are teaching and modelling to their people.

The Bible says, *"Pure and lasting religion in the sight of God our Father means that we must care for orphans and widows in their trouble, and refuse to let the world corrupt us"* James 1:27 NLT. Jesus said that at the judgment he will separate the people according to whether they have shown mercy to the poor and needy see Matthew 25:31-46. He said, *"When you refused to help the least of these my brothers, you were refusing to help me"* v 45 TLB. Judgment will be meted out accordingly. We don't know what this does to your doctrine, but it certainly shows what is important to the heart of God.

Justice and Mercy: God's Other Prescription for National Healing

Most Christians today are aware of God's gracious promise, in 2 Chronicles 7:14, of the healing of a land in answer to self-humbling, prayer, seeking God's face and repentance. But we need to understand another vital Scripture as well.

In Isaiah 58: 6-12 (greatly condensed and paraphrased) God says to Israel, "You've been praying and fasting, and you wonder why I haven't been answering." He continues, "If you want me to hear you, you must do these things: Put away quarrelling and pointing the finger" (of division) "break every yoke" (of injustice and oppression,) "feed the hungry, house the homeless, clothe the naked." Does that sound like a word to the modern Church? And do our failures in this regard hinder the hearing of our prayers and the healing of our land?

God goes on to say, "*Then* – when you do these things – you will call, and I will say, 'Here I am!' And your light will break forth like the dawn, and your *healing* will quickly appear. And you will raise up the *foundations* of many generations and rebuild your walls and cities."

For too long one part of the Church has said, "The gospel is concerned only with individual salvation," while deriding another for "the social gospel. "Isn't the Holy Spirit saying, "God is concerned with both?" Instead of saying to a poor mother worried about feeding her children, "God loves you; be warmed and filled," (while handing her a tract) isn't it better to say, "God loves you, and he has sent us in Jesus' name to help you and to bring you good news"?

Isn't it better to support those ministries that minister to HIV/AIDS victims and AIDS orphans than to pretend the problem doesn't exist?

God calls us not only to show mercy but to show justice as well: *"Speak up for those who cannot speak for themselves, for the rights of all who are destitute. Speak up and judge fairly; defend the rights of the poor and needy"* Proverbs 31:8,9 NIV. That first line: *"Speak up for those who cannot speak for themselves"* could also be a mandate for us to speak up for the most defenceless of all – the pre-born.

Pastor Rick Warren sent an open letter to President Bush saying, "I deeply believe that if we as evangelicals remain silent and do not speak up in defence of the poor, we lose our credibility and our right to witness about God's love for the world." Billy Graham and John R Stott endorsed the letter, which was sent to more than 150,000 evangelicals throughout the US. The National Association of Evangelicals in the USA is urging members to begin addressing global poverty and all its related ills.[7]

Many may be surprised to read that the sins that caused God to destroy Sodom were more than just the one sin that takes its name from that city: *"Now this was the sin of your sister Sodom: She and her daughters were arrogant, overfed and unconcerned; they did not help the poor and needy. They were haughty and did detestable things before me. Therefore I did away with them as you have seen"* Ezekiel 16:49-50 NIV.

Can't the affluent suburban church come alongside the inner-city ministries and *together* be about the business of healing and winning our society? Can't we help them help the needy, defend the weak, bind up the wounded, and by doing this, present the gospel to people who might not otherwise receive from us? As *together* we become "God's love in the flesh," we fulfil his conditions given in Isaiah 58. *Then* we will cry, and our fasting and prayers will be heard. *Then* we will see renewal in the church, awakening in our society, and the healing of our land.

Prayer or Action? How About Both?

In the struggle for righteousness, intercessory prayer and Spirit-led action are two sides of the same coin – action initiated and covered by prayer; prayer backed and followed by action. What if a farmer knelt and prayed for a crop, but never planted; or a general prayed for victory, but never fought; or a runner prayed to win, but never ran? There are situations where we're only called to pray, but somebody (not everybody) has to be on the front line. There are times when we may find it's our turn.

Thank God for the brave souls who have thrown themselves into the arena to wrestle against the forces of moral decay. But activism without prayer cover is like infantry without air cover. It's like David going to fight Goliath, but without the power of God to make his arm strong and his aim sure.

In short, activism without prayer is a battle plan for a losing battle. This is because our real foes are not flesh and blood (human influence and ingenuity) but ancient and crafty beings who have waged their war against mankind since the inception of the race, and who are equipped with a formidable array of weapons, snares and deceptions see Ephesians 6:12.

So before we enter the fray brandishing placards, shouting slogans and bristling with righteous indignation, we need to learn to fight the spiritual battle in prayer. There we receive strategy, armour and air cover for our daily ground skirmishes, and the weapons of wisdom, grace and love to defeat our spiritual foes. Only as our actions are covered by persistent prayer will they accomplish the purposes of God.

We see an Old Testament picture of this in Exodus: When the Israelites were attacked by the Amalekites, Joshua led the counterattack while Moses stood on the top of the hill holding the rod of God in his hand.

> "And so it was, when Moses held up his hand, that Israel prevailed; and when he let down his hand, Amalek prevailed. But Moses' hands became heavy; so they took a stone and put it under him, and he sat on it. And Aaron and Hur supported his hands, one on one side, and the other on the other side; and his hands were steady until the going down of the sun. So Joshua defeated Amalek and his people with the edge of the sword" Exodus 17:11-13 NIV.

This is a picture to us of two layers of intercession: Aaron and Hur interceding for Moses by holding up his hands, and Moses interceding for Joshua and his men by holding up his rod, the embodiment of the authority of God. Without this "air cover" the entire Jewish race, all of whom were present there in the desert, might have ceased to exist. God will move just as surely for us, too, if we work together in determined prayer and righteous action.

Getting Involved

The Lausanne Covenant calls us to practical ministry with the words: "We affirm that evangelism and socio-political involvement are both parts of our Christian duty. For both are necessary expressions of our doctrines of God and man, our love for our neighbour and our obedience to Jesus Christ. The message of salvation implies also a message of judgment upon every form of alienation, oppression and discrimination, and we should not be afraid to denounce evil and injustice wherever they exist."

We *must* get involved in the struggle for righteousness and justice in our nation. To do the job, we must be aware of what's happening in our churches, schools, courts and governments. Intercession is not a cop-out that allows us to remain safely at home, praying, if God is calling us to carry the struggle to the streets, the courts or the political arena. When we don't do our part in the process of running our society, we get just what we deserve. When we don't set the standards and determine the game plan, we find ourselves operating under someone else's agenda.

Then we have to dig out entrenched and determined opponents. We, the citizens, are still the deciding voice in our country, but if we're not informed, we won't know who the good guys are and which rascals to throw out.

Politics: A Dirty Word?

Politics... There's that dirty word again. Many Christians have said, "Politics is dirty. Let's stay out of it." We believe the Holy Spirit is saying, "Politics is dirty. Let's get in it and clean it up."

"But," some say, "this world is not my home – I'm only passing through." That's a warm fuzzy thought, but it's not entirely true. For the time being this world is your home, specifically the country where God has placed you, and you have some responsibility for what happens in it.

The great nineteenth century evangelist Charles Finney wrote, "Politics is a part of religion in such a country as this, and Christians must do their duty to the country as a part of their duty to God... He will bless or curse this nation according to the course they take [in politics]."

Bill Bright, founder of Campus Crusade for Christ International said, "Citizenship in a free country is a blessing from God. Self-government assures every Christian a voice in the affairs of the nation. God wants us to do his will in government, just as in the church and in the home. But we have disobeyed our Lord... As a result, the moral fibre of our country is rotting away – and our priceless freedom is in grave jeopardy... We are in danger of losing our nation by default, and with it our individual freedoms and possibly our very lives. If that should happen, our opportunity to help fulfil the Great Commission throughout the nation and the world will also be lost. And hundreds of millions will never have the opportunity to receive our Saviour."

The very least we can do is vote. This is not a privilege to be taken lightly; it's a right that has been bought and sustained for us with much blood and sacrifice. To disdain and ignore it is to dishonour those who have paid that price. If we don't study the issues and vote for righteous leaders, we have no right to complain when unrighteousness is legislated.

President Thomas Jefferson wrote, "We in America do not have government by the majority. We in America have government by the majority of those who participate." This is true of every democracy. We choose our government. It is our chance to stand up for righteous leadership. If professing Christians neglect to vote they have little right to complain.

Many younger citizens, except for the "usual suspects" – the university radicals – especially are intellectually and emotionally divorced from what is going on in the world. They're more likely to watch TV soaps than the news, more likely to vote for a "Britain Has Talent" or a "Strictly Come Dancing" contestant than vote at the polls to help save our national soul. Apparently many of them get their news from talk show comedians.

Too many people, young and old, are obsessed with fashion, music, sports, computer games and making money. Unfortunately, that includes many in the Church.

Can you imagine what your country might be like by now if all Christians had decided to forfeit the running of it because politics was dirty? On the other hand, can you imagine what it would be like if all Christians became informed and participated? Can't we begin right now? Right here? Of course we can! We have wonderful opportunities to transform our society.

It's vital for Christians in a democracy not only to pray for those in authority, but also for many educated, righteous and prepared people to become those in authority.

But why does it matter if an elected person is a Christian? Isn't it enough if he or she is a sincere, well-meaning, intelligent person trying to do what's right? That's certainly a great start, but isn't it better to have people with a biblical worldview that underlies their decision-making?

There are some fine people in government who don't profess to know Christ but who are people of good will. But good will, without the rudder of the will of God, can become tolerant of laws and lifestyles that directly oppose God's will. And God is very serious about his principles. He made sure they were written down so there would be no mistake. Yet in the name of good will toward all, some of our lawmakers have agreed to abandon that sure rudder and, as a result, the ship of state sails on toward the rocks.

Especially in times of great national crisis, leaders who hear from God and are able to receive wisdom from above are essential. An ungodly person might say, "No way! I don't want some crazy religious crank who claims to hear from God representing me!" But we wish every public servant would talk with God and hear from him. Isn't that what prayer is – asking and receiving? God says, "Call on me and I will answer you, and show you great and mighty things which you do not know" Jeremiah 33:3. God offers wisdom to those who ask for it. He offers to guide our leaders in the governing process.

Do we really want public officials who consider themselves so wise that they don't need God's wisdom? Do we want leaders to whom their faith means so little that they would leave it out of their decision-making? Although a person may have great learning and wisdom in the eyes of the world, the Scripture says, *"The wisdom of this world is foolishness with God"* 1 Corinthians 3:19 NKJV. *"The fear of the Lord is the beginning of wisdom, and the knowledge of the Holy One is understanding"* Proverbs 9:10 NKJV.

Looking Through the Right Lens

Why is it that two reasonably intelligent people, given the same facts, can come to opposite conclusions where matters of righteousness are concerned? The Bible gives us an answer:

"A man who is unspiritual refuses what belongs to the Spirit of God; it is folly to him, he cannot grasp it, because it needs to be judged in the light of the Spirit. A man gifted with the Spirit can judge the worth of everything" I Corinthians 2:14, 15a NEB. *"But we can understand these things, because we have the mind of Christ"* verse 16b NLT.

The Holy Spirit is the instrument or means by which we understand the things of God. If you were a scientist trying to convince a sceptical layman of the existence of microscopic life, you would be hard put to do it without a microscope. But once he has the proper instrument, a whole new world opens up to him. Just so, the Holy Spirit, who comes to live within us when we open our hearts to the Lord, is given to reveal the things of God to us. see 1 Corinthians 2:9-16.

The Scripture explains: *"Satan, the god of this evil world, has blinded the minds of those who don't believe"* 2 Corinthians 4:4 NLT. Another Scripture calls Satan *"the spirit that works in the hearts of those who refuse to obey God"* Ephesians 2:2 NLT. Contrast that with *"It is God who works in you to will and to act according to his good purpose"* Philippians 2:13 NIV. People without Christ may have brilliant minds; they may understand the legalities and business aspects of running a government, but they lack the ability to recognise the spiritual realities behind the visible, and they don't have access to the guidance of the indwelling Holy Spirit. They aren't looking through the right lens.

Think of some of the society-forming moral issues facing our country right now, and the international perils that menace us. All other things being equal, would you rather have a believer or an unbeliever representing you? Your vote will help make that choice.

This, of course, is not always possible. In some elections there is no believer standing for office. It also makes our decision more difficult when a candidate professes to be a Christian but continues quietly to espouse unrighteous causes. We pray; we vote – but sometimes we get fooled. If you don't know where a candidate stands spiritually, at least find out where he or she stands righteously. Look beyond the rhetoric and check the record.

We don't mean to imply that God can't use the unconverted to bring about his will. God can use anybody or anything. He might raise up an unbeliever and use that person in an unexpected way, with or without conversion, and with or without that person's understanding that God is using him. No Christian would have had the prescience to vote for Saul of Tarsus (who was later to become the great Apostle Paul) if he had been standing for office. But God knows things that we don't. So our job is to ask him for his leading as we study, check it out, and vote.

Check It Out

Too many election campaigns deteriorate to the level of food fights and dirty tricks. Not only are they childish and uncivil, but also they make the truth hard to find. We need to take those election-time rumours with a grain of salt, especially the stuff that gets forwarded to us by email or published in garish capitals on the internet.

For example, during one American presidential election, several of these "news sources" reported a true story about a speech that our daughter, Jamie, actually saw on television. Evidently the candidate's polls – or his tea leaves – told him it would be to his advantage to appear religious, so he piously shared that his favourite bible verse was John 16:3. Obviously he meant John 3:16, which every Christian recognises: *"For God so loved the world that he gave his only begotten son, that whosoever believeth in him should not perish but have everlasting life."* But the numbers came out wrong. In John 16:3, Jesus says, *"And these things they will do to you because they have not known the Father or me."* Oops.

The report of this blunder was circulated gleefully far and wide by word of mouth and email. The only problem was... the same story, in the same words, was also attributed to the offending politician's opponent and two candidates in other elections.

We should pray over our elections – that God will help us elect legislators who are righteous and wise; that he will save those who are lost, that he will pull down those who adamantly refuse his grace and legislate ungodliness. If we do this with faith and patience, just watch! God will work!

Government and the New Testament

What does the New Testament say about government? Apart from exhortations to obey the government because God has put it there, and to pay taxes and honour rulers, it doesn't say much. The apostles didn't write inflammatory things about the Roman government that might have got them and their people into unnecessary trouble. Some Christians question the need of involvement, citing the Scripture, *"Don't get tied up in worldly affairs"* see 2 Timothy 2:4 TLB. But abdicating our responsibility for our government is not what that Scripture means. Where we are free to influence government, God holds us to account for our nation's wellbeing.

Some insist, "But Jesus didn't get involved with government." No, he didn't. Jesus' calling was far greater than challenging Rome. He came for the express purpose of dying and establishing a Kingdom that would ultimately rule over all the governments of earth. He explained that clearly to people who wanted him to be a revolutionary. But Jesus' influence was powerful in the physical and political world. His life brought his witness before governing authorities and its influence eventually triumphed over the Roman Empire.

"But the apostles and the early church didn't try to affect government." No, because they had no voice in government. They were subjugated by a foreign power. They were not called to overthrow Rome, but to spread the Kingdom of God to the uttermost parts of the earth. Soon after the birth of the Church, they were few, scattered, and persecuted, and their efforts were focused on survival and on this one cause.

"But," some argue, "the Apostle Paul came with one purpose only – 'to know nothing except Christ and him crucified.'" True. We are all to share our faith, but this doesn't mean that every believer is to specialise in nothing but evangelism.

God has distributed different gifts and callings among us see 2 Corinthians chapter 12. The Church as a whole is called to permeate every area of society. We are responsible to maintain righteous influence and to blockade corruption and darkness.

Paul told Timothy to have the church pray for government so they could have conditions conducive to the spread of the gospel see 1 Timothy 2:1-6. Timothy's people had no voice in government; prayer was their only resource. In any country prayer is our most important resource, too; but in a democracy we also have a choice and a voice! We need to use them so we won't lose them. If we remain silent and evil overtakes us, are we not as guilty as the servant who hid his talent and lost everything? see Matthew 25:14-30. If we see corruption growing and don't try to stop it, are we not like the farmer who sees his field being taken over by weeds but does nothing about it? Soon there will be no harvest. His field will be taken from him and given to another.

We are responsible for preserving the freedoms God and our forefathers gave us. We are to spread the Kingdom of God by pushing back the kingdom of darkness wherever it manifests itself. In government, entertainment, education, or wherever it rears its ugly head – that becomes our spiritual battlefield.

Joseph and Daniel were sovereignly placed in government by God. Esther was given a place of governmental influence. John the Baptist raised his voice against corrupt government and lost his life in the struggle. But he was acting under the calling of God. Many of the prophets spoke against corruption in government. God gave each of these a voice and authority to affect a nation: many were persecuted and some died for it. We Christians in democracies have it easy. If we fail because we've chosen not to try, how will we answer for it?

Praying for Our Courts

The courts are another vital prayer consideration for the Church. They have to deal with agencies fighting with all their might to legalise every evil under the sun, including child pornography and pederasty.[8]

Some say that Christians are so sexually repressed that they can't stand to see other people enjoying sexual freedom. But sexual "freedom" has led to disease, violent abuse and slavery. God has clearly explained the way sex is supposed to work in order to bring joy and fulfilment rather than addiction, ruined lives and death. And God isn't kidding about his rules. When our lawmakers and judges ignore him, they are opening up the nation for judgment. Christians know this. Therefore, to "rebuild the wall of righteousness, which guards the land" they oppose laws and interpretations that give free rein to immorality.

And the battle goes on. One illustrious American senator has stated publicly: "Candidates with deeply held Christian beliefs are unfit and disqualified for serving as federal judges". Actually, it was this senator who had things backwards. God, who created us and ordained the formation of America, made the rules long ago.

We find them in the last words of King David: *"The Spirit of the Lord spoke by me, and his word was on my tongue... **He who rules over men must be just, ruling in the fear of God.** And he shall be like the light of the morning; when the sun rises; a morning without clouds; like the tender grass springing out of the earth; by clear shining after rain."* 2 Samuel 23:2-3 NKJV

According to the Word of God, it's the person who does not have the fear of God who is unfit to be a ruler, which is in a sense what judges and officials are – they rule (make rulings) over men. This senator, by his own words, has revealed himself as unqualified to rule. Shall we Christians stay out of politics "because it's dirty" and leave it to people like this to make and interpret our laws? Or shall we do what we can to replace them with those who will rule in the fear of God?

Laws are meant to build protective walls around a society. No law can make people righteous; but laws are necessary to restrain unrighteousness and influence public behaviour. Sin will spread as far and as fast as it is allowed to. So when the law says, "Anything goes," the walls come down and we soon have moral anarchy, because people have sinful hearts. Only God can change what's on the inside.

But the law is there to protect us from our own worst selves and from one another. We can't afford to have ungodly judges and officials with the power to take down those walls.

We can pray for God to "pull down the ungodly and raise up the righteous" see Psalm 75:7. On the other hand, we can simply pray that he will save and bless them.

That's even better, and God, who wants all to be saved, will love that prayer. We must answer to God for how we vote. If we elect ungodly rulers, they will make ungodly rulings, and the ungodliness could go on for decades, long after their terms of office are over.

What Price Homosexuality?

What is God's attitude toward the homosexual lifestyle? see Romans 1:24-28, 1 Corinthians 6:9-11. God wants to see us freed from our sins and he offers forgiveness to all of us, regardless of what our sins are. *"The Lord... Is being patient for your sake. He does not want anyone to perish, so he is giving more time for everyone to repent"* 2 Peter 3:9 NLT. A repentant homosexual who turns from his or her ways will be saved through the grace of God as surely as any other sinner. So those of us whose sins fall into other categories should feel compassion for those who are caught up in this bondage, but we must not minimize its peril.

We can't repeat too often that the struggle with corrupting influences in our world is really against spiritual enemies, unseen and unrecognised. They still present us with all manner of forbidden fruit. All of us are susceptible to temptation and at some point we all fail. Nobody is free to cast stones. In 1 Corinthians 6:9-11 the Apostle Paul points to some of the sins that keep people from the Kingdom of God. Then, before Christians can get self-righteous, he points the finger in our direction: *"and such were some of you!"* and so would we still be except for the forgiveness and cleansing that Jesus brings.

It doesn't mean we can't name sin for what it is; it means that we don't pronounce *sentence* on (judge) one another, because God hasn't finished redeeming people yet.

Our purpose isn't to bring a tirade against sinners. God actually does love sinners, all of us, and he looks for us with open arms. What we want to address here is the political machine of radical activists who want a society where they are free to pursue, and to perpetuate, their forbidden lifestyles. Legalised sin is the goal. At this point, the church needs to let her voice be heard in heaven, and in the public arena as well. There are a number of organisations doing everything possible to prevent that from happening.

They want laws that will:

- *change the very meaning of marriage and family*
- *compel adoption agencies to place children with same-sex couples*
- *force indoctrination of all school children in the homosexual lifestyle... "Don't knock it until you've tried it. Here's how", without parental consent or notification.*
- *compel churches to hire homosexual staff and perform same-sex "marriages"*
- *Criminalise any public criticism of homosexual behaviour as "hate speech." (Unfortunately, some of it is hateful. People who are guilty of this don't understand the heart of Christ who ate with sinners and got rough only with religious hypocrites). If this "criminalisation" plan succeeds, your pastor could be fined and imprisoned for reading*

aloud an anti-homosexual passage from the Scriptures! At least two pastors, one in Sweden and one in Canada, have already had to defend themselves at great cost against this charge. In Britain our Parliament came within a single vote of passing such a law and there is no doubt that the homosexual lobby will try again at some point. Christians need to be alert at all times – to watch and pray.

This axis represents a grave danger to our culture.

In Britain the homosexual lobby issued a 'manifesto' in 1972 stating that "the family, as the chief source of our oppression, must be destroyed".

In America those who dare oppose the demands of this agenda have been threatened with expulsion from school, loss of employment, fines, prison, loss of sole custody of their children, and other violations of our inalienable, God-given rights.[9]

This should be a wakeup call like the blaring of a klaxon. It's one of the most serious assaults our religious freedoms have ever faced, and it is already happening in some other countries. Concerned citizens must fight this fight for the sake of our nation and our children.

But what, you ask, can I do about all these ills of society? Be encouraged; together, we can do a lot. We'll make concrete suggestions in coming chapters.

---

[7] Religion Journal.com 6/13/06.

[8] sex between a man and a boy.

[9] Alan Sears, Alliance Defence Fund.

Talk About This:

1. How would you define "life intercession"? p67

2. What are some of the concerns in our society that we could be involved in solving? How? Do you think these concerns matter to God? p67

3. Does your church support Christian Concern for Our Nation? Go on line http://www.ccfon.org/ and request their weekly newsletter and pray through current issues.

4. Ask to be put on the mailing list of the Christian Institute http://www.christian.org.uk/ and pray about the issues they highlight in their newsletters.

5. Should Christians be involved in the struggle for righteousness and justice in our nation? How can we do this? p69

6. Should Christians be involved in the political system? How? p72

7. Has the book enhanced your understanding of the structure and power of our court systems? How do you feel about that? p74

8. How should we pray for our judges?

Pray About This:

a. Ask God for wisdom and instruction as to how you (or your group) can become engaged in the "life intercession" that is so important to him. Tell him you are available!

b. Pray for the men and women everywhere who are giving their lives to winning the lost and ministering to the poor.

c. Pray for God to raise up truly righteous people in our political system, and to pull down those who actively legislate ungodliness.

d. Pray for the Judges in our nation, by name, if you can

PART 4

FIGHTING THE FIGHT

Who can snatch the plunder of war from the hands of a warrior?

Who can demand that a tyrant let his captives go?

But the Lord says, "The captives of warriors will be released, and the plunder of tyrants will be retrieved. For I will fight those who fight you, and I will save your children."

Isaiah 49:24-25 NLT

The monks have no sadness. They wage war on the devil as though they were performing a dance.

John Chrysostom

Chapter 10 - Intercession: A Call to War

Onward, Christian soldiers, marching as to war,

With the cross of Jesus going on before.

Christ, the royal master, leads against the foe;

Forward into battle, see his banners go!

Sabine Baring-Gould

When we commit to evangelism, prayer and life intercession, it means we're interfering radically in the plans of God's great enemy. Isn't that wonderful?

It also means we're probably in for a struggle. Statesman/writer SD Gordon said, "The greatest agency [God has] put in man's hands is prayer. And to define prayer, one must use the language of war. Peace language is not equal to the situation. The earth is in a state of war and is being hotly besieged. Thus one must use war talk to grasp the facts with which prayer is concerned. Prayer from God's side is communication between himself and his allies in enemy country."

What is the war in the spirit really all about? Some Christians don't want to hear about it at all. It sounds spooky and frightening. We once met a pastor's wife who flapped her hands and said, "Oh no! I don't want to hear anything about the devil. I just want to hear about Jesus." That would be nice, wouldn't it? But we're all going to hear from the devil whether we want to or not. We'll be better equipped to deal with him if we know more *about* him.

Unfortunately, the term, "spiritual warfare" has got a bad name because of some weird and extravagant behaviour by some of its practitioners. And, truth be known, Satan has probably had a hand in discrediting it as well, even as he has tried to keep people ignorant of his very existence. We hope to bring a balanced perspective to the subject.

The concept takes its name from passages such as 2 Corinthians 10:4, which says, *"The weapons of our warfare are not carnal, but mighty through God to the pulling down of strongholds"* KJV and Paul's vivid description in Ephesians chapter 6 of a believer putting on armour and taking up various weapons of war against spiritual enemies.

The objective of this struggle is not to fight the devil or demon powers but to save souls – souls under siege. These are the spoils we wrest from the enemy and carry home to the King. World evangelisation is the cry of God's heart and the great, unfinished calling of the Church. However, the goal won't be reached without intense struggle. Propagating the gospel is a declaration of war – not against people, but against Satan and his works, and it spawns bitter spiritual opposition.

As in any war, part of our work is offensive and part is defensive. Offence is about taking back territory and rescuing souls in bondage to the devil. Defence is about ridding society of Satan's corrupting influences that lead people into sin, and getting rid of evils that bring the judgment of God on our land.

"Resist the devil and he will flee from you" James 4:7 is defence. So part of our job is to restrain the work of Satan while God's work of redemption is being completed. With proper preparation we can do this job without heaviness or fear.

"On this rock I will build my church, and the gates of hell shall not prevail against it" Matthew 16:18 is offence. Gates are stationary; it's the besieging army, the Church, that's on the move. To use a sports analogy, some of us, according to our gifts and callings, may find the Trainer using us mostly on Offence, and others may find themselves on the Defensive team, although any of us might be assigned to either role on occasion.

The Church has a heritage of hymns about our warfare: "Onward Christian Soldiers," "Am I a Soldier of the Cross?", "Lead On, O King Eternal," "Stand Up, Stand Up for Jesus," but we don't hear them much anymore. That's understandable: some of the music is archaic, but the fact that few modern songs are written or sung on that subject may be testimony to our softness today.

The Holy Spirit, working through the Church, is the *restraining hand* that prevents immediate world control by Satan see 2 Thessalonians 2:3-8. As long as we live in this world, we need to be about our part in this ongoing work, a potent force that is a threat to Satan's plans of world domination. As Professor Peter Beyerhaus said, "Any advancement of the kingdom of Christ takes place by successive dethronement of Satan."

Dethroning the Devil

When we speak of dethroning Satan, we don't mean his final defeat when Jesus returns. We're talking about the dethronement that comes as the Church progressively takes back enemy territory and wreaks havoc in his camp. There is one problem: Most of us are peace-loving souls who prefer God's green pastures and still waters to armies and banners and battlefields. You may even want to take exception to St. Paul, who refers to Christians as soldiers see 2 Timothy 2:3. Certainly few of us are the prepared, dedicated warriors God longs for – ready to give everything and take whatever comes. We'd like to skip the parts about suffering. We'd prefer not to hear God say, *"Do not let yourself become tied up in worldly affairs, for then you can't satisfy the one who has enlisted you in his army."* 2 Timothy 2:1,3-4 TLB.

Real dedication calls for major changes in focus and attitude. Satan is *"the god of this world"* 2 Corinthians 4:4 and *"the ruler of the darkness of this world"* see Ephesians 6:12. The Scripture also calls him *"the prince of the power of the air, the spirit who now works in the sons of disobedience"* Ephesians 2:2 NKJV. He controls how the world thinks and behaves. If we're living by the world's mindset and values, we'll be too vulnerable to the enemy to be useful to God.

The Bible says, *"Don't copy the behaviour and customs of this world, but let God transform you into a new and different person by changing the way you think"* Romans 12:2a NLT. Another translation says, *"Don't let the world squeeze you into its mould."*

Give God control of everything you are and have. Then you can fearlessly resist the devil in Jesus' name. (Martin Luther once heaved an inkwell at him, but we don't recommend that method.) Just tell him who you are, who you serve and who your God is: the creative, sustaining and ruling force of the universe, who is the final authority in heaven and earth. And you are his representative. Say so! Sometimes resisting the devil isn't a matter of struggle and debate but simply of non-response to his first whispers of temptation, avoiding trouble before it starts. Ogden Nash, a poet with a shrewd but cockeyed view of human nature, put it succinctly: "When called by a panther, don't anther."

Recognising the Enemy

It would make our job easier if the devil always showed up instantly recognisable, but he doesn't just walk in and hand us his business card:

**B. L. ZEBUB and Associates
Wrecking Company
Demolition Experts**

"U Build it, We'll knock it down."
Help Wanted 01-666-GET-LOST

But if we look out of our window and see our spiritual foundations being surrounded by hardhats with jackhammers, bulldozers and a wrecking ball, we know whose people they are.

Some see the devil as a cartoon character in a red suit with horns and a tail and a pitchfork. Some believe he is simply a myth or a metaphor for evil, but the prophets, the apostles and Jesus himself say that Satan is a real, live spiritual being. He was once a mighty archangel, who led a host of angels into rebellion against God, and was cast out of heaven see Revelation 12:3-4, 7-9.

"How you are fallen from heaven, O Lucifer, son of the morning!' Isaiah 14:12 NKJV. 'Lucifer' was the devil's name when he was a part of God's heaven. It is a regal name of splendour, but he is no longer worthy of the name. He is now Satan, and in our dealing with him we should never give him the dignity of the heavenly name"! [10]

Satan is the ruler of a cosmic kingdom, a hierarchy of evil beings bent on destroying the work of God. He introduced evil to the human race and continues to incite anarchy and hatred among men. He stirs enmity between individuals and instigates wars that kill millions. His life work is chaos and destruction.

Once we accept what Satan is, we must understand what he is not. Satan is not the opposite of God: the dark counterpart of The Force, all-knowing, all-powerful, ever-present evil. He is a created being with limited powers, who can be in only one place at a time.

Only rarely will he bother personally with most of us. Unless we're doing major damage to his kingdom, we'll probably be relegated to the attentions of lesser spiritual entities. In this book, however, we'll use the terms "Satan" or "the devil" in the generic sense of referring to any or all of his subordinates. To illustrate: In ministering deliverance to a sick woman, Jesus said that Satan had kept her bound for 18 years. Obviously, he didn't mean that Satan himself had spent 18 years harassing that one lady, but the spirit of infirmity that bound her was a representative of the devil's kingdom.

Unwelcome Company

Before we move on, let's mention a subject that has troubled many. Some years ago an argument raged among theologians over the question, Can a Christian have a Demon? Jack Hayford's witty response to this question was, "I suppose you could if you really want one." He then went on to defuse the argument by giving an answer so simple and logical that proponents of both sides of the question said, "That's what I've been trying to say."

He simply drew three concentric circles, like a target, representing – from the inside out – spirit, soul, and body. Then he drew a wedge through the two outer circles with its point touching but not penetrating the inner circle, or spirit. He made the point that a human spirit inhabited by the Holy Spirit cannot be possessed by a demon. But even a Christian may open the door to all kinds of satanic disturbances of the body and mind if we venture into Satan's territory through the occult, or drugs, or sexual sin, for example. Then the day may come when the devil, like a spider, springs the trap and says, "Gotcha!" We might not be Satan's "possession," but he will mercilessly oppress and harass us until we may need heavy-duty spiritual help in getting free. Avoid this at all costs.

But know that if you have fallen into this snare, as many in the church have, there is still hope. Read prayerfully the book of 1 John, more than once if necessary. You have a gracious God, who wants you to be free. The fear and darkness you feel is for your own good. If he allowed you to go on in that path without correction, the consequences could be catastrophic see Proverbs 3:11,12.

House Cleaning

Once we recognise the presence and work of this very real enemy, we can deal with him firmly and effectively and see tangible results.

We had just bought a broken down house at a bargain price. The former owners gave new meaning to the term "dysfunctional family": the rebellious, always-in-trouble teenagers had seriously trashed the place, the father had gone bankrupt and needed open-heart surgery, and finally, the mother had died there. The father and the kids were moving to Florida to start over.

We liked the house from the start, but the atmosphere was heavy, oppressive and uneasy. When we found occult books that had been left behind, we called in the troops – our church elders – to help us give the place a spiritual housecleaning.

This was our method:

- *We claimed the benefits of the blood of Jesus over us.*
- *We put on our spiritual armour* see Ephesians 6:10-20.
- *We went through all the rooms telling the enemy, in Jesus' name, that the Kingdom of God was moving in and he must move out.*
- *We invited the Holy Spirit to take up residence wherever any demonic powers had made their habitation.*
- *We took time in each room to give praise to God.*

A few days later two of our new neighbour ladies, one Jewish and one Catholic, dropped in for a get-acquainted visit. After some polite preliminary remarks, one of them burst out with, "What have you done in here?"

"What do you mean?" we asked.

"Well," said the other woman, "we don't mean to say anything out of line, but this place used to be... I don't know... creepy!"

"You did something, didn't you?" the first lady persisted.

We told them about our "housecleaning" method with the church elders. It all made perfect sense to them. They could feel the difference and they accepted it without question.

Then we had a visit from the eldest daughter of the previous owner. She had stayed in town to finish her senior year in high school. "I'm getting ready to go to Florida," she explained, "and I wonder if I could come in for one last look at the house before I go."

"Of course," we said, "Come on in."

The girl walked into the entry hall, chatting about her plans, then suddenly stopped dead in her tracks. Her eyes and her mouth flew wide open.

"You did it," she whispered.

"What? What did we do?"

"You did it. I can't believe it! You broke the jinx in this house, didn't you?"

She was dumbfounded that the demonic powers that had "jinxed" her family were bound and gone, and we were amazed that she had so instantly sensed their absence. Although she wasn't a Christian, she readily acknowledged that the power of Jesus Christ had radically changed things in that house. Our family lived there for four years, and it was a haven of peace, love and productivity. However, Satan's scope goes far beyond dysfunctional families and demon-infested houses. His influence is global and the battle is cosmic.

A Cosmic Confrontation

Like something straight out of a Frank Peretti novel, the mighty archangel Gabriel wages a titanic struggle to reach the prophet Daniel with an answer to prayer. You can almost hear the shriek of steel and see the flares of cosmic light as the mighty angel of God struggles with "the Prince of Persia," the powerful, malevolent spirit who rules over that kingdom. For three weeks Gabriel fights, but he can't break through. Then Michael, the "Prince of Israel," one of God's chief angelic warrior princes, streaks out of heaven to join Gabriel in the battle. Together they smash through the spiritual blockade. Moreover, after delivering his message to Daniel, Gabriel prepares to battle his way back again, past both the Prince of Persia and the Prince of Greece, where the angel prince, Michael, again will join him in the warfare, read Daniel chapter 10.

The Apostle Paul says that our enemies are not *"flesh and blood, but... persons without bodies – the evil rulers of the unseen world, those mighty satanic beings and great evil princes of darkness who rule this world, and... huge numbers of wicked spirits in the spirit world"* Ephesians 6:12. That's *The Living Bible's* version. Other translations refer to them as "world rulers," "despotisms," "cosmic powers," "potentates of the dark world," and "organisations and powers that are spiritual."

These titles affirm what Daniel learned – that Satan's kingdom is organised. So is God's angelic kingdom. Within each of these kingdoms there is a powerful and dedicated support system for the warfare. (The Church seems to be the one spiritual force that hasn't quite got the unity and cooperation principle sorted out.) Ephesians 6:12 says that we wrestle with spiritual principalities, or with the chief ruling spirits over those principalities. A physical principality is a territory, such as Monaco, ruled over by a prince. It's the same in the spirit realm. Isn't it reasonable to suppose that today, as in Daniel's time, nations have satanic princes assigned to them whose purpose is to control their people and affairs?

The Prince of America

One of Jimmy's most vivid experiences of this kind of spiritual encounter took place on the west steps of the U S Capitol. He was conducting our musical, *If My People*, with a huge choir on Flag Day of our bicentennial year. He was caught up in the message of the lyrics:

Keep looking down; we're seated in the heavenlies;
God's mighty power has raised us over all!
Keep looking down, above all principalities,
For we have died and risen with the Lord!
And in his name we have authority
And in his name we shall prevail.
And in his name we dare to face the enemy
And in his name we cannot fail!

Next, lots of Scriptures on the Church's warfare were read over the pulsating music and then, Bang! straight into the next song:

You are the children of the Kingdom of God,
You're the chosen ones for whom the Saviour came.
You're his noble new creation by the Spirit and the blood,
You're the Church that he has built to bear his name!
And the gates of hell shall not prevail against you!
And the hordes of darkness cannot quench your light!
And the hosts of God shall stand and fight beside you
Till your king shall reign triumphant in his might!

Jimmy explains, "As I conducted, I was feeling the strength and truth of the songs and gazing upward with a tremendous rush of love at the great capitol dome with its flags flying against the sky. "That dome is the symbol of the seat of government of the country I love. Then, like a bolt, the awareness hit me: it also represents the seat of the Prince of America, the very front lines of the battle for the soul of my nation. Here he and a hierarchy of evil persons without bodies are working tirelessly, trying to control the minds of government officials, staff workers, lobbyists, strategists, advisors and other people of influence. There are probably more demons and angels doing their work in that building than anywhere else in the country.

"Suddenly I was conducting, praying and warring in the spirit all at the same time. What was happening in my spirit somehow connected with the choir – you could hear it in their voices and see in on their faces, and they rose to magnificent heights. It was a hair-standing-on-end moment of spiritual awareness, written in my heart forever. When I pray for our government, I often look back on it with awe."

No Cause for Fear

While Satan and other great spiritual authorities are never to be taken lightly, neither are they to be feared by those who belong to Christ and walk in obedience to God. The Bible says, *"God has not given us a spirit of fear, but of power and of love and of a sound mind"* 2 Timothy 1:7 NKJV.

Never be intimidated; we've been authorized to fight this fight and we don't need to be afraid to do it. We can pray confidently and with authority against all the works of the devil. The most effective thing we can do to dislodge him and destroy his strongholds is to glorify and honour God, acknowledging his supremacy over all other powers, and inviting his divine presence. When God really shows up, all other powers release their prisoners and flee. *"Where the Spirit of the Lord is, there is liberty"* 2 Corinthians 3:17 KJV.

If we see ourselves as too puny to stand up to evil forces, we need to understand how those forces see us; that puts a whole new frame around the picture:

Identification with Christ

> *Well, you know I'm not a fighter, Lord*
> *And the hosts of hell are strong.*
> *So fill me with your Spirit,*
> *Help me put my armour on.*
> *And when I face the enemy,*
> *All that he will see*
> *Is me standing there in you*
> *And you standing there in me.*
> "The Warrior" Jimmy and Carol Owens © Fairhill Music

Mark Twain's classic, *The Prince and the Pauper* is the story of a royal mix-up – a case of mistaken identity. A beggar, the living image of a young prince who has run away, is mistakenly taken from the streets, scrubbed and groomed and put on the throne.

He's scared stiff. Surely they can see I'm nobody, he thinks. Surely I'll be discovered and executed. He soon realises, however, that because everybody identifies him with the real prince, all the prince's authority is at his disposal. He is now the man with the power.

We, the Church, are like the pauper. Our authority is not in ourselves, but in our identification with our Prince. In the eyes of both God and Satan, we are one with Christ. The Church fathers experienced that "identification authority" and used it to change the world. Having known its reality and dynamism, the Apostle Paul shares it with us: *"We were dead and buried with him in baptism, so that just as he was raised by the Father's power, so we, too might rise to life on a new plane altogether... Let us never forget that our old selves died with him on the cross that the tyranny of sin over us might be broken – for a dead man is immune to the power of sin"* Romans 6: 4-8 PH.

There is one passage of Scripture so powerful that St Paul prayed a special prayer that his readers would really get it. In Ephesians 1:19-23 NLT he writes:

> *I pray that you will begin to understand the incredible greatness of his power for us who believe him. This is the same mighty power that raised Christ from the dead and seated him in the place of honour at God's right hand in the heavenly realms. Now he is far above any ruler or authority or power or leader or anything else in this world or in the world to come. And God has put all things under the authority of Christ, and he gave him this authority for the benefit of the Church. And the Church is his body; it is filled by Christ, who fills everything everywhere with his presence.*

Now (and this is what Paul prayed we wouldn't miss) compare that with a verse further along in that same discourse, in chapter 2:6: *"For he raised us from the dead along with Christ, and we are seated with him in the heavenly realms – all because we are one with Christ Jesus."*

We suggest you take a few moments to pray and ask the Holy Spirit to implant the meaning of those verses deep in your heart, then go back and read them again, and meditate on them until they take root. If you get nothing else out of this whole book, other than a deep-seated grasp of that truth, it will have been worth it.

In the reality of the spiritual world, the head (Christ) and his Body (the Church) are crucified, resurrected, ascended and enthroned together in the place of highest spiritual authority. If we (the Church) are already *"seated with him in the heavenly realms,"* where does that place us in relation to our enemies? This should always be our point of view: *above* every power and principality that is named.

In addition to being seated *with* Christ, we are told repeatedly in the book of Ephesians that we are *in* Christ. And in Colossians 1:27b Paul proclaims: *"Christ in you, the hope of glory."*

If we don't understand that position, Satan will take advantage of us regularly. But once we put our identification authority to work by faith, we begin to *"reign in life through . . . Jesus Christ"* Romans 5:17 NIV. Then our lives are changed forever. And Satan's will be changed, too, as he is progressively challenged and dethroned.

If you declare this truth right out loud every day of your life, it will cause your faith to soar and it will demoralise the enemy. You can declare, *"It is written: I am dead indeed to sin, but alive to God in Jesus Christ my Lord"* see Romans 6:11 or, *"It is written: I have been crucified with Christ; it is no longer I who live, but Christ lives in me"* see Galatians 2:20. When we claim our death to sin and stand in Christ, claiming his purity and power as our own, we're ready to go to war under God's flag.[11]

Restraining the Enemy

Now thanks be to God who always leads us in triumph in Christ 2 Corinthians 2:14a NKJV.

On the cross, Jesus defeated Satan by pouring out his blood and his life to ransom mankind from the dominion of darkness. On the cross, he discarded the spiritual potentates and powers like so many old clothes and made a public display of them by leading them as captives (in other words, bound up) in his triumphal procession see Colossians 2:15. What a cosmic upheaval!

Then why does Satan still rage through the earth, causing havoc and destruction? One reason is that unrighteous people keep invoking him and his rulership by the way they live. Ungodly people make ungodly decisions and do ungodly things that hurt other people. But we can't blame the lost for all of it. The truth is, Satan is defeated, but enforcement of that defeat is left to the Church, through prayer and spiritual warfare. If we don't do it, it won't be done until the Lord comes back. One reason it isn't done is that few Christians understand this privilege and responsibility. Christ has delegated authority over Satan in earthly affairs to the Church. Therefore, "the praying people are the body politic of the world, and the Church holds the balance of power in world affairs."[13]

Another reason for our failure to assume our responsibility is divided loyalties. If we have a conflict of interest – trying to walk with one foot in the enemy camp and one in the Kingdom – we are ineffective as worshippers, witnesses and warriors. Paul Billheimer told of the 18th Amendment to the US Constitution (later repealed) which prohibited the sale of alcohol:

"It was indeed the law of the land. But its enforcement was entrusted to Andrew Mellon, then Secretary of the Treasury, head of one of the largest brewing syndicates in the world. It became a dead letter through non-enforcement.

"This is an illustration of what happens in the matter of Satan's legal destruction. Calvary was indeed a victory. It in actual fact destroyed all of Satan's legal claims. Nothing is lacking there. But the enforcement of Calvary's victory was placed in the hands of the Church, Christ's corporate Body on earth. The Body with hands and feet is the vehicle that carries out the commands of the Head. If the Body fails to respond, the will of the Head becomes a dead letter."[13]

So then, why does evil continue, and why hasn't the Lord come back? Jesus said, *"This gospel of the Kingdom shall be preached in all the world as a witness to all the nations and, then the end will come"* Matthew 24:14 NKJV. God never intended for Christianity to be a spectator sport, but an active participation in the work of his Kingdom.

If the gospel has not yet been preached in all the nations, whose responsibility is that? Is it not ours? It's within our power to see the gospel preached in every nation in our generation. The technology is there, if only we will use it; the money is there, if only we will give it; and the manpower is there, if only we will go.

Using the Leash

"Although Satan's work is not yet finished and his doom still in the future, God has put a leash on him. He can go only so far and no further. There is the mystery of why God permits Satan to continue for as much as another hour, or why he fits into the cosmic plan of salvation. Nevertheless, God assures his people that he is for them and greater than the one who is against them, that Satan's doom is sure, that he is to be resisted by the people of God see James 4:7, and that for them there is victory over the wicked one."[14]

God has put this restraining leash in the hands of the Church, and he means for us to use it. The inevitable question is how in the world do we do it?

Jesus said we can't rob a strong man's house without first binding up the strong man see Matthew 12:29; Mark 3:27. *"Whatever you bind (declare to be improper and unlawful) on earth must be what is already bound in heaven; and whatever you loose (declare lawful) on earth must be what is already loosed in heaven"* Matthew 16:19 AB.

How do we know what has already been bound and loosed in heaven? Well, we have some strong scriptural clues. At Jesus' ascension *"he led captivity captive – he led a train of vanquished foes – and he bestowed gifts on men"* Ephesians 4:8 AB. Matthew Henry's commentary on this verse is, "He conquered those who had conquered us."

Then, to add insult to Satan's injury, Jesus shares with us weak, fallible mortals who believe in him the benefits of his victory over the powers of darkness by giving us the authority to bind them on earth as they have already been bound in heaven.

The Church is an occupation army, an alien, ruling agency within a nation, enforcing the will of our absent King and restraining the opposition. We do this through intercessory warfare prayer. We bind the enemy by *declaration*, made by faith in Jesus' victory.

Part of Jesus' messianic call was to release the prisoners – those who are bound by Satan – from the dungeon see Isaiah 42:7. We loose the prisoners of sin through the gospel. Where there is enemy oppression, we can invoke the presence of the Lord and his liberating authority, for *where the Spirit of the Lord is, there is liberty* 2 Corinthians 3:17 KJV.

Oh God, Most High, Almighty King!
The Champion of Heaven, Lord of everything!
You've fought, you've won, Death's lost its sting,
And standing in your victory we sing:
(Chorus)

You have broken the chains that held our captive souls
You have broken the chains and used them on your foes
All your enemies are bound, they tremble at the sound of your name!
Jesus, you have broken the chains!

The power of hell has been undone
Captivity held captive by the Risen One!
And in the name of God's great Son
We claim the mighty victory you've won!
(Repeat chorus)

"You Have Broken the Chains" Jamie Owens Collins © 1984 by Fairhill Music.

Our Legal Authority

Here are some simple spiritual legalities:

- *Satan's Cease and Desist warrant has been signed by Jesus Christ, but he has appointed the Church to serve it.*
- *The court of heaven has approved Satan's eviction notice, but the Church has been appointed to deliver and enforce it.*
- *The legalities of divine jurisdiction have been established by the resurrected Lord, but he has appointed the Church to put them into action.*

In giving us such authority, God is teaching us how to reign with him. We may speak to demonic forces just as a policeman would speak to people with bodies, binding their work by stating his authority. Picture the officer directing traffic at the crossroads: he is physically no match for the cars and lorries, but the drivers obey him because of the authority he represents. Just as he says, "Stop in the name of the Law!" we say, "Stop in the name of the Lord!" By doing that, we enforce God's written judgments see Psalm 149:6-9 and invoke his presence into the situation. For instance you may pray something like this:

> *I acknowledge and invoke the overruling power of Jesus Christ in this matter. He is Lord over all and his word is the final word! In his almighty name, I resist and bind the forces of Satan who are at work in this thing that is against the expressed will of God. And I give the Lord glory.*
>
> *Amen.*

Then PUSH – Pray Until Something Happens, or until you feel free in your heart to stop praying. In extreme situations you may feel led to fast as well, but fasting isn't something we do lightly.

Be aware that God sometimes allows drastic things to happen to bring the Church and the nation to their knees. Praise him in that, too. We must acknowledge that even his disciplines and judgments are good and righteous. He does hear us and honour our prayers, but we must leave the results to Him. Our part is to *persevere* and pray.

No matter how powerful or entrenched the enemy may seem, don't come at this with a heavy, discouraged, or fearful attitude. We serve a mighty, awesome, triumphant God.

Like the monks, perform your dance. *For the joy of the Lord is your strength* Nehemiah 8:10.

Even a child who believes in Jesus can bear his authority. When our son was eight or nine years old, he began having trouble sleeping. He told us someone was in his room, talking to him – someone he couldn't see. We didn't take him too seriously at first. But when this went on for a couple of nights, we decided to take him seriously after all. We went into his room, explained to the devil that this child belonged to God and then told him to leave. Our son went peacefully to sleep.

But the very next night it happened again. At that point, we explained to our son to whom he belongs and whose kingdom and power protect him. *"You are of God, little children, and have overcome them because he who is in you is greater than he who is in the world"* 1 John 4:4 KJV. We told him to declare it himself. He sat up in his bed and did it with surprising conviction and authority. And that was the end of that problem.

Authority is not only a defensive weapon, but also it's an aggressive and powerful one that enforces God's will in matters of intercession.

It's a method of rulership, to be used by mature and wise people. Here is another sample prayer: *"In the name of Jesus and through the power of his cross and resurrection, I take authority over Satan's interference in this situation. I declare that Jesus Christ has won the victory over all the works of the devil and that his will shall be done here and now."*

In the first two verses of the Book of Acts, Luke refers to his Gospel as an account of *"all that Jesus began both to do and to teach, until the day in which he was taken up..."* Why does he say Jesus began? Because the work is unfinished. And who is doing the work now? Jesus is – when the Church does it, Jesus is doing it. In this way, living in his earthly Body the Church, he rules in the midst of his enemies see Psalm 110:2.

It's our responsibility to see that his will is done on earth, as it is in heaven, through sensitive spiritual discernment, authoritative intercession and unwavering spiritual battle. And always with the spirit of joy that is our strength.

This Present Madness

Picture the scene as one fine day the police try to stop a suspicious looking car that, instead of pulling over, speeds off into the woods and hits a tree. Then the people start piling out like one of those clown acts in the circus. They just keep coming and coming, twenty of them, including five from the car boot. To add a further bizarre touch, they're all stark naked. Their leader, a preacher, explains that they're fleeing from the devil. On the way they've decided their clothes are demon-possessed, so they've abandoned them along with three cars that have run out of fuel. The preacher is arrested, the rest escape into the woods.[15]

This kind of thing is both funny and incredibly sad. These folks were obviously terrified, and their example can make people think that all spiritual warfare is nutty. It isn't; however, it can lend itself to some strange behaviour. For some Christian thrill seekers, it's a sort of glorified Dungeons and Dragons game in which the imagination is fired and emotions run high with a perceived sense of power.

Some prayer groups spend more time yelling at the devil and generally throwing up dust than in declaring God's sovereignty. Some folks who are really on the fringe have even tried beating the devil out of each other, a dangerous and futile practice that can land its victims in the hospital and its practitioners in jail.

While we believe in the reality of demonic spirits, we don't for a moment blame Satan or demon powers for all of society's woes. Much of the ugliness in the world is caused by rebellious people who simply have chosen to sin see James 1:14. We need to figure out the difference and then be careful not to go off the deep end. To do this, we can ask God for spiritual discernment. And our greatest protection from error is always the Word of God.

Both theology and demonology consist of gathering facts and formulating doctrines from the Bible. Trouble starts when we form doctrines and practices based on experience without checking to see if they line up with the Scriptures. These doctrines can become laced with enough error to make them dangerous – exciting, but dangerous.

They also raise unrealistic expectations, as in the case of the fledgling missionary who gets off the plane at his new station and immediately binds Satan and every spirit in the country, (like lassoing a whole herd of cattle all at once), then proceeds on the assumption that this has been successfully done. His first encounter with the local witch doctor may be an eye-opener.

Our young missionary will learn firsthand that the battle in the spirit is not a mind game. It's a real war in which we wrestle with a determined enemy and in which people sometimes get hurt. We must be determined, too. And courageous.

If you answer the battle cry, don't be surprised if you get some dents in your armour and accumulate some wounds. Jesus certainly did, and in Matthew 10, he tells us not to be surprised if we receive the same treatment. The Apostle Peter says, *"Dear friends, don't be bewildered when you go through the fiery trials ahead, for this is no strange, unusual thing... Instead be really glad – because these trials will make you partners with Christ in his suffering, and afterwards you will have the wonderful joy of sharing his glory...."* I Peter 4:12 TLB

Remember, ultimately, you will win! And because of your courage and endurance, many will be saved from a fate worse than death.

You don't need to be afraid. If you've done your best to fulfil God's "ifs", you're on winning ground. You can face God with faith, and the devil with confidence. You'll come to rejoice in the struggle even when it gets tough, because you'll understand that you're making inroads into an evil kingdom and shaking up its leadership.

When we took our musical *Come Together* into Britain, we realised we would get into a serious spiritual battle because Satan fears nothing more than unity in the Church – and that's what the presentation was all about. We knew we were right when a friend called and said, "I woke up at three o'clock this morning hearing the Lord say, 'Pray for the Owens'; the devil is very angry with them.' I don't want you to be afraid, but you should be careful to keep one another covered."

We were gratified to hear this, because we were glad to think we were upsetting Satan and his kingdom and making a difference in the world.

We had the same sort of message as we toured with *If My People*. God gave us the assurance that he would bless powerfully, but that it would cost us more than we knew. But there are churches functioning today that had their beginnings in the teaching of those musicals. Roger Forster, founder of the International March for Jesus events, said the marches had their start when the British took *Come Together* to the streets.

We did have some memorable adventures on those tours: the witches' coven who tried to put a curse on us; the out-of-control man who tried to keep Jimmy from conducting and chased the overflow crowd away; the sniper in the attic, caught just before a meeting; the four thugs who ran one of our vans off the road and were breaking in when they suddenly fled in terror; the approaching mob with torches, swearing to "burn everything in sight", who, as we prayed, suddenly were scattered by a blinding rainstorm – but these things were nothing compared to what the persecuted saints and martyrs have gone through throughout history.

Interceding spiritual warriors should always focus on God rather than on the satanic. Nevertheless, there's a need to be constantly alert. Satan has more than one arrow in his quiver and he uses them all. He tempts us not only with the sins of the world and the flesh but also with the age-old pull of idolatry – the occult.

---

10 *Hayford's Bible Handbook*, Jack W. Hayford, General Editor. Thomas Nelson, Inc.

11 This truth of identification is so important that it needs a book of its own – we've only touched the edges of it here. It's the scriptural way to victory over sin. See Andrew Murray's classic book *Covenants and Blessings* [Whitaker House]. It will absolutely change your life.

12 Paul Billheimer, *Destined to Overcome*.

13 *ibid*, p33

14 Harold Lindsell, *The World, the Flesh, and the Devil*, Canon Press, 1973.

15 Newsweek, August 30, 1993

Talk About This:

1. What does the Bible say about Satan and demon powers? Who and what are they? p82

2. What do you believe about spiritual warfare? Is it real? How do we fight both an offensive and a defensive war? p80

3. What is the Church's objective in this spiritual struggle? Who are the "souls under siege" and where are they? p80 Do you know any?

4. What does "dethroning the devil" mean? p81

5. Do you see any satanic influence at work in human governments? p86. In the seven mind-moulders listed in Chapter 8? p64

6. What does declaring your position in Christ, claiming his purity and power as your own, do for you in keeping you from sin and in waging your warfare? p86-87

7. How do we restrain the enemy and loose his captives? p88

8. How do we know the difference between satanic influence and plain old human rebellion?

Pray About This:

a. Take a private time to confess and lay down every relationship and practice that would make you vulnerable to Satan.

b. Declare Romans 6:11 aloud: "I am dead indeed unto sin, and alive unto God through Jesus Christ my Lord."

c. Declare Galatians 2:20 aloud: "I have been crucified with Christ; it is no longer I who live, but Christ lives in me; and the life which I now live in the flesh I live by the faith of the Son of God."

d. Declare Jesus to be absolute Lord over your life, your church, your community and your nation.

e. Ask God for spiritual discernment, courage, wisdom, and faith to be a good soldier for Christ.

f. Take time to worship the Lord. Use the Psalms if they will help get you started.

Chapter 11 - The Occult: Enemy Territory

Then the Lord God asked the woman, "How could you do such a thing?"
"The serpent tricked me," she replied.
Genesis 3:13 NLT

Even Satan can disguise himself as an angel of light. So it is no wonder his
servants can also do it by pretending to be godly ministers.
2 Corinthians 11:14 NLT

It's evening in a small city in England as our friend Jean Darnall addresses a large home meeting. As Jean stands in front of the enormous fireplace in the vicarage, she's aware of a big black dog stretched out on the hearth. He belongs to an exotic lady, all in black, who sits on the front row. As Jean begins to speak, the dog raises his head, stares at her, and begins to growl. His attitude becomes threatening, but nobody moves a muscle to stop him. Finally, Jean says, "I think this dog is unhappy with me. We both might be more comfortable if he were somewhere else. Would you mind taking him out?"

With a malevolent glance at Jean, the lady in black stands, collars the dog, and flounces out of the house. The vicar looks miserable and Jean is baffled. She finishes her message feeling that she has made a huge mistake, but is unable to figure out what it is.

After the meeting the vicar says, "Oh, dear, I wouldn't have had that happen for the world. It's very awkward."

"What do you mean?" Jean asks.

"Well, you see, she's a very special lady," says the vicar. "Actually, she's a spiritualist medium who is such a help in my healing ministry."

Talk about putting the fox in the hen house!

As Jean and her husband Elmer minister to the vicar, they find he doesn't know one spiritual kingdom from another. If it's spiritual, he thinks, it must be God. As they patiently teach him from the Word, he is appalled. No wonder, he says, that so many weird things have been happening to him and his family and his church. Later, they all try to minister to the medium, but she will have none of it. Thoroughly outraged, she leaves the church and takes with her a load of oppression.

Romancing the Serpent

Amazingly, many Christians, sometimes through ignorance, are involved in the occult. They're unaware of its subtleties. They don't recognise it when they see it, or understand its dangers, or know how to combat it. But they need to learn because God hates it.

In the Old Testament God took drastic action to keep his people free of occult things so they wouldn't pollute the land with satanic wickedness. His judgments were catastrophic: idolaters, astrologers, mediums, wizards and witches were to be stoned to death.

While this is no longer the case in this New Testament Age of Grace we live in, God is still just as offended by these practices as he was in Old Testament times.

God killed King Saul, a man he had earlier anointed, *"for his disobedience... and because he consulted a medium, and did not ask the Lord for guidance"* 1 Chronicles 10:13-14 TLB. He also warned Babylon, a heathen nation, that because of its occult sins he would bring terrible judgment. No supernatural powers could help; their astrologers and prognosticators would burn up like stubble see Isaiah 47:13-14. God told Israel that if they inquired of idols instead of Him, He would *"rush down upon them like fire and devour them"* see Amos 5:4-8. That's an extreme reaction from a God who means business and who means to be obeyed.

He means business with us, too. He says that we are to ask only him for spiritual wisdom. If we do, he will give it to us liberally see James 1:5.

"Well now, hold on," you may say. "Do you really believe that just having my horoscope done is going to irritate the Lord?"

Yes, we do. The early Church understood this, and Christians who had practised "curious, magical arts" confessed their sin and burned their books and charms publicly see Acts 19:18-20. No matter that the paraphernalia was expensive; they feared God, and keeping their relationship right with him was all that mattered.

Acceptance of occult practices is sin, and may be a determining factor in our fate as a nation. God said to ancient Israel, *"Do not let your people practise fortune-telling or sorcery, or allow them to interpret omens, or engage in witchcraft, or cast spells, or function as mediums or psychics, or call forth the spirits of the dead. Anyone who does these things is an object of horror and disgust to the Lord. It is because the other nations have done these things that the Lord your God will drive them out ahead of you"* Deuteronomy 18:10-12 NLT.

If in Old Testament times the Lord punished nations and individuals because of these sins, will he not punish nations and individuals today for doing the same things?

The Occult in Modern Society

There is an amazing depth and breadth of occult influence in Western society. Its greatest danger is that much of it seems so innocent at first.

Take the case described in *The Exorcist*, the first in a line of major occult-horror books and films. In this story, based on a case history, a young girl becomes grossly demon-possessed. Her downward spiral begins with a Ouija board. Unfortunately, these spirit boards, by which people try to communicate with the dead or with disembodied spirits, have been a popular parlour game in many homes for years. But they aren't a game to God. We know of schoolgirls attempting levitation and séances at their slumber parties. They usually do it in ignorance, and amid giggles and glasses of pop it all seems harmless. But it isn't.

We even saw a book displayed prominently at the checkout stand of our local supermarket, called *Tarot for Dummies/Tackle Life's Biggest Questions*. Right. "Dummy" is a pretty good description of folks who tackle life's biggest questions with a deck of fortune-telling cards.

Housewives sit over their morning coffee reading their daily horoscopes in the local newspaper and offending the God who has commanded them not to do it. (If anyone ever asks you, "What's your sign?" tell them, "Agnus" [pronounced og´noos, or ahnyoos, which means the Lamb]. "The Lamb of God cancels out all the others."

Mystics, witches, occult "prophets," mediums and psychics are popular guests on television talk shows, thus bringing the doctrines of devils right into the homes of our nation. David Wilshire, a Member of Parliament, lobbied for the return of witchcraft laws that had been repealed in 1949. He said, "Once you open up the mind to the sorts of ideas and imagery and history of witchcraft, where is the dividing line between committing something which is a bit of a giggle and something which slips very readily into full-blown Satanism?"

The New Age and Old Lies

Many gullible people are involved in some form of the New Age movement, which is nothing more than a modern name for an ancient error. It has some worthy goals: get in tune with nature, clean up the air, save the planet. It brings encouragement to discouraged people by teaching them that they simply haven't discovered their limitless human potential – and that may often be true. But then the other shoe drops and they are dazzled by the revelation that each of them is actually God!

The spiritual goal of New Age is the deification of humanity and the entire created order. There is no fixed moral code, no guilt and no judgment. Perfection of humanity comes, not through repentance and redemption, but through a sudden, staggering evolutionary transformation called the "quantum leap" whereby man will become entirely recreated and freed from old evils.

Many New Agers, following the lead of celebrities seeking repentance-free religion, have adopted reincarnation: If at first you don't succeed, try, try again... and again... and again.

These teachings of reincarnation and the deification of humanity bring us back to the original lie: *"You shall not die... You shall be like God"* Genesis 3:4-5 KJV.

There are also New Agers who consult trance channellers, or spirit mediums. Some of them claim to receive instruction from extra-terrestrial guides who visit them via UFOs. Some are so immersed in this they probably believe it.

Though not all New Agers believe the same doctrines, they are united by a mystical, occult world view that's permeating our culture, especially through our entertainment media and educational systems, both of which powerfully influence our young people.

What's Up, Kids?

What are we to make of the Harry Potter phenomenon – the series of books and films that has captivated the minds of children everywhere? It's about a young man in training to be a wizard – a male witch. (That should tell us something right away. Consider what God says about witchcraft in Deuteronomy 18 and magical arts in Acts 19, which we discussed earlier.)

Some would argue that C S Lewis *The Chronicles of Narnia* and J R R Tolkien *Lord of the Rings* wrote fantasies about magic and witches as well, but there is a difference. In their stories we know who the good guys and the bad guys are. Their heroes aren't trying to be wizards and exercise occult powers; more often they're ordinary people who are trying to save others from those dark powers.

David Kinnaman of Barna Research reports that four out of five teenagers have read or watched Potter, including three quarters of all church-going teens. But very few Christian teens report receiving any spiritual input on it from their church or their parents. Most Christian leaders and parents have responded by either condemning the series or ignoring it, leaving the kids to process it on their own.

One out of eight teenagers – nearly three million – said that the Harry Potter chronicles increased their interest in witchcraft. Whether or not the series alone leads young people into practising witchcraft is up for speculation, but we've seen it open the door into other occult avenues. When the books came out, some book stores surrounded the Potter displays with entire collections on the study of witchcraft and the occult. The Wiccans (witches) must be delighted to get this much free publicity, and doubtless the powers of darkness are, too.

Kinnaman suggests: "The teenage years are an important transition from the leadership of parents to independence and reliance upon God. Instead of simply trying to isolate children from all the spiritually dangerous material available in our media-saturated culture, parents could prepare their kids to be missionaries to their peers and to our society.

"The Bible notes that believers should always be ready to answer questions about their faith whenever people ask. While not minimizing the spiritual danger of stories like Harry Potter, the upside of such content is that it raises questions of purpose, destiny, relationships, isolation, redemption, spiritual power and more – the very topics that are so important to the message of Christianity. But, as things stand, many parents and church leaders are letting those spiritual opportunities go to waste."

Guarding the Children

The Barbarians are no longer at the gate. Now they're in the living room and the schoolroom, entertaining and educating our children.

Parents have the responsibility before God of being guardians over their children. In state schools, teachers have been forbidden to teach Christian principles, and in fact may be commissioned to teach some things designed to destroy faith in God. If you're a parent, your job therefore is not only to guard your children against the untruths being fed to them, but also to indoctrinate them in the truths of the Bible and the Christian faith so they can answer for themselves. This means you need to check regularly the materials they're being taught and be able to rebut those teachings that are anti-God or otherwise harmful. This will take time, study and dedication, but considering the stakes, it will be worth it.

There is a serpent behind all occult activity. It's like a swaying cobra – sleek, beautiful, exotic, beguiling, but subtle, deceptive, and deadly. It will let you play with it for a while, but ultimately it will turn and poison you. And it is after your children. The Word of God is the light that can expose its lie and the rock that can break its fangs.

Their world is full of smiling heroes
Who will take them by the hand
And lead them to the serpent
And defend them from the Lamb.

"Where Have the Children Gone?" from the musical Heal Our Land,
by Jimmy and Carol Owens © Fairhill Music

Television shows and films about the supernatural, aimed at young people, are more prevalent than ever these days. Parents should also be very aware of the video games their kids are playing. Many of them are innocent pastimes (although for some they can become unhealthily addictive) but some are filled with witches, spells, demons, monsters, psychic powers, and even human sacrifice. The Scriptures specifically forbid any involvement with the practices in many of these games.

Spiritual Guides in the Classroom

Occult teaching permeates not only films, TV and games, but schools as well. The United States now offers to many school children courses in Eastern meditation ("relaxation techniques") and the calling up of spirit guides ("old souls" or "wise old teachers") through imaging and listening to "inner voices" and this could come to the UK soon.

Be alert. If you find occult practices such as this in your children's classrooms, see that either the practices or your children are removed. Don't think these teachings are nonsense and not worthy of notice. They are an alluring and exciting spiritual trap and seriously anti-Christ. None of us can afford to make them a part of our lives.

For our older young people, some universities offer courses in witchcraft, ESP, clairvoyance and transcendental meditation. This last technique may be called by different names, but it's still the same old Eastern practice leading to altered states of consciousness. New Age variations of transcendental meditation are religious, no matter what its practitioners may say. The writings of Maharishi Mahesh Yogi, one of the earlier and more influential of its teachers and the Beatles' guru, called these techniques "a path to god... a most powerful form of prayer; a way that will enable men to find their god within themselves."

In some forms of Yoga, the participant is given a mantra to intone, the sound of which is the name of a Hindu deity to be invoked.[16] Many people who do this have no idea they're taking part in an occult Hindu rite intended to get their minds into an altered state of receptivity to the gods or goddesses that are being summoned. Yoga is marketed in the West as a holistic practice to improve mental and physical health.

Here are religious movements without redemption, teaching doctrines of demons under various names, in the same schools where all references to our God and Saviour are systematically being silenced.

Beware, too, of transpersonal psychology that encourages psychic phenomena. Although this has been labelled with respectable scientific terminology by some universities, it is devilish.

Nations that permit or promote these practices bring down the wrath of God on their own heads. Not only do they have God's wrath to fear, but the one they have turned to is already rewarding them with the harvest of their sin: violence, disease and destruction.

This is a good time for a check-up on occult practices in your life – hangovers from the past perhaps, such as witchcraft, necromancy, sorcery, astrology, or communion with spirits. You can repent of them and renounce them right now. Then destroy any paraphernalia such as charms, books and horoscope charts. There will never be a better time to make sure this is taken care of once and for all and to be set free. Don't give them away – destroy them, so they can't ruin somebody else's life.

When we play around in any enemy territory, we play by his rules and he will take quick and terrible advantage of us. But as long as we give him no place in us, we're on safe and solid ground. A praying Church, moving in purity and spiritual authority, is fully equipped and qualified to wage warfare against the demonic doctrines of the occult.

For the sake of our nation, we must do it now.

---

16   Source: Hinduism info centre home website

Talk About This:

1. How does God view the occult? Is this serious? What does he want us to do if we've been involved in it? p95

2. Do you think most Christians really understand the dangers of playing with "harmless" occult practices such as horoscope reading? p96. What should the Church be doing about this?

3. Have you broken with all past occult practices? If not, you can do it right now, either privately or with the help of your fellowship.

4. What are the goals of New Age teaching? How are they contrary to Christianity? p97

5. What do you think of David Kinnaman's suggestion that, rather than trying to isolate kids from all spiritually dangerous material (an impossible task in this day and age), parents should prepare them to use the material to bring the gospel to their peers? How would you do that? p98

6. Has the book given you new light on some of the occult practices in local schools? What steps will you take to make sure this isn't happening in your local school?

Pray About This:

a. Repent of and renounce any occultism in your life. Destroy any occult paraphernalia, literature or games you possess.

b. Pray against occult influences in the lives of government leaders and in the "mind-moulders" of our society.

c. Pray for the Church to awaken to the reality of satanic influence in all our public places, and to rise up in purity and spiritual authority to pray against the demonic doctrines of the occult.

d. Pray for your local schools: the governors, the head teachers, the teachers and the pupils.

PART 5

THE SPIRITUAL ARMOURY

A sound of battle is in the land.

Jeremiah 50:22 NKJV

Chapter 12 - The Weapons of Our Warfare

Onward, Christian soldiers, marching as to war,
2 Corinthians 10:4 NLT

"All right, people – we're at war," the general shouts as he reviews a vast throng of new recruits. Packed onto the parade ground of the army base, they shiver in the midnight cold. Jerked from their beds by a besieged and desperate military, they are still in civilian clothes, confused, unprepared and unarmed.

"We're being invaded from all sides by a well organised, well armed enemy who is moving fast," the general informs them. "This is no foreign battle; this is here, now. Your homes, your families are already under attack." Even as he speaks they see the first flare of rockets and hear the sound of shellfire.

The initial babble of alarm turns quickly to a roar of outrage. Spines stiffen, fists clench and adrenaline flows. They look expectantly at the general, waiting for orders, for arms.

"All right!" he roars. "About face!"

The massive gates of the compound swing open.

"Now!" shouts the general to his weapon-less recruits, "Go get 'em!"

Like these fictional recruits, we have been thrown, unsuspecting and unprepared, into a cosmic war. But unlike the fictional general, our commander has provided us with powerful and holy equipment for the battle: First, the filling and empowering of the Holy Spirit and the equipping with spiritual gifts; next, protective armour; then an arsenal of spiritual weapons and prayer techniques. We've already discussed some of these, such as declaring our own identification with Christ, speaking the word of authority, and binding and loosing, but there are a few more. Learn to use them all, and you'll be a dynamic intercessor.

The Armour

Protection – that's what we need. God has tailor-made a suit of armour for intercessors:

In Ephesians 6:10-18 Paul the Apostle tells us to put on the whole armour of God, so that we may resist evil and stand our ground. Put the armour on by faith. When your feet hit the floor in the morning, say: "In the name of Jesus I put on the helmet of *his salvation* over my mind and the breastplate of *his righteousness* over my heart. I gird myself with *his truth*. I take *his Word* as the sword of the Spirit, *his gospel* as my message, and I shield myself with *his faith* – the faith of the Son of God who lives in me and is greater than any other power that exists." Pastor Rick Warren says he does this every time he gets up to preach.

All this is summed up in one terse phrase in Romans 13:14 NKJV: *"Put on the Lord Jesus Christ."* You don't have to go through the whole list every time you have a battle to fight. Simply say to the enemy, "I stand here covered by Jesus Christ the Lord. In his name I assume his authority over you." Then tell him what he must do and keep at it until he does it.

We also need protection against our own natures as well as against Satan. We've just quoted from Romans 13:14, *"Put on the Lord Jesus Christ,"* but that's only half the verse. The rest of it says, *"and make no provision for the flesh, to fulfil its lusts."*

We are vulnerable wherever we are sinful. Keep yourself armoured daily against sin this way:

1. Submit yourself to God.
2. Reckon (consider) yourself dead to sin and alive to God through Jesus Christ.
3. Claim the righteousness of Jesus Christ as your own.

The Holy Spirit will then progressively *impart* the righteousness already *imputed to you* through Christ. This is powerful protection.

The Sword

Jesus used the sword of the Word as his personal weapon of choice when Satan goaded him to demonstrate his divinity see Matthew 4:1-11 NIV:

When Satan suggests he turn stones into bread, Jesus doesn't bluster or debate; he simply says *"It is written: 'Man does not live on bread alone, but on every word that comes from the mouth of God.'"*

When Satan proposes he jump off a pinnacle of the temple to see if the angels will rescue him, Jesus replies *"It is also written: 'Do not put the Lord your God to the test.'"*

When Satan offers him the kingdoms of the world in exchange for his worship, Jesus has had enough. He says, *"Away from me, Satan! For it is written, 'Worship the Lord your God, and serve him only.'"*

There is no answer from the devil. He has heard "the judgment written" Psalm 149:9, and there is nothing left to say. He simply goes away.

Jesus used *"God's mighty weapons, not those made by men, to knock down the devil's strongholds"* 2 Corinthians 10:4 TLB.

God's weapons can pull down strongholds for us, too. These strongholds may be political, spiritual or personal – wherever Satan has gained a foothold.

One of the devil's most debilitating personal strongholds is condemnation. As one lady said wryly, "For most of my life, I thought guilt was one of the five senses." She's not alone.

Satan uses vague feelings of unworthiness or condemnation to rob us of faith and power and make us feel unworthy to pray for ourselves or for others. The Holy Spirit, on the other hand, clearly pinpoints problems so we can confess, repent and accept our cleansing. Guilt over sins already forsaken is not from God. He never condemns a repentant heart.

The Blood of the Lamb and the Word of Our Testimony

Two powerful weapons against condemnation or any other satanic ploy are listed together in Revelation 12:11 KJV: *"They overcame him by the blood of the Lamb and by the word of their testimony."* The word of your testimony is your confession of faith see Hebrews 3:1; 10:23. When condemnation hits you, or when you need to assert spiritual authority, simply declare to the enemy what the Blood of Jesus Christ has done for you:

- *I am* cleansed from sin and have peace with God.
- *I belong* to Christ. I am his possession.
- *I am* a citizen of the Kingdom of God.
- *I am* under his protection.
- *I am* acting under his authority.

The enemy may resist that authority, but if you know your rights and assert them, he has to give way.

Actually make these confessions out loud. There is a question about whether demons can read our minds. Nowhere in Scripture are we plainly told that they can, but obviously they can see what we do and hear what we say, and they can influence our thinking. And besides, these declarations increase our faith and declare our freedom from bondage and satanic bullying. Speak them often – they really work!

Just as you testify to the enemy of what the blood has done for you, you also testify to people of what the blood has done for them. The word of your testimony is also the means of leading people to the Lord, and leading a soul to Christ is a major victory over the devil.

The Power of Agreement

If two of you agree down here on earth concerning anything you ask, my Father in heaven will do it for you. For where two or three gather together because they are mine, I will be right there among them. Matthew 18:19-20 TLB.

The First Century Church was, at first, small and faced with opposition from both the Jewish leadership and from the ruling Gentiles. All they had was one another; if they couldn't walk in agreement, they would quickly be decimated.

But they had a secret. Right from the first they found they had power with God when they agreed together in prayer. Look at these examples:

*"These (disciples) all continued **with one accord** in prayer and supplication"* Acts 1:14 KJV. This was the first thing they did after Jesus ascended into Heaven. It was the first of many **"with one accord"** prayer meetings that brought dramatic response from God as he gave them direction and power for their calling. It was a precursor to Pentecost.

*"When the day of Pentecost was fully come, they were all with **one accord** in one place."* Acts 2:1 KJV.

In response to their oneness of heart and purpose, God poured out the Holy Ghost in fulfilment of the ancient prophecy of Joel 2:28, 29.

Again *"... they lifted up their voice to God **with one accord.**"* Acts 4:24 KJV. They worshipped and prayed for courage and power, and *"... when they had prayed, the place was shaken and they were all filled with the Holy Ghost, and they spoke the word of God with boldness."*

In Acts 12:5-18 Peter was in prison, awaiting trial for preaching Jesus, and the church was having another fervent **one accord** prayer meeting for him. Peter was asleep, guarded by sixteen soldiers and chained between two of them (He had worked so many signs and wonders that Herod must have thought he was an escape artist, too). Suddenly an angel showed up, slapped him on the side and said, "Quick! Get up! Get dressed and follow me." Peter's chains fell off and he followed the angel right through two guard posts and out through the gate, which opened by itself. He thought it was a vision, until the angel left and he found himself walking down the street a free man. He went to the prayer meeting and knocked on the door. A servant girl named Rhoda went to open it, but when she heard Peter's voice she got so excited that she forgot to let him in, but ran back inside and told everyone, "Peter is standing at the door!" They answered her, "You're out of your mind!" But when she kept insisting, they decided, "It must be his angel." Meanwhile Peter kept knocking, until they finally unlocked the door and were amazed to see their prayers answered.

As you see from Jesus' words in the Matthew 18 Scripture above, agreement between even two of us gives us a winning edge. Jesus sent out the twelve and then the seventy, two by two see Matthew 10:1; Luke 10:1. They strengthened, encouraged, helped and covered each other, and doubtless held each other accountable, and came back rejoicing.

King Solomon observed this principle centuries earlier, and he wrote: *"Two people can accomplish more than twice as much as one; they get a better return for their labour. If one person falls, the other can reach out and help. But people who are alone when they fall are in real trouble... A person standing alone can be attacked and defeated, but two can stand back to back and conquer. Three are even better, for a triple-braided cord is not easily broken"* Ecclesiastes 4:9-12 NLT.

The Power of Song

Praise – sung or spoken – binds spiritual kings and destroys strongholds, because it invokes the manifest presence of God see Psalm 22:3.

A case in point is Nepal, the world's only nation where Hinduism was (until 2006) the state religion. Its atmosphere is dense with the influence of a million gods. Religious proselytising is illegal. Nevertheless, an intrepid Youth With A Mission team goes in determined to tell people about Jesus. They soon find that no one will even listen. It looks as if they will have to get arrested to get some attention. They are out of ideas and discouraged.

Then one morning they hold their praise and worship time outside on their rooftop patio. As they sing their praise to God, they hear voices drifting up from the street below and they take a look over the edge. There is a crowd of Nepalese neighbours looking back at them.

"What are you doing?" somebody calls up to them.

"We're worshipping God," they reply.

The crowd buzzes awhile among themselves, talking it over. Then the spokesman calls back. "We've never heard people sing to their God like that before. Come down and tell us about him."

The Hindus, accustomed to repetitive chants and mantras, want to know what kind of god could evoke such joyous, spontaneous song in his worshippers. The YWAMers are delighted to tell them.

Their songs of praise have become a formidable force that breaks through the spiritual powers that have kept the Nepalese from receiving the gospel.

"Let the high praises of God be in their mouth and the two-edged sword the Word – Ephesians 6:17. *in their hand... to bind their kings with chains and their nobles with fetters of iron, to execute upon them the judgment written. This honour have all his saints."* Psalm 149: 6-9 KJV

In 2 Chronicles 20 there's a remarkable story in which King Jehoshaphat learns that three enemy nations have formed a coalition army against Judah and are only days away. He is terrified. But he does the right thing: he seeks the Lord with prayer and fasting. With God's assurance of deliverance, Jehoshaphat shows his faith by devising one of the more amazing military strategies on record: he sends the singers out in front of the army (Being in the choir in those days was a real adventure). The victory comes when the singers begin to sing and praise God. Then the Lord turns the enemy armies against each other and they destroy one another. Praise goes before the Lord's people like a consuming fire.

Talk About This:

1. Do you really believe there is a spiritual war going on? If so, how do you think it affects you?

2. Have you tried putting on your spiritual armour using the method described in this chapter p104

3. What results have you seen? Do you feel this will become a regular part of your life?

4. How can you keep yourself armoured daily? p105

5. Which of these spiritual weapons do you use most often and find most effective: The Sword of the Word; the Blood of the Lamb; the Word of your testimony; the power of Agreement; the power of Song?

6. If these weapons haven't been a regular part of your prayer life, do you believe they will be helpful? Which ones are you most willing to try? Why?

Pray About This:

a. Ask for wisdom and courage as you take on the warfare challenge.

b. Ask for cleansing as you prepare your heart for intercession.

c. Put your armour on, right out loud!

d. Use the weapons and prayers you've been studying to tackle some obviously ungodly problem in your community or nation. Make it an ongoing prayer project.

e. Take time to listen. God may want to alert you to a strategy that will help solve the problem.

f. Submit yourselves totally to God and take time to worship! Give him praise for his power and his wonderful works.

Chapter 13 - Fasting: Supercharged Prayer

Prayer links us to heaven; fasting separates us from earth.
Charles H Spurgeon

We've all experienced times when our prayers seem to bounce off the ceiling or extreme situations where prayer alone doesn't seem to be getting the job done. It's for these times that God has given us fasting – both private and united public fasting – with prayer.

Fasting is calculated to bring a note of urgency into our praying, and to give force to our pleas in the court of heaven... When a man is willing to set aside the legitimate appetites of the body to concentrate on praying, he is demonstrating that he means business, that he is seeking with all his heart, and will not let God go unless he answers. Arthur Wallis

Fasting helps to express, to deepen, and to confirm the resolution that we are ready to sacrifice everything, [even] ourselves to attain what we seek for the Kingdom of God..
Andrew Murray

The reason many do not live in the power of their salvation is because there is too much sleep, too much meat and drink, too little fasting and self-denial, too little [taking part in] the world and too little self-examination and prayer. William Bramwell, Wesleyan preacher, 1809

Eating is the granddaddy of all appetites. Fasting is a commitment to bring about self-control and overcome every other conceivable temptation. Neil Anderson

My agitation was the proof of the grip it [food] had on me. Rees Howells, intercessor

Fasting is a tremendous lesson in establishing who is the master and who is the servant. Remember, your body is a wonderful servant, but a terrible master. Derek Prince

Fasting burns out our selfishness. In fasting we willingly submit to the cauldron of renunciation as we give up one of life's greatest pleasures. Fasting is the foundry in which we are purified. Its fires refine our faith; its flames separate the base impurities from our true character in Christ; its hot blasts purify our hearts. Lee Bueno

Compiled by Pastor Wendell Smith, City Church.org.

Angry Prophets and Fasting Kings

Imagine the traumatic experience of the prophet Jonah: God had sent him on an assignment – to prophesy to a people he feared and hated. But Jonah ran from the Lord and tried to sail as far away as he could. And now here he is, back on shore: a wild apparition, vomited from the sea, bleached white from his sojourn in the belly of a fish, but humbled and thankful to be alive. Jonah sets out on his four-hundred-mile trek to Nineveh, the capital of his nation's worst enemy. He enters the city and shouts his terrifying message: no wasted words, no offer of hope, simply, *"Forty days from now Nineveh will be destroyed!"* Full stop! Jonah 3:4 TLB.

Lo and behold, the Ninevites believe him. They declare a fast, and all of them, from the greatest to the least, put on sackcloth. Their heathen king sits down in the dust and issues a proclamation: "Nobody eat or drink anything! Turn from your evil and call urgently on God for mercy!" see vv.7-9. God hears them and graciously rescinds his sentence of destruction.

Jonah is furious. *"I knew you'd do that; that's why I didn't want to come!"* he rails at God. *"I knew you were a gracious God, merciful, slow to get angry, and full of kindness; I knew how easily you could cancel your plans for destroying these people! Please kill me, Lord. I'd rather be dead than alive [when nothing that I told them happens]."* Then the Lord said, 'Is it right to be angry about this?... Why shouldn't I feel sorry for a great city like Nineveh with its 120,000 people in utter spiritual darkness... ?'" 4: 2-3, 11 TLB.

It would be hard to find a better example than Nineveh's of the effectiveness of fasting. As a powerful measure for answered prayer, nothing beats it. Used according to God's conditions, prayer with fasting has seldom failed to bring about restoration, deliverance and victory.

For another instance of fasting, let's look again at that siege of Jerusalem we just read about, when King Jehoshaphat sends the singers out in front of the army. When he hears of the approaching army, he holds a nationwide prayer meeting and proclaims a fast throughout the kingdom – including men, women and children.

Before all the people he cries out to the Lord, *"We don't know what to do, but our eyes are on you!"* God's answer is swift: the Spirit of the Lord comes on a prophet, who shouts out, *"Don't be afraid! The battle is not yours but God's! You will not need to fight! Stand still and see the salvation of the Lord!"* What a thrill for Jehoshaphat and his people! They recognise those words! They were spoken by Moses to the children of Israel long ago, when they stood with the sea before them and the Egyptian army behind them: *"Stand still and see the salvation of the Lord!"* Exodus 14:13.

The king and all the people fall down to worship, then the Levites stand up to sing praise. They go to the war zone (led by the singers), to find that God has turned the invaders against one another. Instead of a sea of glittering spears, Judah faces only a vast army of corpses. They spend three days gathering up the spoils and then live on in peace for years afterward see 2 Chronicles 20: 1-25. Not every battle, of course, is this easy. God is sovereign; he can deliver by many, or by few – or by himself.

By the way, we mustn't make a doctrine out of this story; there is no "one size fits all" battle plan. True, sometimes praying is all we can do, but it would be presumptuous, if not disastrous, to assume that we can always just pray and praise and watch what happens. In most instances, Israel had to fight their battles; in these two rare cases God told them just to let him do it. The lesson here is to say what Jehoshaphat said: "We don't know what to do, but our eyes are on you," then do whatever God shows us.

Fasting was a familiar practice to all the Old Testament Jews. Through years of experience, they learned the effectiveness of fasting and prayer in times of both personal and national crisis.

Old and New Testament believers fasted and prayed for several reasons:

- *Affliction of the soul as a sign of mourning or distress* see 2 Samuel 12:16, Psalm 35:13-14
- *Restoration of the nation* see Nehemiah 1: 3-4

- *Deliverance from enemies* see 2 Chronicles 20:2-4, Esther 4:16
- *Deliverance from God's judgment* Jonah 3:4-8, Joel 2:12-18
- *Guidance for ministry* Acts 13:2

Follow the Leader

The sun refracts the water into a million prisms as Jesus stands in the Jordan, praying, and a divine dove soars downward through the glory of the opened heavens. As the Holy Spirit settles upon him, the audible, awesome voice of God declares, *"You are my Son, my Beloved! In you I am well pleased and find delight!"* Luke 3:22 AB.

Surely this breathtaking empowering at his baptism should launch him straight into his miraculous ministry. But it doesn't. First comes the fast – forty days and forty nights. Only when he has overcome his appetites is he ready to overcome the challenges of Satan and face his own destiny. see Luke 4:1-2.

In the Sermon on the Mount see Matthew chapters 5-7, Jesus takes for granted that his followers will fast, even as he takes for granted that they will pray and give alms to the needy:

When you do alms... (6:3)

When you pray... (6:5)

When you fast... (6:17)

Notice he says **when**, not **if**. These are directives, not suggestions.

The apostle Paul disciplined his body by fasting often. He knew he couldn't have victory over the enemy until he had victory over his flesh see 1 Corinthians 9:27.

The early Church fasted to lend weight to their worship and to receive revelation and direction from God see Acts 13:1-3. If all these leaders needed it, surely we do, too.

Unfortunately, the practice of fasting has been all but lost to large segments of the Church. Because it's been associated with legalism and asceticism on one hand and with meaningless ritualism on the other, "thinking" Christians have tossed it out completely.

But today the Holy Spirit is calling the Church to fast. We see it happening all over the world. Considering both the crisis times we live in, as well as the possibility of imminent and perhaps unprecedented revival, every intercessor needs a balanced biblical perspective of this powerful exercise, and the know-how to use it under the Holy Spirit's guidance, both to derail the plans of the devil and to undergird the moving of God.

How Do We Do It?

For our fasting to be effective, we need to do much more than just abstain from eating. The fast – the self-denial – that impresses God, according to Isaiah 58, includes life intercession:

- *Freeing the oppressed*
- *Feeding the hungry*
- *Housing the homeless*
- *Clothing the naked*
- *Speaking the truth*
- *Walking in humility*
- *Providing for our families*
- *Refraining from gossip*
- *Being just, fair and righteous*

Justice, mercy, and humility: all these can be summed up in one verse, found in Micah 6:8: "*He has shown you, O man, what is good; and what does the Lord require of you but to do justly, to love mercy, and to walk humbly with your God?*" NKJV.

In return for our obedience, God promises us revelation, healing, guidance, protection, provision and promptly answered prayer. A generous return on our investment, wouldn't you say? If we're not receiving these blessings and can't understand why, it might be wise to go back and use "God's chosen fast" see Isaiah 58:6-12 as a personal checklist. It may provide some clues.

What exactly do we mean when we refer to fasting? Let's look at some definitions and then move on to some practical suggestions for effective fasting. A dictionary definition of fasting is: "To abstain from food; to eat sparingly or to abstain from some foods." Here are three types of biblical fasts:

- **The total fast:** abstaining from all food and water see Deuteronomy 9:9, 18; Ezra 10:6; Esther 4:16; Acts 9:9.
- **The normal fast:** abstaining from food but not from water see 1 Kings 19:8; Matthew 4:2.
- **The partial fast:** eating sparingly or abstaining from some foods see Daniel 10:2-3.

Know that however you choose to begin fasting, it won't be easy. These tips will help you prepare and hang in there:

- **Be ready for a struggle.** *Take, for example, the preacher who had been on a long fast and was having a battle with a serious appetite. Staunchly he stuck with it. As he got up to speak at a meeting on the last day of his fast, his stomach had finally had it and put up loud and vociferous protestations during his message, a borborygmic cacophony, from low grumbles to high migratory yowls, which his lapel microphone duly amplified. The audience thought it was hilarious, but the preacher was not amused. As soon as he got off the platform, he and his stomach had a showdown. "All right, you," he snarled, glaring down in the vicinity of his navel, "That kind of behaviour will get you nowhere. Just to teach you a lesson, we're going to fast an extra day!" And they did.*
- **Begin with short fasts,** *perhaps only a meal or two, and graduate to longer ones. Try partial fasts, such as Daniel's, at first.*
- **Don't go without liquids for more than three days.** *This seems to be the biblical limit. Longer abstinence may seriously harm your body. Moses abstained from*

water for two periods of forty days each, but he was supernaturally sustained in the immediate presence of God.

- **Consult your physician** before fasting if you have serious physical problems such as diabetes.

- **Break your fast carefully.** *Eat lightly at first. If you've been on a long fast, begin by taking only liquids. Then take a few days to get back to normal eating patterns. This is a good time to break the habit of overeating. You may be like the food-loving fellow who gets a headache and feels faint if he misses lunch. But it's no joke when the body begins to react to some real food deprivation. People who use a lot of sugar or caffeine often have the hardest time. It's a good idea to cut down gradually for a few days before you begin to fast.*

- **Don't try extremely long complete fasts unless you have a special revelation from God.** *Remember, those achieved by Moses were undertaken only by special revelation and divine empowerment.*

- **All fasting should be led by the Holy Spirit.** *Be careful not to let it become ritualised or legalistic.*

- **If you're fasting to receive guidance, it's wise not to act on any decisions until you have broken the fast,** *especially if it's a long one. You'll then be able to evaluate more clearly what the Lord has shown you.*

- **Don't fast for show.** *Jesus said, "When you fast, don't make it obvious, as the hypocrites do, who try to look pale and dishevelled so people will admire them for their fasting. I assure you, that is the only reward they will ever get. But when you fast, comb your hair and wash your face. Then no one will suspect you're fasting, except your Father, who knows what you do in secret. And your Father, who knows all secrets, will reward you"* Matthew 6:16-18 NLT.

- **When you fast, pray for the hungry.** *Once you've experienced a little of how they feel, you'll be able to pray more effectively for them. And how about interceding with the money you would have spent for food by giving it to Christian relief organisations that will use it to feed those who are starving? You'll be fulfilling part of God's chosen fast.*

Victory in this battle with our appetites stands us in good stead as we push on toward victory in the battle with Satan.

Talk About This:

1. After reading this chapter, can you name some of the biblical purposes for fasting? p111

2. Do you think fasting is a valid, spiritually powerful practice for the Church today? Why or why not? p112

3. If you haven't tried fasting before, are you willing to try it? What kind of fast would you start out with? p113

4. What are some health issues you should consider before you fast? p113

5. Do a check-up using "God's chosen fast" listed on p110. How do you think you rate personally? As a group? As a church?

6. How could you or your group help your church understand the value of fasting?

Pray About This:

a. Ask God for wisdom and willingness to use fasting as a power tool in prayer, both for yourself and your church.

b. Ask God to give you and your group a greater determination to pray faithfully for your nation. Plead for God to heal your land.

c. Pray for the national news media. Because of their places of influence, pray for salvation for the news directors and commentators. Pray for their accuracy and honesty. Here is another place to ask God to pull down and raise up according to his will.

d. Pray for a great ingathering for the kingdom across the nation. Ask for a revival within the church that will refresh God's people and bless the Lord.

WINNING ATTITUDES

Your attitude should be the same as that of Christ Jesus...

Philippians 2:5 NIV

Chapter 14 - Its All About Attitudes

Now your attitudes and thoughts must all be constantly changing for the better. Yes, you must be a new and different person, holy and good. Clothe yourself with this new nature.
Ephesians 4:23-24 TLB

Even though we fast and pray and know how to use our spiritual weapons, if our attitudes are wrong we can still find ourselves flat out on our backs on the battlefield. One of the most essential attributes of a Christian soldier is the willingness to put God and his business first.

Single-mindedness: Going for the Goal

The Apostle Paul wrote to his young disciple Timothy, *"Endure suffering along with me as a good soldier of Christ Jesus. And as Christ's soldier, do not let yourself become tied up in the affairs of this life, for then you cannot satisfy the one who has enlisted you in his army"* 2 Timothy 2:4 NLT.

Paul compared himself to a runner, saying, *"I am focusing all my energies on this one thing: Forgetting the past and looking forward to what lies ahead, I strain to reach the end of the race and receive the prize for which God, through Christ Jesus, is calling us up to heaven"* Philippians 3:13b-14 NLT.

James encourages us not to waver in asking God for anything: *"But let him ask in faith, with no doubting, for he who doubts is like a wave of the sea driven and tossed by the wind. For let not that man think that he will receive anything from the Lord; he is a double-minded man, unstable in all his ways"* James 1:6-8 NKJV.

Patience: Waiting for God to Move

A speaker at a pastors' conference began by putting on an exaggerated ecclesiastical tone. Solemnly he pronounced:

    "God ... is omnipotent.
    God ... is omniscient.
    God ... is omnipresent.
    God ... is slooooooooow."

Everyone burst out laughing. He had struck a common nerve. How often have we all prayed, and waited... and waited... ? How often have we thought, "Lord... ? Lord... ? What's happening? You have all the time in the world, but I don't. I have deadlines. And there's so much I want to do. And I'm not getting any younger! The Scripture says a day with the Lord is as a thousand years see 2 Peter 3:8, and right now it certainly seems that way. You said, *'The trying of your faith worketh patience'* James 1:3 KJV but what doth the trying of my patience work? Lord...?

He knows all about it. But he operates on his own timeline, and he's not about to let us get ahead of it. He can see the end from the beginning, and we can't. He knows what his plans are for us, and we don't. He is God, and we're not. And besides, he insists on teaching us patience because in our agitation and anxiety, we forget that he's in charge. This is surely one of God's most important and difficult lessons, but it's a key to a victorious, faith-filled life. "Hold on," God is saying; "I'm here. If you trust and wait, you'll see my plan unfold.

Anthony DeStefano writes, "God is a God of *perfect timing*. Since he is able to see the "big picture," he knows just when you should move on and when you should stay where you are. And sometimes before you move on he has to "arrange" a thousand different details in order to make that move possible. That arranging takes time".[17]

Obedience: Finding God's Will

Some decisions are easy; we make many of them each day. Sometimes we have to make spur-of-the-moment decisions when there's no time to deliberate. All we can do is shoot up a quick dart of prayer and do what feels right before the moment passes. The better we know the Lord and his ways, the more likely these decisions are to be right. The Holy Spirit guides us and even in certain situations puts words in our mouths see Luke 12:11-12.

Sometimes God makes decisions for us without our knowing. He steers us out of the path of the danger that we didn't even know was there. Or he places us in exactly the right spot at the right moment to meet someone he has prepared for us to help, or work with (or marry). Superstitious people may call this coincidence, or fate, or luck, or serendipity, but we like to think of it as God's engineering.

Some decisions are make-or-break ones; if we take a wrong turn here we may be a long time getting back on track. So how do we go about finding the will of God in important situations where there are several possible ways to go?

Our chief source of revelation is, of course, God's Word. Not only is it a formidable weapon, it's also the most important faith-building, error-avoiding tool God has given us. But there are times when we can't find scriptural revelation on the solution for a here-and-now problem. James 1:5 says that if we need wisdom, we can ask God for it and he will give it to us. And in Psalm 32:8 God promises: *"I will instruct you and guide you… along the best pathway for your life. I will advise you and watch your progress"* TLB.

We believe God lines up **guideposts** pointing the way for us. Here are the ones we look for, not necessarily in this order:

- Circumstances: open doors and divine appointments
- Sensing the leading of the Holy Spirit, or inner conviction
- Confirmation of that conviction through trusted counsel
- God's will revealed through his Word
- Provision

For us, none of these indicators by itself is sufficient for long-term, life-impacting decisions.

An open door alone doesn't give us the go-ahead (it depends on who opened the door). Neither does a closed door indicate that we're not to keep on knocking.

A feeling that we're to take an exciting new direction may be a word from God, a momentary enthusiasm, or something we ate. Feelings alone can be dangerous because *"the heart is deceitful above all things, and desperately wicked"* Jeremiah 17:9 NKJV. Our own desires can masquerade as the leading of the Holy Spirit.

A word from a prophet that we're to pull up stakes and move to the desert isn't necessarily the word of the Lord; if so, God will confirm it in other ways. But wise counsel from others whom we trust is important: *"In the multitude of counsellors there is safety"* Proverbs 11:14b NKJV. See also Proverbs 24:6.

Sometimes passages we're reading in the Bible come alive and whisper or shout the word of the Lord specifically to us. But opening up the Bible (or any book) at random and putting your finger on a verse is called "bibliomancy" and is akin to fortune telling. We once heard of a man, looking for guidance, who tried this. He closed his eyes, opened his Bible, and his finger fell on *"Judas went out and hanged himself."* Alarmed, he closed it quickly and opened it again, only to find his finger resting on *"Go thou and do likewise."* Not exactly the kind of guidance he was hoping for.

Provision – now there's a delicate one. Sometimes provision for a project we feel called to, comes ahead of time; sometimes it requires an act of faith to step out, and if God is in it, provision comes as we begin to obey. When the Israelites started to cross the Jordan, the river didn't begin to part until the priests stepped into the water.

If at least adequate provision doesn't come, stop and question your leading. The Lord may be directing you into another path. *"And if you leave God's paths and go astray, you will hear a Voice behind you say, 'No, this is the way; walk here'"* Isaiah 30:21 TLB. Time for course correction.

Sometimes lack of provision can be a clue to one of three things:

1. We've stepped off the track.
2. We're on the track but God is signalling a change of direction.
3. We're on the track but the time is not yet.

Moving ahead before God has prepared the circumstances ahead can be fruitless if not disastrous. Many years ago Carol worked at a Christian-owned recording studio.

Most secular customers paid on time, but sometimes it was the Christian ministries that got into trouble.

Someone would "sense" a calling from the Lord to make a radio broadcast or an album and would take a leap of faith and run up a big studio bill. When they couldn't pick up their master tape because they didn't have the money to pay for it they were shocked. But if God hadn't really called them to do it, he was not responsible to provide for it.

One of these guideposts alone is not enough for us to act on, but when they start to come together and line up; we begin to feel we're onto something. And often we are. To mix a few sports metaphors: sometimes we get into trouble by jumping the gun, or jumping offside, as soon as we sense the first indication of something we really want to do. The Bible says, *"Let the peace of God rule in your hearts"* Colossians 3:15a NKJV. That word for rule, in its noun form, means umpire – *"Let the peace of God umpire in your hearts."* When enough signals fit together to give you peace about it, you can say, "Yes! I'm convinced that's what the Lord is saying." Then go for it!

All this requires praying, listening, patience – and coming to know the Word of God. Although the Lord does lead us by his Spirit, no "leading" or "feeling" or "sensing" is from God if it violates any of the principles revealed in his Word. That's why it's so important to learn the Word well so the Holy Spirit can bring it to your remembrance when you need it. The psalmist wrote, *"Your Word I have hidden in my heart, that I might not sin against you"* Psalm 119:11 NKJV. (If you've never done any disciplined Bible study, start with classes at your church. Then try the Navigators' memory system. Or take a Bible school extension course).

Here's how all this worked for us: An important turning point in our lives came when we sensed God had something new for us to do. (This was to desist from writing which went on for a year and a half.)

It was a strange time for us. We couldn't see it then, but looking back now, it seems the Lord was engineering some life-changing circumstances to make us more dependent on him and to prepare us for a new direction. As the Scripture says, *"A man's heart plans his way, but the Lord directs his steps"* Proverbs 16:9 NKJV.

First, we stumbled into attending a (then) tiny but blossoming new church pastored by our old friend, Jack Hayford. Although we didn't realise it yet, this was our *divine appointment*. But, about that same time, Jimmy developed a serious health problem, and almost immediately after that his major source of income all but failed. Although just enough work came knocking on our door to keep food on the table, we still felt strongly that we were not to write anything new until we heard from God. Our job was to wait on him. It took a long time.

Because writing was a significant source of our income, by the end of a year and a half we had reached the bottom of the moneybag.

By the time we had to sell a piano to pay the bills, we were getting a little concerned. Still we waited... and wondered: Had we heard right? Were we crazy? (By the way, all this was done with the knowledge and encouragement of our pastor and fellow church council members. Then the thought did occur: Maybe we're all crazy!)

Our family never missed a meal or failed to pay our bills while all this was going on. If that had happened, we would have known we had heard wrong and immediately done something to remedy it. We were willing; we were just waiting for our specific path, and finally we found it.

The break-through came when our pastor casually remarked over Sunday dinner, "Maybe God wants you to write a musical about our church." Then he laughed. We didn't take it seriously at the moment, but by morning Jimmy awoke with the thought, "That's it!" A musical, not about our church, but about what God had been teaching our church for the past year and a half. Carol agreed, and we went to work. Through a trusted leader, we had heard wise counsel from God, even though he didn't realise the importance of what he was saying! But, we heard God anyway. The results were amazing to us.

From that time of waiting and praying and listening sprang our musical, Come Together, with ministry more far-reaching than all our previous twenty years of ministry combined. It was videotaped at the Los Angeles Forum and shown as a television special throughout the United States and Canada, and hundreds of churches performed it. Jean Darnall met with church leaders in Great Britain and organised a national British tour. Then thirty cities formed their own touring troupes and mass choirs and presented several hundred performances, filling many of the largest halls and cathedrals throughout Britain. Some of those groups stayed together for ten years.

Two Members of Parliament who attended one of the first performances went to the Archbishop of Canterbury and urged him to issue a public call to the nation to return to God. He did, and the queen backed him up. A cover article about Come Together appeared in a leading British Christian magazine in 2000, subtitled, "How One Musical Changed the Way We Worship."

Our next musical, If My People, followed in those same venues, plus a 70-city American national tour that brought over 120,000 commitments to intercede for the nation. 30,000 attended its opening events in Los Angeles alone. Writing musicals for ministry became, for many years, our chief calling.

We were stunned by all this. When we had started trying to find out what the Lord had for us to do next we had no idea where he would take us, or of the whole new turn our lives would take because of it.

If the Church will wait on the Lord until we hear his instructions, we will be dramatically more effective in intercession and action. Ephesians 2:10 sheds clear light on this:

> For we are God's handiwork, recreated in Christ Jesus, that we may do those good works which God predestined (planned beforehand) for us [taking paths which God prepared ahead of time], that we should walk in them [living the good life which he prearranged and made ready for us to live] AB.

- **Not just any good works...** but those good works.
- **Not just any paths...** but those paths.
- **Not just any life...** but that life... planned, prepared, prearranged.

Finding a need and trying to fill it isn't always the best plan. God has promised to bless only what is in his will. There is a master plan (prepared by the Master), and we need to find our place in it as we intercede with our prayers and lives.

So, we have to learn to wait, watch and listen.

Some things, such as family and church, are plainly part of our prayer and action assignment. We've also been given both these responsibilities for our government. The most effective way to fulfil these assignments is to ask God to bring specific situations and people to our attention. Then we'll pray his prayers in his will. Our intercession brings God's intervention.

To make sure you're hearing God's voice in your heart, begin by practising James 4:7, which says, *"Therefore submit to God. Resist the devil and he will flee from you"* NKJV. Our friend Joy Dawson uses this Scripture to point out a powerful three-step procedure:

- **Submit yourself to God** *Tell him you're submitting your will, your opinions, and your desires to Him.*
- **Resist the devil** *and he will flee from you. In Jesus' name forbid Satan and demon powers to speak to you.*
- **Wait and listen patiently.** *God may bring someone's name or face into your mind. It will keep coming back, nagging at you until you pray.*
- **Search the Scriptures** *as you pray. If you find any contradiction to what you think you're receiving from God, go back and start over! The Spirit and the Word agree. Always. The Word is your safeguard and the light on your path.*

When you're confident that you're praying in God's will, you'll be able to ask in faith and speak with authority.

You may say, "I feel certain that what I'm asking for is in the will of God, but I don't see any progress with my problem. Is that a blockage? What now?"

When progress is slow, stand fast. Maintain your attitude of authority, praise and patience. Keep the faith! You're in a warfare that's fought skirmish by skirmish. Your opposition is real and your job is to stand fast. Ultimately you'll win.

Proper Protocol: Speaking of the Devil

If we don't maintain the proper attitudes in our spiritual conflict, we'll find ourselves in deep and murky waters. This is not the place for smart-alecks. Although we may not understand why, we're told to follow spiritual protocol in dealing with our satanic enemy. While we may operate with utmost boldness, arrogance is out of place. It's not scriptural and it's not wise to deride or scorn the devil. God says not to do it, so we don't.

People who encourage you to adopt this attitude are either uninformed or disobedient to the Word. Jude, in warning the Church about false teachers says, *"Their dreams lead them to… insult celestial beings. In contrast, when the archangel Michael was in debate with the devil, disputing the possession of Moses' body, he did not presume to condemn him in insulting words, but said, 'May the Lord rebuke you'"* Jude 8-9 NEB. see also 2 Peter 2:10-11.

You don't need to use abusive words against the enemy. All you need is the knowledge of your authority in union with Christ's power. Refer the devil to Calvary; he knows he lost the battle there. Refer him to the empty tomb and to the ascension; he knows he was stripped of his authority then. Now he knows that we know it, and that puts things on a different footing.

However, while it's true that we're identified with Christ in his authority and righteousness, we can't use that as a haven to harbour deliberate, known sin. If we try it, the devil will laugh in our faces. So, before we charge in with bared bayonets, we'd better have the humility to check – often – for our vulnerable areas. We need to keep short accounts with God, turning quickly to confession and repentance. To be able to say with Jesus, "Satan, you have nothing in me" see John 14:30 puts us in the position of safety and power.

Vigilance: Watching, Working, and Winning

The book of Nehemiah in the Old Testament tells of the rebuilding of the walls of Jerusalem after the Jewish exile in Persia. Bitter enemies plotted to come and fight against Jerusalem and kill them and stop the work. *"But we prayed to our God and posted a guard day and night to meet this threat."* Nehemiah said to the people, *"Don't be afraid of them. Remember the Lord, who is great and awesome, and fight for your brothers, your sons and your daughters, your wives and your homes."* Nehemiah relates: *"From that day on, half of my men did the work, while the other half were equipped with spears, shields, bows and armour... Those who carried materials did their work with one hand and held a weapon in the other, and each of the builders wore his sword at his side as he worked."* God protected them and gave them the victory.[18]

The Apostle Peter wrote, *"Be sober, be vigilant; because your adversary the devil walks about like a roaring lion, seeking whom he may devour. Resist him, steadfast in the faith, knowing that the same sufferings are experienced by your brotherhood in the world"* 1 Peter 5:8-9 NKJV.

But Satan doesn't always come on as obviously as a roaring lion – in his wily ways he makes more subtle approaches. Your knowledge of God's Word and your sensitivity to the Holy Spirit will keep you from being blinded by false doctrines and religions (or from developing your own doctrines from isolated Scriptures pulled kicking and screaming from their proper context).

Boldness and Humility: a Winning Combination

Spiritual warriors need balanced attitudes: *boldness* through our authority in Christ, and *humility* to keep us aware of our total dependence on Him. Jesus meant it when he said, *"Apart from me, you can do nothing"* John 15:5 NIV. Boldness is an attitude that keeps us on the offensive, that preaches the Word and wins battles. Humility keeps us clinging to Jesus, saves us from spiritual independence and leads us into the covering of submission.

Submission: For Protection and Correction

Independence is a dangerous attitude in the Christian life, and especially in spiritual battle. A good, solid covering shield by our allies is vital.

Remember this old familiar movie scenario? Nigel and Trevor are frantically clawing their way through the jungle, heading for cover after setting explosive charges to blow up a strategic enemy bridge. The success of their mission will, of course, determine the entire outcome of World War II. From a safe distance, they stop to watch the explosion. Nothing happens. Looking through their field glasses, they find the problem: the fuse has gone out.

Nigel loses the coin toss, so he goes back to relight the fuse. By this time, enemy troops are approaching the bridge from the other side. Nigel's chances of remaining undetected are nil. His only protection is Trevor with his rifle, popping away at the enemies. Nigel, of course, blows up the bridge but, overwhelmed by the enemy's firepower, dies a hero's death.

What the poor man needed was the covering of a whole platoon of heavily armed soldiers. There are some things you just shouldn't try without the proper protection.

No matter how strong or important we may think we are, every one of us needs a covering – a shield. We find it in our submission to the Church. These are our fellow warriors. Just as soldiers in physical battle cover one another with protective fire, so Christians are to constantly shield and defend one another by intercessory prayer. We need trusted pastors, spiritual mentors and prayer partners, not only for their help in the heat of battle, but also for their wise correction, which may save us from disaster along the way.

Every Christian soldier – even those in positions of high authority – needs the counsel and aid of experienced warrior-leaders. Even the apostles answered to one another for how they lived, what they taught, and how they ministered. This protected them and the Church from error. When Paul and Peter were opposed by other teachers, they submitted to the conclusions of a council of apostles and elders at Jerusalem. If they operated in the attitude of submission to the Church, how much more should all of us?

Because the two of us have travelled for extensive periods, we haven't been constantly under the eye of a local body. Instead, we have a group of mature, spiritually seasoned men and women – some are on our ministry board and some are pastors – who are only a phone call away. These are the people we talk things over with before we make major moves. They pray with and for us and ask God to speak to them on our behalf. Sometimes they call us with advice. They have given us encouragement, direction and correction for years. There's no way to tell you how grateful we are for them. *"For by wise counsel you can wage your war, and in an abundance of counsellors there is victory and safety"* Proverbs 24:6 AB

Expectancy: Believing for the Best

The Bible says, *"But without faith it is impossible to please him, for he who comes to God must believe that he is, and that he is a rewarder of those who diligently seek him"* Hebrews 11:6 NKJV.

Jesus said, *"All things, whatever you ask in prayer, believing, you will receive"* Matthew 21:22 NKJV. Knowing the promises of God and the character of God helps us to grow in faith and have our prayers answered.

James wrote, *"ask in faith, with no doubting"* James 1:6b NKJV. One thing that causes us to doubt is an unclear conscience. That's why it's so important to search our hearts and make sure there is no hindrance to our prayers. *"Beloved, if our heart does not condemn us, we have confidence toward God, and whatever we ask we receive from him, because we keep his commandments and do those things that are pleasing in his sight"* 1 John 3:21-22 NKJV.

We come to a God *"who by his mighty power at work within us is able to do far more than we would ever dare to ask or even dream of – infinitely beyond our highest prayers, desires, thoughts, or hopes"* Ephesians 3:20 TLB.

Persistence Pays

A persistent attitude pays off. Jesus said, *"Ask and keep on asking and it shall be given you; seek and keep on seeking and you shall find; knock and keep on knocking and the door shall be opened to you* v 9 AB.

For instance, once when we sold our house, we ran into all the usual delays with lenders and estate agents. Transferring papers between neighbouring offices apparently required an act of parliament. At the same time, an acquaintance of ours was also selling a house. In the twinkling of an eye, it seems, all the papers were signed, the deal was closed and he had moved out.

"Wait a minute here!" we protested. "How'd you *do* that?"

"I drove them crazy," he said. "I called two or three times every day, checking them out. At the end, I parked myself in their offices till they signed the papers I needed, and then I hand-carried them to the next guy on the agenda." He smiled smugly. "They couldn't get rid of me fast enough."

Jesus seemed to recommend a similar method of getting what we need through prayer. His story goes something like this: A man has an unexpected midnight visit from a friend who is passing through town. The friend is not only tired but also hungry. But there's a problem: the cupboard is bare. Our man rushes over to his neighbour's house and knocks on the door. When the neighbour, looking cross, peers out from the bedroom window, our man asks him for three loaves of bread.

The neighbour says, "It's midnight! Can't you see the lights are out? We're all in bed, where all decent people should be. Go away!" And he shuts the window.

But our man is shamelessly persistent. He knocks again and waits for his neighbour's head to pop out of the window so he can repeat his request. This goes on until the neighbour decides that our man is not going away and nobody is going to get any sleep until the three loaves of bread are handed over. Jesus said that although the neighbour wouldn't supply our man out of friendship, yet because of the man's persistence he got up and gave him as much as he needed see Luke 11:5-8.

That's the key. After you've prayed in faith, keep on giving thanks for prayer already heard and answers already on the way. Keep on standing firmly on the promises of God's Word.

Then let patience and perseverance complete their work.

You might pray like this: "Father, here I am to remind you again. I thank you that you always hear me and that you're moving in my behalf. I just want you to know that I'm still asking and I'm still waiting with confidence and peace for you to move – and I'll be back."

This was the attitude of the Church in Riga, Latvia, under Soviet domination. A letter was smuggled out to us saying that our music had reached them several years previously and they had risked doing a performance of *Come Together* in an attempt to unify a divided and demoralised Church. They had no idea what kind of response they might receive but, happily, the venue was packed. "So the work began," they said.

Our next musical, *If My People* followed. This called the people to ongoing intercession for their beleaguered nation. For years they steadfastly prayed and built a wall of righteousness for the land. For years nothing happened. Then, when God's time finally arrived, the walls of communism crumbled so fast that the whole world watched in awe.

Soon after the communists were deposed, we went on an outreach to the Baltic countries and Russia with Loren Cunningham and other YWAM leaders.

In Tallinn, Estonia and Riga, Latvia, the churches collaborated in big public productions of *If My People*. The performances were emotional and powerful as the people gave thanks, worshipped and prayed. Then they pledged themselves to keep right on praying for their land and, now that the walls of righteousness had been established, to guard its gates.

Maybe you've been praying for a long time for ungodly government officials, or against unrighteous or oppressive laws, without seeing any change. Never give up. Let the perseverance and victory of the Baltic people give you courage. God still moves in human affairs and when the time is right, he does a quick work.

Spurgeon wrote, "Let your faith be more resolved... Let your cry grow more vehement. ... Bring your prayers as some ancient battering ram against the gate of heaven and force it open with a sacred violence... Besiege the mercy seat and you shall prevail."

Joyfulness in All Circumstances

"The joy of the Lord is your strength." Nehemiah 8:10b KJV

"Dear brothers and sisters, whenever trouble comes your way, let it be an opportunity for joy" James 1:2. How can this be? The Apostle James goes on to say, *"For when your faith is tested, your endurance has a chance to grow. So let it grow, for when your endurance is fully developed, you will be strong in character and ready for anything"* verses 3-4.

Can you image a more desolate situation than that of Paul and Silas – chased by an enraged mob, then arrested, stripped, severely beaten with wooden rods and imprisoned with unwashed wounds in the blackness of an inner dungeon with their feet clamped in stocks, facing a trial and an unknown future? So how do they react?

"Around midnight, Paul and Silas were praying and singing hymns to God" Acts 16:25. Singing? The mind boggles! Suddenly a great earthquake shakes the prison to its foundations, blows open all the doors and knocks off all the chains. But do Paul and Silas run to escape? No – they stay behind to stop the jailer from suicide and lead him and his whole family to the Lord. The next morning they're set free. Read it in Acts 16:22-40.

In 2 Corinthians 11 Paul describes his years of hard labours, jailings, whippings, beatings, stonings, shipwrecks, floods, muggings, mobbings, weariness, pain, hunger, thirst, and cold. Besides that, he had "a thorn in the flesh", an ongoing physical infirmity that the Lord wouldn't take away, lest he get swollen-headed because of the revelations he had had. Yet this is that same Paul who wrote, *"Rejoice in the Lord always. I will say it again: Rejoice!"* Philippians 4:4 NIV.

This is the same Paul who wrote, *"In everything give thanks; for this is the will of God in Christ Jesus for you"* 1 Thessalonians 5:18 NKJV.

This is that same Paul who wrote, *"I have learned how to get along happily whether I have much or little. I know how to live on almost nothing or with everything... with a full stomach or empty, with plenty or little. For I can do everything with the help of Christ who gives me the strength I need"* Philippians 4:11-13 NLT.

The Apostle Peter wrote: *"Dear friends, don't be surprised at the fiery trials you are going through, as if something strange were happening to you. Instead, be very glad – because these trials will make you partners with Christ in his suffering, and afterward you will have the wonderful joy of sharing his glory when it is displayed to all the world"* 1 Peter 4: 12-13.

For years we've kept an old cartoon of a scene where devils with horns and pitchforks are driving people at hard labour. In the midst of flames and smoke, one man is pushing a wheelbarrow filled with coal, whistling, smiling, and happy as can be. In the caption, one demon says to another, "You know, we're just not reaching that guy." We have a long way to go, but that's the way we want to be. The lives of the apostles set a standard for us all.

A Matter of Life and Death

One last vital attitude: *"They did not love and cling to life even when faced with death"* Rev.12:11 AB. Jesus said, *"I am the resurrection and the life; he who believes in me will live, though he dies. And whoever lives and believes in me will never die"* John 11:25-26 NIV.

In Estonia we met people with this attitude. It's the attitude of overcomers. We spoke in Estonia's largest church on the day after all laws restricting religious freedom in the Soviet Union expired, after seventy years of oppression. The church is just down the street from the former KGB headquarters where some of their people had been imprisoned and tortured. But they had come back out and kept on going, knowing that their lives were on the line. This is what Christianity is all about: It is a faith so strong, an eternal future so sure, that there is no risk in laying down our lives in life intercession, for there is no death for the believer in Christ.

Our son experienced that when he was in his teens. Did you ever get one of those phone calls that begins with, "I'm all right ... ", and every hair on your head stands up, waiting for the "but ..." We had a call like that from our teenaged son.

"But... ? what?! Where are you?"

"At the hospital."

"The hospital! (Dear Lord... !) "What are you doing at the hospital? What happened? Are you hurt?"

"No, I just had my ear sewed up."

"Your ear? What happened to your ear?"

"Well, it was like this... Scott and I were hiking... "

"Yes?"

"And... well, we took a shortcut through that long narrow train tunnel. A train had just gone through, and we figured, surely there wouldn't be another one for a while, but there was."

"A train! What... ?"

"Yes. We were about halfway through when the tracks started to ring and there was this terrific noise behind us and this vibration and this light swinging and growing. We started running as fast as we could, but I could see there was no way we were going to beat that train. All I could see ahead was that little bright hole that was the tunnel exit, way, way off."

"What happened? How did you hurt just your ear?"

"Well, I had my scout knife in my scabbard on my belt and it was loose and started flopping around and I grabbed it and just then my elbow hit the wall and well . . ."

"Well?"

"Well, it knocked my arm up and I ran the knife through my ear, front to back. I'm really okay... except for a few stitches."

"Thank God!"

"But you know, Mum, Dad... with that horrendous noise and vibration gaining on me by the second, it dawned on me, I am really going to die – right now! And then I thought, Dear God, I'm going to see Jesus. In just a few seconds I'm going to see Jesus! And that's when I started to get excited."

In spite of his spiritual excitement, his legs kept on running until he and his friend fell into a shallow escape niche carved into the side of the tunnel. There they pressed themselves into the wall while the train slammed past only inches from their faces.

Since they came through relatively unscathed, our first reaction – after bear hugs from his dad and kisses from his mother – was to scathe him ourselves. But he had already learned a lesson. He said, "I found out the most important thing in the world in that tunnel; I found out that I really believe all the things I always thought I believed."

For those moments at least, he had experienced the certainty of eternal life and freedom from the fear of death. Jesus died to break the bondage Satan holds over you through that fear see Hebrews 2:14-15.

When you *know* you have eternal life, you can follow the arrows wherever God leads you because you have nothing to be afraid of. When you recognise that, you're totally liberated.

There is no fear in love; but perfect love casts out fear, because fear involves torment.
1 John 4:18 NKJV

"NO FEAR" – We've all seen the tee shirt. Usually it's meant as a macho display of hubris – a pretentious flaunting of the wearer's supposedly indomitable spirit in the face of whatever he may face, including God himself. It's the same attitude we find in *"Invictus"*, the poem by William Ernest Henley, which we first encountered in English Lit 101, in which he thanks "whatever gods there may be" for his unconquerable soul: "I am the master of my fate, I am the captain of my soul." In other words, "I don't need God or anybody else, and you'd better not mess with me." The chilling part of this is that Timothy McVeigh quoted the poem as his last words before his execution in 2001 for the Oklahoma City bombing. And this was presented to us high school lit students as an example of nobleness?

"No Fear" is also a slogan of "extreme sports" enthusiasts. Our daughter Jamie was watching one of those Evel Kneivel-type daredevil motorcycle stunts on TV. The rider swaggered up to his bike, VROOM VROOM VROOMed around the arena before the crowd with his fist raised triumphantly, then launched himself into the air and unfortunately reached the other side before his bike did. Carol walked in just in time to see him come a cropper. "Who in the world was that?" she asked. Jamie's dry reply was, "Stupid Knupid." Maybe he should have listened to his fear.

But in the spiritual realm, God does say to us, "No fear." We are to fear God, of course, but when it comes to man, Jesus himself said it over and over: *"Do not be afraid."* This is a seemingly impossible attitude to drum up on our own. In fact, seasoned soldiers will tell you that courage in battle is not the absence of fear, but heroic acts committed in spite of fear. Fear is a gift of God, to protect us from danger; we learn early that fear of being burned protects us from touching a hot stove.

But our lack of fear in fearsome circumstances has to be based on something other than our own determination. It must be based on our belief in the immutable promises of God and the empowering of the Holy Spirit. Why should we not fear if we are about to face danger, or even death, for our testimony? Because Jesus said so.

In the same discourse where he told his followers that some of them would be killed for their witness, he said to them (and by extension, to us): *"Not a hair of your head shall be lost"* Luke 21:18 NKJV. Obviously the truth he was teaching, as was often the case, was spiritual not physical.He didn't say he would keep us from suffering (although he often does); he said that he would be with us in it:

"I am with you always, even to the end of the age" Matthew 28:20 NIV. In another place he said, *"Be of good cheer. I have overcome the world"* John 16:33 NKJV.

He has been there before us, and even he sweated great drops as of blood in contemplation of it, and he is with us in our ordeal, whatever that may be. Anthony DeStefano writes in

"Ten Prayers God Always Says Yes To", that in virtually every book of the Bible God tells his people to be brave. He points out: "The words 'fear not,' 'be not afraid,' or variations on that phrase appear 144 times in the sacred Scripture! And they aren't just suggestions – they're commands. The Bible doesn't say, 'Try not to be afraid,' it says, 'Don't be afraid.' It doesn't say, 'Do your best to be strong,' it says, 'Be strong and fear not, for I will help you.' God never gives a command unless he also gives us the ability to follow that command."

Corrie ten Boom, in *"The Hiding Place"*, told of her fear, as a young girl, that she wouldn't be able to face martyrdom if necessary, if she and her family were caught hiding Jews from the Nazis. As she and her father were waiting to board a train, she asked him about her ticket. He told her he was holding it for her and would give it to her when she needed it. He told her that God held such a ticket for her, and if a time for persecution ever came, he would give it to her then. Her father called it her "grace ticket." In the meantime she was to live without fear.

Even so, we can say, *"I know whom I have believed, and am convinced that he is able to guard what I have entrusted to him for that day"* 2 Timothy 1:12 NIV. When we need our "grace ticket," it will be there for us, too.

Prayer for the Battle

When you use your armour, wield your weapons, and get your attitudes in order, you're ready to win spiritual battles. Use this prayer as a jumping-off place from which you can expand on any and all of these urgent prayer points.

Mighty God, we put on your armour: your salvation, truth and righteousness. We take the shield of faith to repel Satan's fiery attacks. We lift up your sword – the living Word of God – and with your high praises in our mouths we come to do battle.

We are the temple of the Holy Spirit – the repository of your authority in our world. We are the ambassadors of Jesus Christ, who has all authority over the devil and his works. We are cleansed and made righteous by Jesus' blood, and we declare to the powers of darkness that they have no place in us and no power over us.

In Jesus' name we resist the dark spirits that pervert justice and fill our streets with fire and blood. We plead for equal justice for all people in our nation. Lord, replace hatred and violence with your spirit of peace, compassion, repentance and reconciliation. In the name of the Lord, we lift up the banner of the Kingdom of God and pray for the Spirit of grace over our land.

We resist the deceiving spirits who encourage the slaughter of our unborn children. Give us love, wisdom, and godly strategy as we confront this evil. Bring revelation, conviction, and repentance to those who defend and encourage this terrible sin in our nation.

Lord, break the power of gross immorality and perversion that brings bondage, degradation and death to thousands of our countrymen.

Open the eyes of the spiritually blind. Let them see that truth, life and real freedom are in Jesus Christ.

We lift your triumphant name up over the lying spirits of occultism and idolatry in our land. Expose them with your truth and free those who are entangled in a lie. Protect the minds of your people from these deceptions and keep them pure through your Word.

Lord, you are the Truth. You are the Spirit above all spirits, King above all kings and Lord of heaven and earth!

We hold a defensive umbrella of prayer over our national decision-makers. Protect them from the enemy's influence. Give them wisdom and courage to make righteous decisions so that your blessing, rather than your curse, may rest on our country.

We resist the spiritual principalities of darkness that rule in our city. Make us prayer warriors who will persevere until Satan's strongholds crumble.

Protect us from the weapons of our enemies, who want to conquer not only our country but all of Western Civilisation. Scatter them, Lord, and bring confusion to their plans and failure to their cause.

Renew the Church in wisdom, faith, holiness, love, courage, and power, so the world may see you in us and believe.

Move the whole Church to take the whole gospel to the whole world so that we may see in our time the final great harvest that will signal the return of our Lord Jesus Christ!

In that mighty Name we pray!

Amen.

---

[17] Anthony DeStefano, Ten Questions God Always Says Yes To [Doubleday]

[18] excerpted from Nehemiah, NIV

Talk About This:

1. How do you feel you score on the first three attitudes listed in this chapter: single-mindedness or determination; patience; and obedience? What might you need to work on? p121-123

2. How important is it to find those good works which God predestined for us? p122

3. What are some directional guideposts leading to God's will? Have you had occasion to try these? How have they worked for you? p119

4. Are you discouraged when you don't see immediate answers to prayer? Have you seen good results from perseverance? How can your group encourage one another in persevering prayer?

5. How important is searching the scriptures as you pray in order to find God's will? Why?

6. If you ever have to deal directly with a satanic situation, what should your attitude be? How should you speak to the enemy? p123

7. Moving at your own pace, discuss the important attitudes covered by the rest of the chapter. If you are in a group which ones created the most discussion?

Pray About This:

a. Pray *The Prayer for the Battle* p131. If you are in a group take turns in reading paragraphs. As one reads, let the others agree. Do we hear an "amen"?

b. Pray for personal requests and blessing for your families.

PART 7

LIGHT OUT OF DARKNESS

Behold, the darkness shall cover the earth, and deep darkness the people; but the Lord will arise over you, and his glory will be seen upon you.

Isaiah 60:2 NKJV

Chapter 15 - Lions in the Street

It is high time to awake out of sleep; for now our salvation is nearer than when we first believed.
Romans 13:11 NKJV

Years ago a musical called *Cabaret* came to our stages and screens. It was vulgar indeed and we aren't recommending that you rent the video! But it's a powerful allegory. Much of the action takes place inside a cabaret in Germany during the beginnings of the Nazi movement. The cabaret patrons are a microcosm of pre-war society, given over to a pursuit of material, emotional and sexual fulfilment. God doesn't even enter the picture. Their philosophy is "Eat, drink and be merry, for tomorrow we die." Come to the cabaret!

While all the wild partying is going on and the empty relationships are building inside the cabaret, we have occasional flashes of what is happening just outside the doors: young, arrogant brown-shirted Storm Troopers are strutting through the streets. They're only a small radical group. The cabaret performers make fun of them; the customers ignore them.

Gradually, we glimpse the Troopers' behaviour becoming more aggressive as they begin to hassle the citizens. Finally, they start tormenting the Jews. Few in the cabaret protest this behaviour or speak out. After all, it isn't their responsibility; why get involved?

Before long, however, these same brown-shirts are filling the cabaret itself. Now they are the majority and can no longer be ignored. At that point it's too late to protest. The Nazis are in power. The party is over for everyone.

Likewise, if we don't want to subject ourselves to the authority of the "children of disobedience" and lose our freedoms, we must do something about it right now see Ephesians 2:2. If we don't pray for our government, use our courage and our rights to make our voices heard for righteousness' sake, and exercise our blood-bought right to vote, the Church may still find herself with her mouth gagged and her hands tied. We must not sleep during the seasons of seeming peace, because though the enemy may lie quietly, he only waits for us to close our eyes or to leave our posts to play and he will be upon us. This is not paranoia; it's history.

We needn't constantly be looking over our shoulders or peering into dark corners. But we need to be informed and to make prayer for our nation and its leaders a lifestyle, setting our faces for the long haul. Then we won't find ourselves desperately trying to deal with the consequences of what could have been prevented in the first place.

Had the Church been awake, praying powerfully, vital in her witness and courageous to speak out against unrighteousness in the name of the Lord, Nazism or communism or other tyrannous governments might never have reached their pinnacles of power. But the Church was either uninformed of her privileges in intercession or uninterested in exercising them. Her witness weakened, and the nations forgot God. The consequences were war and oppression.

Within those nations, however, a core of persistent prayer warriors continued to cry out. Gradually, intercessors in other nations heard God's commission to stand in the gap on behalf of their brothers and sisters and joined the spiritual fray. As a result, we have seen these despotic governments fall one by one. What if the cry had gone up before the tyrants were entrenched and the nations overcome?

Turning Up the Heat

A polarization between good and evil is growing in Western nations, as those who cry out to them that their ungodliness is bringing the judgment of God down on the nation are faced by those who cry out for their right to be ungodly.

Here's a story that makes the point: A group of people push off in a rowboat. When they get out to sea, one of them brings out a big drill and starts to drill a hole in the bottom of the boat under his seat. When the others realise that the boat is filling with water, they protest. The man says, "Hey, you can't tell me what to do. It's my seat!"

The enemy is patiently drilling holes in our boat, with a persistent, insidious attack on Christianity. So far it consists mostly of ridicule, especially in the extreme media and entertainment arenas. To them "a Born-again" means a person who is out of the mainstream, politically incorrect, and intolerant. Tolerance is the mantra of a permissive generation – tolerance of every life-style, philosophy and religion – so long as it isn't Christianity.

TV comedies mock Christians and portray us as misfits, hypocrites and homophobes. Columnists and television personalities have compared us to Nazis, book-banners, witch-burners and the Taliban. We're called arrogant and narrow-minded for saying Jesus is the only way to God, although we didn't make that up – Jesus said it himself see John 14:6, so we don't need to apologise for it.

We Christians in democratic nations have taken for granted our long season of relative peace. And as long as we go along with the tide of secularisation, we can go on living that way. But as we resist in greater numbers the encroachments that corrupt our children and bring the displeasure of God on our nation, some persons (with and without bodies) will feel their backs up against the wall and will lash out at us. Like tarantulas – they may be fun to watch, trundling around harmlessly. You can move in pretty close as long as you don't menace them. Some people even keep them as pets. But get one pinned in a corner and it can jump straight up and nail you.

This is more than religious bigotry or ideological debate. Already some Christians have been threatened, arrested, jailed, sued, ostracised, fired, and kicked out of schools for exercising their freedom of conscience and religious expression. This clash of kingdoms will lead to more and more overt persecution. God's enemies are trying hard through the political system to criminalise Christianity.

Persecution is foretold in the Bible, and has happened throughout history and throughout the world. Paul wrote, *"All who desire to live godly in Christ Jesus will suffer persecution"* see 2 Timothy 3:1, 12 NKJV.

But Jesus said, *"When the world hates you, remember that it hated me before it hated you. The world would love you if you belonged to it, but you don't. I chose you to come out of the world, and so it hates you... The people of the world will hate you because you belong to me, for they don't know God who sent me"* John 15:18-19, 21 NLT. In another place he said, *"What happiness there is when others hate you and exclude you and insult you and smear your name because you are mine! When that happens, rejoice! Yes, leap for joy! For you will have a great reward waiting for you in heaven. And you will be in good company – the ancient prophets were treated that way too!"* Luke 6:22-23 TLB.

And what should be our response to our persecutors? The Apostle Paul wrote, *"Don't get involved in foolish arguments which only upset people and make them angry. God's people must not be quarrelsome; they must be gentle, patient teachers of those who are wrong. Be humble when you are trying to teach those who are mixed up concerning the truth"* 2 Timothy 2:23-25a TLB. Jesus said, *"Love your enemies, bless those who curse you, do good to those who hate you, and pray for those who spitefully use you and persecute you"* Matthew 6:44 NKJV. Only a working of grace in our hearts can make this happen. Our natural response to aggression is to lash back, but as the Holy Spirit weaves into us the character of Christ, we may find ourselves rejoicing as Jesus told us to, and praying, as he did, *"Father, forgive them, for they don't know what they're doing."* Persecution will try and test us, and if we let it, will steel our resolve. God will give grace, and we will find we need each other more than ever.

Actually, these anti-God attacks are beginning to unite the church in its purpose. As Japanese Admiral Isoroku Yamamoto said after the attack on Pearl Harbour, "I fear all we have done is to awaken a sleeping giant and fill him with a terrible resolve." As the assaults on God, our children, the church, and the gospel increase, our prayer is that the church will arise and pursue the enemy to the gates of his domain, not with weapons made by man, but with spiritual weapons and Spirit-led actions.

A Battle for a City

In Jeremiah 29 the captive Jews in Babylon were told to "occupy" in the midst of their enemies and were given prayer responsibility for their city: *"Seek the peace of the city... and pray to the Lord for it; for in its peace you will have peace"* verse 7.

As an example of successful destiny shaping, take the experience of Antelope, Oregon. In 1981 the Bhagwan Shree Rajneesh, an Indian guru, with his 7,000 devotees and his 93 Rolls Royces moved into that rural Oregon community and began buying up the town.[19] By 1984 the cult took over the local government and school system and changed the name of the town to "The City of Rajneesh". They began to hold mass free-love rallies, which included sexual perversion, and to offer free accommodation to like minded people from all over the country. By the time the press got wind of the goings-on and made it public knowledge nationwide, it seemed too late to change things.

However, the cult made some mistakes. First, they purchased a Christian church and used it for storage and trash disposal. Then the Bhagwan publicly announced that Jesus Christ was a madman who had failed by dying on the cross.

When that hit the papers, Evangelist Mario Murillo read it, and it was just too much for him to swallow quietly. Immediately, he had his crusade director contact the local Christian organisations in nearby Madras and booked the local high school auditorium. Then Mario flew in to preach a sermon titled, "Did Jesus Fail by Dying on the Cross?"

The auditorium was packed. After preaching the gospel and leading a host of souls to Christ, Mario told the people that now was the time to stand and pray for their city in intense intercessory warfare and to keep on praying until the job was done. The Holy Spirit gave him three specific things to pray for:

- First, that someone of high rank in the cult would turn against the Bhagwan and expose him
- Next, that the Bhagwan would incur a government investigation leading to criminal charges
- Finally, that he would be deported.

They prayed that these miracles would be complete within six months. Almost to the day, these things came to pass in startling detail as the Bhagwan's right-hand leader exposed him and caused irreparable damage to the organisation. Then the unrelenting media assault forced state and federal investigations of cult activities, leading to criminal indictments. And last, the Bhagwan was fined $400,000 for immigration fraud and deported to India. The dump became a church again, and the properties were reclaimed by their original owners.

Mario says, "It was none of my doing that wrought this miracle. It was the army of God who took their rightful place in prayer and, through intercession, literally recaptured their community."

This is a picture for us of what can happen when somebody leads out and does something: when the Church rises up and says, "We're mad as hell and we're not going to take it anymore!"

The battle fought in the heavenlies worked itself out in the press, law enforcement and the courts, and an outpost of Satan's kingdom was shut down. The postscript to this story is that the whole compound was purchased by Young Life, and is now one of Oregon's premier Christian conference centres! Is there anything in your city that needs fixing?

By Many or By Few

Look at King Saul and his band of six hundred men, with only two swords among them (the rest have only farm implements) as they face the Philistine army, which boasts thirty thousand chariots and six thousand horsemen. A narrow pass between two rocky crags separates the armies. So far no one has made a move.

While Saul's army rests in their camp, Jonathan, Saul's son, who has one of the two swords, decides to do something about the situation. He says to his young armour bearer, *"Come on, let's go over to the garrison of these pagans; it may be that the Lord will work for us; for there is nothing to prevent the Lord from saving by many or by few"* 1 Samuel 14:6 AB.

The Philistines see the two Israelites coming and shout, "Come on up here and we'll show you a thing or two!" Jonathan, having the Lord's assurance that he is with them, accepts the invitation, climbs up to meet the enemy and slaughters about twenty men. The Philistines panic. The earth quakes and it becomes a terror from God. The Philistines turn their swords on one another in wild confusion.

When Saul and his napping army awake and look across the pass into the enemy camp, they finally realise what is happening and join the battle. Then the Israelites who have joined the Philistines turn back to fight for Israel. Even the Israelites who have hidden in the hills come out to fight when they hear that the Philistines are fleeing. So God delivers Israel see 1 Samuel 13:16-14:23.

Victory begins with only two brave men. Since in Old Testament typology, Israel is a model of the Church, we can picture from this story what can happen if a few Christians full of faith begin to attack the enemy.[20]

- There will be casualties in the enemy's camp and panic in his ranks as he reacts in confusion to the unexpected attack.
- Many in God's sleeping army will wake up, see what is happening and join in the battle.
- Christians who have joined the enemy's camp will renew their allegiance to God's cause as it goes from victory to victory.
- Those who have been fearful and have hidden from the warfare will take heart and join in pursuit of the enemy.

Many people are waiting for someone to step out and lead the way. You might find it easier than ever now to find willing warriors, because this is a movement borne on Spirit-wings. More and more believers are hearing the call to prayer and action as the Holy Spirit lifts up a standard rallying the Church to battle. Once you and a few "armour-bearers" have begun the work, share your vision with churches and pastors other than your own. As pastors call their people to united intercession with others, you can stand together, an army of light raised up against the onslaught of darkness.

You don't have to let the devil devour your family or your community. Don't lose the war by default. Stand up! Put on the armour! Pick up your weapons – and fight the spiritual fight! Whether we're many or few, let us "wage war on the devil as though we're performing a dance" – with confidence and joy.

God is listening – and it is *not* too late!

---

[19] Associated Press, 10/19/2001

[20] Note that we called Israel a model, or type, of the Church. We are not implying that the Church has in any way replaced Israel in God's scheme of things. Israel, in Scripture, means Israel. The Church is the Church.

Talk About This:

1. Whom do you see as "the children of disobedience" in our world? What are the three basic things you can do to keep from losing your freedoms to them? p136

2. Can you think of current examples of the polarisation between good and evil in British society? What can you do about it? p137

3. If we should face ridicule or persecution, what should our attitude be? Should you expect that to happen at some point? How should you feel about that? p137-138

4. Is there anything in your city or town that needs fixing? What can you do about it?

5. Many people are waiting for leadership in prayer and action for the nation. Might you, your group, or your church be willing to speak out and rally the troops? How? When?

6. This is a good time to recap any areas of the book you may not have had time to fully discuss or pray about earlier.

Pray About This:

a. Pray for the nation and its leadership, using the instructions and prayer points in the Epilogue on pages 173-176. You won't get it all done in one session, but you'll get a good start! Allow plenty of time for this.

Chapter 16 - The War We Face: Praying Against Terrorism

You shall not be afraid of the terror by night, Nor of the arrow that flies by day, Nor of the pestilence that walks in darkness, Nor of the destruction that lays waste at noonday. Psalm 91:5,6 NKJV

Today our western world is in a war unlike any other we have ever fought. In addition to moral decay from within, we face a new but ancient enemy from without, as jihad has been declared against us by fanatics who have used their scriptures as a rationale for a rampage of murder and destruction. Although the scale of this war is still small compared to other wars, its potential is ominous. The clash of nations is a manifestation of the clash of spiritual kingdoms: light against darkness, good against evil and freedom against bondage. Osama bin Ladin has called this "the beginning of World War III."

The events in the Middle East are inseparable from the terrorists' war on America, the United Kingdom, and other western countries. As intercessors we need to understand the connections and pray for those nations as we do for our own. Our enemies' specific goal is to kill and destroy (sound familiar?) not only Israel, but America as well, and ultimately to subjugate the entire world. Their final aim is the destruction of Western Civilisation, the forced conversion or annihilation of all "infidels" (non-Muslims), and the establishing of Islam as the one, uncontested world religion. This is not a new idea; it has been their purpose, written in their scriptures since Mohammed set the goal fourteen centuries ago, but only recently have their leaders felt it was time to step up the offensive on a global scale. But God's people are not to be afraid; God is firmly in control. Remember the sting operation he pulled off to achieve our redemption? Well, we can be assured by the prophetic Scriptures that the trap is set, and he is again watching Satan engineer his own downfall.

The present world conflict had its roots 4,000 years ago, when Abraham sired two sons: Isaac was the child of faith that God had promised Abraham; Ishmael was the child of impatience, born earlier because Abraham and Sarah lost faith in God's promise that Sarah would bear a son in her old age, and Sarah pressed Abraham into having a child by her Egyptian servant Hagar. God had Abraham send Ishmael and his mother away, but promised that both sons would give rise to great nations.

From Ishmael's line grew the Arab race, from Isaac's line the Jewish race, which in time brought forth Jesus, the God/Man, the Messiah, the Saviour of mankind.

But we must be careful not to disrespect Ishmael. God didn't. He sent his angel to miraculously rescue him and his mother in the desert. Arabs are not the enemies of mankind; terrorists are.

Six hundred years later Mohammed planted the religion of Islam and sowed the seeds for animosity to flare between Muslims and Jews in the last days. The Jews were scattered throughout the world from 70 AD, but God, as he had promised, began drawing them back to their homeland after the holocaust of World War II. This re-ignited ancient enmity with their Arab brethren.

Today both sides claim the Holy Land was given them by God and is home to sites sacred to both, as well as to Christians.

Here are excerpts from the Palestinians' HAMAS Covenant, issued in 1988:

"The land of Palestine is an Islamic Waqf [Holy Possession] consecrated for future Moslem generations until Judgment Day. No one can renounce it or any part, or abandon it or any part of it... Israel will exist and will continue to exist until Islam will obliterate it, just as it has obliterated others before it".[21]

A rabbi explains the Jewish side of the conflict – God promised Abraham that he and his descendants (through Isaac) would inherit the land of Israel as an eternal possession. "Our people flourished here for thousands of years. Our right to the land did not expire because we were forced to leave. We are required to *protect* ourselves and we are not permitted to give away land so that terrorism can be cultivated! In Jewish law, a Jew is not allowed to hand over *any* parts of the Holy Land to a non-Jew".[22]

That's what you call the ultimate standoff. There is no human solution. The nations of the world can't solve this; it's a family feud. But when this conflict explodes, the entire world will be drawn into it. Ultimately, the end-time events prophesied in the Bible will play out on the world stage. The time could be soon.

We see on our screens the faces of hatred and hear the voices of fury screaming, "God is great! Death to Israel! Death to America!" We have been attacked, not by Islam, but by *radical, militant* Islam: most Muslims want to live and let live, but these extremists want to die and kill. They consider themselves holy warriors; this is their war of faith. It takes a lot of faith to want to blow yourself up, believing you will be assured of heaven in the process. They are sincere in their faith, but sincerely wrong. And their zeal has made them heartless, with no qualms about murdering innocent women and children, and the more the better. Their leaders issue fatwas – religious edicts – to all the faithful, to kill Israelis, Americans, the British, and others who stand with them, at any opportunity.

These radical warriors sincerely believe they can win and, in time, rule America. One of their bellicose leaders boasts, "We will raise the flag of Islam over the White House and rule the world." They dream of enforcing their Sharia (religious) law on mankind and demanding that the rest of us convert or die. They think America will collapse under its own weight, as did the Twin Towers, if they can get a few weapons of mass destruction into its borders to ignite the process. Unless America as a nation is on our God's side, their dream is not impossible.

Radical Islam's strategy for Britain is somewhat different. They have set their sights on making the UK the first western Muslim nation. Already there have been attempts, some successful, to establish Sharia law in British courts for dealing with disputes between Muslims. The ultimate goal, as they grow toward a majority, is to see it established as the law of the land.[23]

When God gave to ancient Israel the horrendous list of curses that would come upon them for disobedience to Him, one of the curses, found in Deuteronomy 28.43-44 NIV was: *"The alien who lives among you will rise above you higher and higher, but you will sink lower and lower.*

He will lend to you, but you will not lend to him. He will be the head, but you will be the tail." Could the Islamic dream come true in Britain? How about other Western nations that are feeling powerful Islamic encroachment in their societies and even in their governments? Unless the churches intercede and the nations stand on God's side, their dream is not impossible.

Perpetuating Jihad

Their next generation of jihadists is being formed now, as little children are taught, not only in the Middle East, but even in the mosques of western countries, to love murder/suicide and martyrdom. It's chilling to see five-year-olds in militaristic garb, brandishing fake rifles, shouting parroted slogans of hate, and declaring that they want to be martyrs for Allah. TV cartoons in Muslim nations depict their "action heroes" blowing themselves up as they take evil Jews and Americans with them.[24] This wholesale brainwashing is reminiscent of the Hitler Youth Movement.

Those citizens who hate Jesus Christ and their country's godly heritage, and are trying to throw the public acknowledgment of God out of their nation, are aiding and abetting this enemy, and digging a deeper grave for their society than they dream. As they weaken the nation's foundations and resolve, they are setting us up for the real possibility of a take-over they may not have considered. If we all wake up some morning and find Mullahs running the town hall, our women swathed in chadors, our churches boarded up and all those "free speech advocates" in jail, they, and we, will have only ourselves to blame.

In 2009 Iran's president, Mahmoud Ahmadinejad, ranted, "We will wipe Israel off the map!" If this sounds familiar, perhaps you've read it somewhere: *"Come, they say, "let us wipe out Israel as a nation. We will destroy the very memory of its existence"* Psalm 83:4 NLT. This was Asaph the Psalmist, quoting to God the threats of Israel's enemies 3,000 years ago.

Today we see the same old enemies, some of them under other names (the area of ancient Persia is now called Iran; the name of the land of the Philistines equates to Palestine, for example), and the same old spirit of revenge and violence still consumes them. The difference today is that instead of swords and spears, they are trying to develop or acquire nuclear weapons to do the job. Israel is armed with nuclear weaponry and will use it if necessary to avert destruction by Iran. America will, of course, defend Israel.

One scenario is that this might then bring Russia and China into the fray on the side of Iran and other nations, which is exactly what the Bible predicts, will happen in the last days. Russia and China have held their first joint war games, and Russia has been supplying arms and nuclear technology to Iran.

The world is in danger of a conflagration, possibly *the* apocalyptic conflagration, and Iran is the fuse.

The Prince of Persia - On the Move Again

We said before that this is a family feud, but it's more than that: the Prince of Persia is on the move again, this time with a new puppet. We described earlier the passage from Daniel, in which cosmic warfare raged between the Archangels Gabriel and Michael on the one side, and the Prince of Persia on the other, with Daniel interceding for Israel. It's important to recognise that, unlike much of the rest of the Middle East, most Iranians are not Arabs. They are Persians. Ahmadinejad is the modern day equivalent of Haman, in the book of Esther, who tried to get every last Jew annihilated.

God loves the Persian people as he loves all the peoples of the world, but he is again at war against this ancient spiritual enemy. Does it seem too much to suppose that the same Archangels might be playing a leadership role in the struggle, as before? Gabriel told Daniel, in describing the great last days Tribulation period, *"At that time Michael shall stand up, the great prince who stands watch over the sons of your people"* [Israel] see Daniel 12:1. We turn to the New Testament description of that same conflict, Jesus' Revelation to John, and there is Michael, leading the armies of heaven in casting out the dragon – *"that serpent of old, called the Devil and Satan, who deceives the whole world; he was cast to the earth, and his angels were cast out with him"* Revelation 12:7-9 NKJV. We know there is again a mighty cosmic struggle going on in heavenly places, and it will affect us all. Looking at the daily unfolding correlation between prophetic scriptures and human events, does it seem we might be nearing that time?

We are about to see great miracles as God moves on behalf of his special people Israel. If we can pray nothing else, we are told to *"pray for the peace of Jerusalem"* Psalm 122:6 KJV. In prayer, you can play a part in this great cosmic battle.

Iran is far from alone in its hatred of Israel: "The leader of Hezbollah in Lebanon, Hassan Nasrallah, has stated that 'if the Jews all gather in Israel, it will save us the trouble of going after them worldwide... It is an open war until the elimination of Israel and until the death of the last Jew on earth.'"[25]

Why Do They Hate the West?

Jihadists' hatred of the Jews has ancient roots, but why their hatred of Western nations? They hate us for several reasons:

1. *We defend and enable Israel.* We stand in the way of their plans to annihilate Israel and claim "every inch of Palestine" for Islam. Iran's ruler promises to destroy Israel, but he knows he will have to go through America and her allies to do it. He has said he would sacrifice half the population of Iran if necessary to get rid of America.

2. *They see the Western nations as Christian nations.* The spirit in them hates the Spirit in Christians – people who believe that Jesus Christ is the Son of God, the Messiah, the Saviour of the world. Nothing inflames them more.

3. *They are jealous of our prosperity.*

4. *They see the West as a decadent culture,* corrupting the world, largely because of the image its entertainment industry projects.

5. **Western troops have dared to invade Islamic soil,** which they consider an attack on all Islam. America is "the Great Satan" in their eyes. So she and her allies are targeted, and Western civilisation is threatened.

The focus of the world is on Israel. Her modern and ancient history is full of stories of God's miraculous intervention and protection from her enemies. It's a miracle she even exists as a nation. After nearly two millennia of her Diaspora, scattered and persecuted throughout the nations, she has not only retained her identity, but has also been re-gathered by God back into her Promised Land. On the day she became a nation in 1948, she was attacked by the heavily equipped modern armies of seven Arab nations, and outnumbered ten to one.[26] With little more than farm implements and some smuggled weapons to defend herself, she won! And she has won all her wars since, at least nine more wars and intifadas, sometimes in the face of impossible odds, with the possible exception of the 2006 incursion into Lebanon, in which both sides claimed victory.

God is on the side of his special people Israel, not because of their righteousness (37 percent of them today claim to be atheists or agnostics) but because of the promises he made to their forefathers. Israel has been blinded in part, but God promises to open their eyes, and eventually, after much bloodshed and loss of life, *"all Israel will be saved"* Romans 11:26 NKJV.

God has promised to bless those who bless Israel and to curse those who curse her. America is Israel's strongest ally and guardian because God has established it in that relationship. But America, because of its position and power, exerts almost irresistible influence on Israel. We must pray that she will never pressure Israel into going against the will of God. Neither do we as intercessors want to be found praying against what God has said will happen.

We don't cite these things to bring fear; that's the job of the terrorists. Ours is to bring hope. Remember, God is in control, and he is able to protect his people and give them peace. *"You will keep him in perfect peace, whose mind is stayed on you, because he trusts in you"* Isaiah 26:3 NKJV see also Psalm 91.

The outcome of the venture we described above, where Russia, China, and other nations come against Israel to destroy it, whether it happens in our time or not, is predetermined. God himself will turn these powers against each other and destroy them with pestilence, hailstones, fire and brimstone, and both the heathen and the house of Israel will know that God is God, and Christ will come and establish his Kingdom on earth. Read all about it in Ezekiel chapters 38-39. If the last days scenario is really shaping up now, as many Scriptures and events lead us to believe it is, we may find ourselves caught up to meet him sooner than we expect!

Prayer in a Time of War

Now, how do we pray about the problems the world faces right now? Here is a suggested prayer you might use as a starting place for your own regular intercession in world affairs:

> Heavenly Father, we come with thanksgiving, and we praise you for your protection over us. We pray for the peace of Jerusalem and of this world, and for our nation's part in this war, which was thrust upon us by the treachery of our enemies.

We don't ask you to be on our side in this struggle: may we as a nation be found on your side. You are the Victor, and the final outcome of history is predetermined and prophesied in your Word.

Grant godly wisdom, guidance, and protection for our government's leaders.

Cause them to be united in their understanding and decision making, for you told us that a kingdom divided against itself cannot stand. Wake more free nations to rise as allies with us in the struggle for freedom.

All-seeing Guardian, give supernatural aid to our intelligence agencies and those of our allies. Expose the hiding places and movements of terrorist leaders, cells and networks throughout the world.

Mighty Warrior, give special wisdom to those who plan the operations of our military forces wherever they must fight.

Protect our protectors; defend our defenders – the troops who are in harm's way for our safety. Embolden and anoint the believers among them and the chaplains who minister to them. Send revival into their ranks.

Establish peace, religious freedom and righteous government in the Middle East.

Strong Defender, continue to stand guard over our homeland. Protect us from the weapons of our enemies, especially weapons of mass destruction. Whatever they are plotting for our hurt, stop them, in Jesus' name. Watch over our most vulnerable points: our airports, our seaports and our porous borders. Give great wisdom and success to our security people. Turn the hearts of the people of Israel to trust in you, Lord, for their deliverance – to remember your promise, **"Not by might nor by power, but by my Spirit, says the Lord of Hosts"** Zechariah 4:6 NKJV. *May the sweet influences of the Holy Spirit and demonstrations of your power draw them to faith in you.*

Raise up evangelists, filled with the Holy Spirit, to carry the gospel to Jews and Muslims, in the power and demonstration of the Holy Spirit.

We pray that the Muslim peoples of the world will come to faith in Christ. We know that you love them as you love all mankind.

May Muslim leaders, including terrorists, experience "Road to Damascus" revelations and conversions like the Apostle Paul's. Use them mightily among their own people.

Raise up intercessors throughout the world to fight this war in heavenly places, with Spirit-directed wisdom in praying.

Give pastors and church leaders courage to speak out boldly in love, to call the Church to intercession, worship and witness, and our populace back to righteousness, the wall that guards the land.

Amen.

God's Biblical Battle Plans

God's ways are infinite and we can't tell him how to do his job, but we can be aware of some of the ways he has answered his people's prayers, even as our forefathers boosted their faith by recounting his deliverances. We may at times feel led by the Spirit to ask him to employ some of his Scriptural battle plans:

1. **God can thwart the plans of the enemy.** *"The Lord brings the counsel of the nations to nothing; He makes their plans of no effect"* Psalm 33:10 NKJV.

2. **God can bring confusion into the enemy's strategising.** King David prayed, *"Let them be turned backward and brought to confusion and dishonour who desire and delight in my hurt"* Psalm 70:2b AB. See also Psalm 109:29. When David heard that his trusted advisor Ahithophel was conspiring with Absalom to overthrow him, he prayed," *O Lord, turn the counsel of Ahithophel into foolishness!"* 2 Samuel 15:31 NKJV. And that's exactly what happened. God caused Absalom to disbelieve Ahithophel and listen to faulty counsel that brought about his own defeat. See 17:14.

3. **God can turn the enemy factions against each other.** Remember Jehoshaphat's great battle in which Judah didn't have to fight, but was told to "stand still and see the salvation of the Lord." God caused the three enemy armies to turn on each other and wipe each other out. 2 Chronicles 20. *"The fear of God was on all the kingdoms of those countries when they heard that the Lord had fought against the enemies of Israel"* verse 29 NKJV. Today there may be enough enmity between radical factions to spark such a fire.

4. **God can cause the wicked to fall into his own trap:** *The man who sets a trap for others will get caught in it himself. Roll a boulder down on someone, and it will roll back and crush you"* Proverbs 26:27 TLB.

Haman, the Persian prime minister and the melodramatic villain of the story of Esther, is like the cartoon character *Wile E Coyote*: his plots backfire on him. He tries to have the Jew Mordecai hanged, but instead is forced to dress him in a royal robe and lead him through the streets on the king's horse, shouting his praises. Haman slinks away with his head covered. Then he tries to have all the Jews in the Empire killed, but his wickedness gets exposed and the Jews are spared. (Curses! Foiled again!) Haman is hanged on the gallows he had built for Mordecai, and Mordecai replaces him as prime minister. These events are still celebrated annually by the Jews in the feast of Purim.

In the 1970s, when we lived in England, news came just before church one Sunday that IRA terrorists, on the way to plant a bomb in London, were killed when it exploded in their car.

No one else was injured. Pioneer church pastor Gerald Coates, said to the congregation, "We've learned to thank God for his goodness; we need to thank him for his judgments as well." No one cheered or laughed or danced. It was a solemn moment of thanksgiving.

5. *God can prompt moderate Islamic voices to rise up against radical jihadists and say, "Enough!* You are bringing disgrace on our religion!" This is already happening: The Jerusalem Post reported, "An anti-Hezbollah coalition is emerging in several Arab countries. The Hezbollah leaders are talking about an Arab 'conspiracy' to liquidate the Shi'ite organisation. The anti-Hezbollah coalition, which appears to be growing, is spearheaded by Saudi Arabia, Egypt, and Jordan".[27]

6. *God, through intercessors, can bind the demonic spirits that drive terrorists*
See chapter 8.

7. *God can raise up and pull down leaders* see Psalm 75:7.

8. *God can protect his people* see Psalm 91. *"The Lord knows how to rescue godly people from their trials, even while punishing the wicked right up until the Day of Judgment"* 2 Peter 2:9 NLT. Ask him daily to cover our leaders, protect our protectors, and shield our country from the weapons of terrorists.

9. *God can send angels to fight for his people.* In 2 Kings chapters 18 and 19 Jerusalem was besieged by Assyria's great army that had crushed everything in its path. King Sennacherib and his general ranted and derided God's ability to save Jerusalem. Oops! They insulted the wrong Person. In answer to King Hezekiah's fervent prayer for deliverance, *"that night the angel of the Lord went out to the Assyrian camp and killed 185,000 Assyrian troops"* 19:35 NLT, and the nation of Judah was spared. "Let us not trust in that which is seen by the eye and heard by the ear, but let us have respect to spiritual agencies that evade the senses but are known to faith. Angels play a far greater part in the affairs of Providence than we realise".[28]

We don't pray for war, but for peace. But if war has been forced on us, we must keep informed and fight the battles in the heavenlies as the Spirit leads. It's a war whose victory must precede any hoped-for victory on the military or political battlefields. We need an army of people who understand what is at stake and who will respond to the urgency and volunteer for the struggle. And we had better be quick about it. The time is shorter than we may think.

With all these possibilities, there is yet another:

10. *God can sovereignly reveal himself to Muslims who are seeking truth.*
Researchers say that 80 percent of new Christians in South Asia come to Christ as a direct result of some kind of supernatural encounter.

In Gujarat, India, church membership jumped from zero to 60,000 in ten years as a result of hundreds of miraculous healings.

At the 1994 Hajj, after several Saudi Christians had prayer-marched around Mecca, Jesus appeared to a group of Nigerian Muslims and declared that he is the Lord.

A group of Sufi Muslims in North Africa who were chanting and dancing and asking Allah to reveal himself say that Jesus appeared and declared that he is the true God.[29] Reports are now coming in from many Muslim countries, including Iran and Iraq, that huge numbers are coming to Christ, not so much through preaching or personal witness, but through personal visitations of Jesus, appearing to them in dreams and visions. One reason for this is that multitudes of peaceable, moderate Muslims are disillusioned by Islam through the blood madness of their compatriots. They look at Christians and see peace in the midst of chaos; so, in spite of the danger of persecution and even death they seek the Christians' God and discover Christ.

"It's estimated that every year in the world some six million Muslims convert to Christianity, even though they face death threats and exclusion from their families".[30] "There are 35 new churches in Baghdad. They're calling it a revival".[31]

We have a photo, clipped from a magazine, of an Arab at a Hajj at Mecca, the pilgrimage that faithful Muslim men try to make once in their lives. This man has a sweet countenance with a look of deep longing. His palms are turned upward as in prayer, and his eyes glisten with tears. He touches our hearts, and we sometimes pray for him, that God will reveal Jesus to him and to innumerable others like him. This is the kind of seeking heart God looks for, although the man is seeking in the wrong place because that's all he knows. This man is not our enemy and will pose us no trouble.

On the other hand we see pictures daily of venomous, hate-filled men brandishing weapons, burning flags and effigies and chanting threats and maledictions at us. There is more than human hatred here; the murderous looks on their faces are the physical manifestation of the puppet masters who inflame and animate them. It's the essence of pure evil. These are our enemies in the flesh. But God can get through even to them. Saul thought he was doing God a favour in rounding up Christians to be killed, until Jesus appeared to him, struck him temporarily blind, and changed him into the great Apostle Paul, who gave us most of the Epistles in the New Testament see Acts 8:1-3.

Let's remember, in our praying for the nations: God so loved the world, not just Israel, not just Christian nations. God loves mankind and is not willing that any should perish, but that all should come to repentance. There's a thrilling passage in Isaiah 19 – a prophecy yet to be fulfilled:

> "In that day the Lord will make himself known to the Egyptians. Yes, they will know the Lord and will make sacrifices and offerings to him. They will make promises to the Lord and keep them. The Lord will strike Egypt in a way that will bring healing. For the Egyptians will turn to the Lord, and he will listen to their pleas and heal them. "In that day Egypt and Assyria will be connected by a highway. The Egyptians and Assyrians will move freely between their lands, and they will worship the same God. And Israel will be their ally. The three will be together, and Israel will be a blessing to them.For the Lord God Almighty will say, 'Blessed be Egypt, my people. Blessed be Assyria, the land I have made. Blessed be Israel, my special possession!'" Isaiah 19:21-25 TLB.

Assyria of Isaiah's time corresponds to modern-day Iraq, Lebanon and Syria. Today, hundreds of thousands of ethnic Assyrians, including many Christians, are scattered as refugees throughout Syria, Jordan and Turkey, in misery, uncertainty and persecution, but the day of their deliverance is coming, too.

Clifford tells us of another remarkable incident...

Miraculous Intervention in World War II

The biblical history of Israel demonstrates the faithfulness of God in keeping his promises. When the nation turned away from the Word of God and times of hardship or oppression from their enemies came upon them; when they cried out to the Lord in humility and repentance, God was faithful to restore his blessing. God is faithful and prayer is powerful!

We've looked at biblical ways the Lord can bring about victory for his people in answer to prayer. Cliff tells us here of God's miraculous moving on behalf of Britain in times of war:

There is evidence that the gospel reached British shores during the Apostolic era and since that time faithful believers have interceded for the land. Many miracles There is evidence that the gospel reached British shores during the Apostolic era and since that time faithful believers have interceded for the land. Many miracles have been recorded in her history since then, such as the winds that blew away an invading Spanish Armada to their own destruction. But what about contemporary history? Is he aware of the fate of modern nations? Does he care? There is no more vivid illustration of God's faithfulness in response to the prayers of his powerless people than that which occurred in more recent history:

The early days of the Second World War brought about a situation similar to that which faced Israel at the time of King Jehoshaphat when a vast army threatened to destroy Jerusalem. Jehoshaphat's prayer was a model of faith and trust in the Lord. *"We have no power to face this vast army that is attacking us. We do not know what to do, but our eyes are upon you"* 2 Chronicles 20.12. So it was, as France fell to the rapidly advancing German Panzer divisions leaving the British Army stranded on the Continent, unable to return across the Channel to defend their homeland from invasion. On 27 May 1940 the German High Command announced, "The British Army is encircled and our troops are proceeding to its annihilation." But the day before the German announcement, King George VI, in a stirring broadcast, called the whole nation to a Day of Prayer. And the nation prayed. Immediately a series of miracles occurred.

For some unknown reason Hitler ordered his generals to halt the advance towards the west coast of France. Secondly, a storm of extraordinary fury grounded the German Luftwaffe on 28 May allowing the British forces to make their way to Dunkirk. Then a great calm settled over the Channel for several days allowing an armada of little ships, many of them only river boats, to cross the Channel and ferry the waiting soldiers from the beaches out to Royal Navy warships for the return to Dover. An amazing 335,000 men were evacuated from Dunkirk in those few momentous days, which were a turning point in world history.

In a speech to Parliament, Prime Minister Winston Churchill said, "I thought, and some good judges agreed with me, that perhaps 20,000 or 30,000 men might be re-embarked. The whole root and core and brain of the British Army seemed about to perish upon the field or to be led into captivity." He told the nation he believed Dunkirk to be a miracle – an answer to prayer.

Unfortunately, the battered army had been forced to leave its weapons and equipment in France and was desperate to rearm and regroup. Amazingly, Hitler hesitated to invade throughout June 1940, giving vulnerable Britain a crucial breathing space. Then Field Marshal Goering told his Air Force Commander that before Germany could invade Britain they had to destroy the Royal Air Force. On 30 August 1940, 800 enemy aircraft darkened the skies over southern England aiming to destroy airfields. Within a week Fighter Command was in serious trouble as aircraft and pilots were being lost at a rate far in excess of replacements. There were no reserves left. Defeat appeared inevitable which would open the way for invasion.

However, Sunday 8 September 1940 had been called as another National Day of Prayer to give thanks for the miracle of Dunkirk, but it became a day of intercession for another miracle to turn the tide in what was already becoming known as "the Battle of Britain". As enemy aircraft swept across the Channel in wave after wave, both night and day, British aircraft were being destroyed on the ground, and landing strips damaged faster than they could be repaired. The situation was desperate. Then suddenly, inexplicably, Hitler ordered the Luftwaffe to switch its attack back to London, which actually saved Fighter Command. Another breathing space for Britain and a catastrophic blunder for the enemy.

Spitfires and Hurricanes took a tremendous toll of the enemy bombers and by mid-September the German Air Force had suffered such great losses that they ceased their mass attacks. On 17 September 1940 the German Supreme Command issued an order postponing the invasion of England "until further notice". The Battle of Britain was won. As Churchill said, "Never in the field of human conflict has so much been owed by so many to so few." But the nation acknowledged that it was not just their tiny armed forces that had repelled the might of the enemy but the power of prayer.

Today, Britain is in great trouble again. So too are all the nations of the West. America, Canada, Australia, South Africa and the nations of Europe, who have had centuries of Christian tradition, are suffering moral decay and corruption. Only spiritual revival can assure their survival.

There is desperate need for discerning leaders to mobilise the church for prayer, because this is not a battle that can be won on the land or in the air with physical weapons of war. We need leaders who will seek the Lord for his strategy for this battle. But they will need to be upheld by the prayers of the people as Moses' arms were upheld. This is a battle that involves every believer and each one is needed to take a position and stand firm, having upon him or her the whole armour of God.

Back to Jimmy and Carol...

A Platoon of Intercessors

The great classic book on intercession is Rees Howells, *Intercessor*, by Norman Grubb (Christian Literature Crusade). Rees Howells was the founder and director of the Bible College of Wales during World War II. He had learned the secrets of deep, Spirit-directed intercession and led his small army of prayer warriors for six years, throughout the conflict.

They followed the war news on the radio and prayed strategically as the Holy Spirit led. They interceded fervently each morning, noon and night, for hours each day, with much fasting, as they fought the war in the heavenlies battle by battle.

As early as 1936 Howells recognised Hitler as more than just a man; he was a demon-possessed tyrant, deeply occult, directed by a "voice" that told him what to do. Howells saw this as a war between kingdoms in the heavenlies, and led his warriors in providing air cover in the Spirit for the earthly battles. Through victory after victory, with occasional setbacks, they kept on until the monster was defeated and peace returned, for a time, to the world.

This is what we urgently need now – all over our country. Most of us have no concept of this depth of prayer; in the insular comfort of our homes, workplaces, shopping malls, supermarkets, churches and entertainment centres, many have been lulled into a careless disregard of what is shaping up in the world around us. But if we don't get serious now about praying against our radical terrorist enemies, we may find ourselves called into more and more of this kind of dedicated, cross-bearing intercession for the survival of our nation.

Make no mistake; our enemies are serious. Very serious. For instance, Osama bin Laden has said, "We love death. The US loves life. That is the big difference between us".[32]

The good news is that because of the understanding, faith and fervency of a few, God has again and again moved into the arena of national and international affairs. In the case of communism he blew down the walls with a suddenness that stunned the world. God may seem to move slowly, but when he moves, nothing can withstand Him.

---

[21] Information Division, Israel Foreign Ministry – Jerusalem

[22] Rabbi Mendy Chitrik. www.askmoses.com.

[23] See various articles on the web on Sharia law in the UK.

[24] Fox TV News Special, 2/10/0725.

[25] www.jewishsoftware.com

[26] Joel Rosenberg, *Epicenter*, p.133

[27] September 12, 2006.

[28] Charles Spurgeon.

[29] excerpted from *Praying Down Miracles*, an article by Bruce Steinbaum
www.thegospeltruthministry.com; www.encountersnetwork.com

[30] Breaking Christian News, 2/6/07.

[31] Faith Network News 2/6/07.

[32] quoted in National Geographic TV special, August 2006.

Talk About This:

1. How serious do you think the radical Islamic threat is to the Western nations? To Israel? To the Christian faith? Could this eventually affect you? p142-143

2. How are atheists and anti-Christian factions aiding and abetting this enemy? p144

3. Why do jihadists hate the western nations? p145-146

4. If you believe that a last-days scenario could be shaping up now, does that influence your life? Who do you believe is ultimately in control in all this? How does that influence your faith? p146

5. Name some of God's biblical battle plans. Will they still work? p148-149

6. Do you believe God still loves everyone in every nation? Why? What effect will that have on your prayers for them? p150

7. Discuss the miraculous interventions of God on Britain's behalf even in times of war. Were you aware of these reports given by Clifford Hill on **pages 151-2** What is your reaction to these answers to prayer?

8. Do you believe God might intervene so dramatically at the cry of intercessors on behalf of the spiritual warfare we now fight?

9. How do you feel about Clifford's statement that "only spiritual revival can assure their (the nations') survival?" Why?

10. Would your group consider the kind of on-going, informed prayer Rees Howells intercessors prayed during World War II? How do you think the Holy Spirit might direct your intercessory targets for prayer today?

Pray About This:

a. Pray the Prayer in a Time of War on **page 146-47**, if in a group take turns and agree this together.

b. Pray for British troops and their allies everywhere in the world. Ask God to defend and protect our protectors.

c. Pray for faith and courage and joy as you persevere in intercession.

RESTORING THE FOUNDATIONS

*When the foundations are being destroyed,
what can the righteous do?*

Psalm 11:3 NIV

Chapter 17 - Plans for Action

The task of the people of God is, as far as possible in a sinful society, to reclaim the cosmos for God's created purpose.
Carl F H Henry

It's time for action, time for plans and strategies. We'll propose specific plans to heal wounds, restore foundations, and advance the Kingdom of God in our society. If all this seems daunting, don't worry. Not all of us will feel called to concentrate our efforts on all of these things. Certainly we're all called to pray, to witness, and to worship, to do justly, to love mercy, and to walk humbly with our God. But even as the Holy Spirit gives certain spiritual gifts to some and not to others, he also apportions different callings to different members of the Body. That way everything gets covered and nobody gets burned out. Find which ones match your gifts and callings and go for it.

Plan 1: Monthly Fasting and Prayer

The year is 1974; In America, a year of national trauma, disillusionment, and bitterness. The Watergate soap opera in the White House is reaching its climax and the country watches and listens with trepidation and sorrow.

On April 30 our church, along with countless others, fasts and prays for the nation at the request of the United States Senate. Our pastor, Jack Hayford, delivers a prophetic message, which says in part: "An era turns on the strength of a day. This day is marked in the annals of eternity, a great turnabout, a day of enormous consequences. An unwritten history of doom and judgment is erased and a new history is being written. The powers of the heavens are being shaken. This is a day of great scattering and confusion among the enemy."

Great things quickly begin to happen. The very next day President Nixon releases the fateful secret tapes, and the rancorous affair is on its way to an end. He steps down and Gerald Ford steps up. At his inauguration, he says, "You have not elected me with your votes, but I ask you to confirm me with your prayers." A good start.

Almost immediately rain falls in the drought-stricken Midwest. A good sign. In our own state and community, notorious terrorist groups and narcotics rings are uncovered and destroyed; the crime rate drops drastically; righteous legislation regarding hard-core pornography passes, along with many other victories.

But there's more to Pastor Hayford's prophetic word of April 30. It goes on: "The battle turns today, but the completion is yet to be carried out. There will be other days and other battles. There are mighty victories to be accomplished. The battle is the Lord's."

At this point, Jimmy senses the Holy Spirit is saying something momentous to him also.

How long, he wonders, before the Church is again called to battle? And who will call her? If once a month we would gather in our churches for fasting and prayer for the nation, we would see major spiritual strongholds crumble and principalities topple.

Jimmy approaches Pastor Hayford who enthusiastically affirms the idea. The church commissions Jimmy to go and meet with leaders throughout the country. These meetings, accomplished primarily through the help of Dr Lloyd Ogilvie, who later became the Chaplain of the United States Senate, lead to "The Summit Conference of Church Leaders in America."

On 12 and 13 September 1975, 130 leaders meet in Chicago – heads of denominations and ministries, media and educational leaders, and other Christian statesmen. Together they pray and strategise on how to mobilise the Church for intercession.

Jimmy proposes that one day each month be designated as a day of corporate prayer and fasting across the country. The leaders approve the resolution unanimously. They agree to urge their constituents, through the bicentennial year, to rally and pray for government and other critical areas of societal influence; to pray against injustice and crime; to pray for revival. It's a critical and far reaching decision.

Within a year we see dramatic results: Christians are elected to major political offices; television noticeably cleans up its sex-and-violence routine; the crime rate drops significantly in major cities; there is awakening and spiritual growth in the churches. Even the Washington Post declares there is "a new spirit abroad in the land."

But prayer itself has a shelf life. Unfortunately, after the bicentennial year only a few ministries continued to intercede as vigorously for the nation. The gravity of the times demanded more. As the Church's vision for intercession faded, America's morality, honour and strength faded too. We now face daily the results of that failure as we struggle for our national soul through crisis after crisis.

The good news is that the Church in America is again rallying to the cause. Prayer ministries are proliferating, and the monthly prayer movement, for so long existing only as an ember, has again been fanned into flame–and it's spreading rapidly.

Shortly before the turn of this century, the AD 2000 and Beyond movement, an offshoot of the Lausanne Committee on World Evangelisation adopted the monthly prayer movement and caused it to spread to many nations.

On the 30th anniversary of the movement, a well-known leader said, "Fads in prayer come and go. What God is looking for is the kind of consistent, persistent prayer that is the hallmark of the monthly call to united prayer and fasting. Every church needs to join in calling their members to monthly prayer and fasting". [33]

Many intercessors for the UK have chosen the third Thursday of each month as the day for fasting and prayer for the nation. Intercessors UK [34] will give you strategic information for prayer needs and offer prayers you may join with in agreement.

Some leaders have taken it a step further, calling for fasting and prayer every week to ask God to contain the very real threat of radical Islamic terrorism.

United intercession may well determine the future of the nations.

Plan 2: Declaration and Invocation: Lifting Up Your Voice!

Declaration is worship that acknowledges who God is and proclaims his love and mercy and power. *Invocation* is worship that invites his great presence into our midst.

Together, these two forms of prayer are keys to spiritual power and blessing. Knowing this, we have to wonder if most of us Christians are being out-prayed by adherents of other religions who also seek the favour of god. It's a possibility.

As Pope John Paul II said of the Muslims, "It is impossible not to admire their fidelity to prayer. The image of believers in Allah who, without caring about time or place, fall to their knees and immerse themselves in prayer remains a model for all those who invoke the true God". [35]

The Muslims can certainly teach us a few things about dedication and about invocation as well. They understand it and practise it. It's a simple form of worship that affects the entire nation where it's observed. Oh, the Christian Church knows the term invocation; we even name it in our church bulletins, but many of us don't understand it very well or practise it much – certainly not as effectively as they do.

In Islamic countries the public call to worship goes forth five times a day as loudspeakers carry the voices of the muezzins from the mosques across the cities. And five times a day, Muslims kneel, faces to the ground, and corporately declare out loud the sovereignty of Allah and their allegiance to him and to his prophet, Mohammed.

The result, as you know if you've been to the Middle East, is that you can literally feel the presence and influence of the deity who is invoked and enthroned there by the worship of the people. Remember, invocation is worship that declares the reality and power of the one who is being invoked, and is an invitation for him to manifest himself. And he does.

This is a major premise in C S Lewis's book, *The Last Battle*, as the villains, in order to terrify the people, invoke the demon god Tash, never believing for a moment that anything will happen. To their unhappy surprise, Tash not only shows up but devours them. They have discovered an interesting spiritual principle: the spirit that is invoked is the spirit that manifests himself. Or herself, as the case may be.

So it is for the Christian Church: The Lord inhabits, or enthrones himself on, the praises of his people see Psalm 22:3. In other words, God manifests himself where he is publicly honoured and welcomed.

Some churches understand the power of declaration and invocation, although they may not use that terminology. They declare Jesus' sovereignty and invite his presence over their families, churches, cities and nations. They sing it, say it and shout it from pulpit and pew. The problem is, they do it only for a few minutes once a week – or twice a week, if the faithful little band that turns out for prayer meeting remembers to practise it.

Meanwhile, Islam is practising it faithfully five times a day, seven days a week – millions of them lifting their voices in concerted declaration and invocation.

We wish more of us Christians had the Muslims' devotion and discipline in prayer. Nevertheless, as Pope John Paul II recognised, "Islam is not a religion of redemption. There is no room for the cross and the resurrection". [36] *Radical* Islam is a rigid religion of forced worship to a god who asks his people to sacrifice their sons to die for him, and so earn heaven. Christianity is a faith whose God has sacrificed his son to die for his people to give them free access to heaven.

But, while Muslims don't have the truth of Jesus Christ and his redemption, they do have spiritual power. So have many other major religions and occultists and New Agers, who are hotly pursuing other gods and familiar spirits who come where they are invited. This is invocation.

We are in a massive spiritual power struggle worldwide. The Church is learning again to declare Jesus' sovereignty and invoke his presence and power over their nation. This being so, what if three times a day, every day, Christians were to exalt the name of Jesus and declare his sovereignty over their nation? What if they were to do it out loud? Together? At home, at school, on the job?

"Well," you ask, "how do we do that?" What if we set a time when Christians could join together spiritually all over their cities to invoke the presence of Jesus there? Let's make it simple: during the normal meal time hours. We could make it part of our mealtime blessing.

Next question: "How do we pray?" *Out loud*. We needn't make a scene, but we need to be vocal. It takes only a few moments. It is short, declarative prayer said with focus, fervour and faith. For example: *Jesus Christ is the risen Son of the Living God. He has all power in heaven and on earth. Let his will be done on earth as it is in heaven. Amen.*

You may choose to put the name of your family, church, community, city, state or nation in place of the word *earth*. Or you can use your own words, so long as you proclaim who he is and his authority in our world. We do it together, not as an obligatory habit, but as a meaningful exercise, and it often draws our attention back from wherever it has wandered, to God's love and goodness to us.

Christians won't have these prayer disciplines forced upon us as most Muslims have; we'll be responsible to discipline ourselves. But can't we who have the aid of the Holy Spirit dedicate ourselves to making strong daily invocation an ongoing, life-long practice? Can't we do it wherever we are without being self-conscious or embarrassed about it? The Muslims do. Surely we can be as dedicated as they!

If we are, God will hear us. Spiritual powers will hear us, too and, as we persist, there will be cracks in the gates of hell, resulting in revival in our churches and changes in our society.

Plan 3: Praying the News

Wouldn't it be wonderful if we had a way to call multitudes of prayer warriors to immediate alert in times of crisis? Well, we have – and it's right in our living rooms.

The two of us always look forward to the TV network news. It has become one of our most intense intercession times. We realised that there must be multitudes of Christians across the nation – even across the world – whose hearts are touched by the daily parade of catastrophe crossing our TV screens. If only we were aware of each other, we could pray as a united army. If one shall put a thousand to flight and two, ten thousand see Deuteronomy 32:30, how many spiritual foes can be routed by the simultaneous prayers of thousands of intercessors? We could pray with new faith and boldness, knowing that we are not alone but are many.

Great spiritual principalities and powers of evil are not routed by loners but by armies of prayer warriors praying strong prayers. And that marvellous last-days technology that God has given us – the ability to communicate images and sound instantly to the whole world from anywhere on earth via television – may be part of God's plan to summon those vast armies immediately to battle.

One of the great values of television is its immediacy. Consider for example:

TV: *"We take you live by satellite to the ____ airport where terrorists have seized hostages." Images flash on the screen. Within moments, prayer warriors are called to battle worldwide:*

We pray: *"In the overruling name of Jesus we resist the spirits of anarchy and violence that drive these terrorists and, as an army we bind them up. Lord, send your angels to confound the powers of darkness. Protect the innocent. Give wisdom to the authorities." Then we stay with it, following the news flashes and responding in prayer until the episode ends.*

TV: *"An attorney for a civil rights advocacy group has asserted today that all speech, even child pornography, is legal."*

We pray: *"O God! Destroy these works of ungodliness in Jesus' name. Defeat the plans of those who corrupt our children! We resist the spirits of perversion and depravity that enslave the innocent and bring your wrath on our country. Forgive us for our apathy, which has allowed this evil to spread across our nation. Show us what you want us to do now."*

Other typical calls to prayer:

Refugees from a natural disaster or war. Bureaucracy holds up relief efforts. Speak against those obstacles in prayer. Ask mercy for the suffering and bereaved, and blessing on the rescue efforts.

Continuing violence between Israelis and Palestinians: Pray for the peace of Jerusalem Psalm 122:6 KJV.

Drugs, crime, abortion, corruption in government and in the Church, AIDS, poverty, injustice. These things and others are daily brought into our homes as instant calls to prayer. All across the time zones of our nation and the world, an intercessory army is mobilised to resist the devil and cry out to God.

When Christian leaders are being interviewed live, ask God to put words of godly wisdom in their mouths. Pray for the news media, too, that God will save those who decide its content or remove those who mock righteousness and promote evil causes. Think what wonders might be accomplished through the *daily* agreement of thousands of Christians "watching and praying."

However, take a word of advice from a pair of inveterate news watchers/pray-ers: Watch the news, understand the times, and pray, but don't immerse yourself in bad news, and don't live in fear. You could work yourself into a depression by soaking in it all day every day. Most news networks make a living by scouring the world for all the bad news they can find and sensationalising it for us. But how much good news gets reported? Not a whole lot. Maybe a warm fuzzy "human interest" story or occasionally the birth of a cute baby panda in a zoo, but most newsrooms don't consider it a story unless it bleeds. Keep your peace by resting in the Lord.

We try to be careful where we get our news. We've skipped back and forth between the major news networks enough to know which ones like to bless our country and which ones like to blast it. We also like to get a Christian slant on what's happening in the world, so we get daily reports from ministries that report on world news by email. We often find sides to the story that most of the secular media don't want us to know.

Here's another, smaller way to be a part of united prayer for a nation: During World War II an advisor to Churchill encouraged people to pray for the war collectively every day at a prescribed hour, for one minute. This idea is now spreading again. If you would like to participate: Every day at 12 noon stop what you're doing and spend one minute praying for the safety of your country, your troops, your citizens, and for the return of godliness to your nation.

Plan 4: "Doing the Stuff"

We want to see the governments do more for the hurting and helpless, not only in times of catastrophe, but whenever help is needed. But as Rick Warren has pointed out, the Church is the largest organisation in the world, the quickest to be mobilised, the most cost effective, and the most compassionate and trustworthy.

Not only are churches needed in times of catastrophe, but also in meeting the continuing needs of the community. Doug Stringer, president of "Somebody Cares" Ministries refers to their outreaches to the underprivileged – feeding, clothing, housing, educating and training – as "doing the stuff." We suggested earlier that not only individuals, but also congregations pitch in and help those who are ministering in our inner cities.

Most of us have no concept of how it feels to be caught in a web of grinding poverty, perhaps trapped in a bureaucratic system that perpetuates it, surrounded by gang wars and drug dealers, denied human dignity, wounded by a lifetime of racial insults, hurting and robbed of hope - or the anguish of a single mother with no food for her family. Where does she go? What does she do? Does she beg? Steal? Sell herself? Many of our inner cities are like tinderboxes of humanity, waiting for a spark to ignite a conflagration. What an opportunity for the Church to intervene!

In cities of any size, you can find ministries trying to meet these needs. They're run by full-time life intercessors who are struggling to help the homeless and the hungry and undereducated while most of us are not aware – or don't care – that these ministries exist. These folks are doing our hard work, our dirty work, for us, but the job is too big now for these few. We are just as responsible as they to minister to the crying needs in our own backyards. They need our support and our strong foundation of intercessory prayer. Then, as together we become "God's love in the flesh," we fulfil his conditions given in Isaiah 58. *Then* we will cry, and our fasting and prayers will be heard. *Then* we will see renewal in the Church, leading to awakening in our society and the healing of our land.

Plan 5: Taking Civic Responsibility

We considered this in detail in Chapter 8. In summary:

- Study the issues.
- Study the party platforms.
- Study the candidates.
- Ask questions if necessary.
- Pray for wisdom and insight.
- Vote.
- Where possible, select those with strong Christian values.
- Pray regularly for those in authority.
- Help the righteous get elected. Urge other believers to vote.
- If God leads, stand for office?
- Churches, provide voter registration tables and distribute voter guides that show which side of moral issues each candidate says he or she is on.
- Pastors, speak out on moral issues.

We now have the numbers to turn things around if we'*ll* do it.

---

[33] Dave Butts, Chairman of America's National Prayer Committee.

[34] www.intercessuk.org

[35] Crossing the Threshold of Hope, New York: Random House, 1994.

[36] Crossing the Threshold of Hope.

Talk About This:

1. As you review the Action Plans, remember no one person is required to do them all! Which ones best suit your personal leanings and spiritual gifts?

2. How do you feel about the plan to make the third Thursday of every month a day of fasting and prayer in the churches nationwide? Without waiting for others, will you be willing to start now? p157

3. Do you find the idea of Declaration and Invocation exciting? Will you and your prayer partners put it into practice? What do you think will happen? p159

4. How would praying the news work as an intercession time for you? p158-160

5. How can you, your group and/or your church be involved in the life-intercession of "doing the stuff"? p161-2

6. As a Christian citizen, do you feel the need to increase your involvement in the political process: In what way? How many of these things do you already practice? p162

Pray About This:

a. Begin with Declaration and Invocation. Invite the Lord to be manifest in your midst and to help you pray.

b. Pray for any important current events that affect the nation. Ask God to oversee these. Pray for his will alone to be done.

c. Ask for instruction for you and your group in "doing the stuff."

d. Pray for God's direction in taking on civic responsibilities. Ask how you and/or your group are to be involved, and how far you are to go.

Chapter 18 - More Action Plans

"All that is necessary for evil to triumph is for good men to do nothing."
Edmund Burke

Plan 6: Knowing and Defending Your Rights

The devil is determined to destroy religious freedom, and he uses human agencies to do it. Those people whom Satan uses to do his work fall into two groups: we call them the troops and the dupes.

The *troops* are Satan's soldiers, and they have deliberately chosen to do evil. They may not even believe in the devil's existence, but they know what they're doing is wrong, and they serve his purposes by doing it for their own enjoyment and profit. They might be pornographers, pimps, prostitutes, drug dealers, criminals, casino operators and the like. Or they might be anti-God activists who have sold their souls to the devil and work tirelessly in their cause because the spirit at work in them genuinely hates God.

The *dupes* don't know they're being used but in some cases may wreak more havoc than the troops. Our dictionary defines a dupe as a person who is used unwittingly to accomplish another's purpose. Dupes are, in their own eyes, sincere in their pursuit of what they see as righteous causes, but because of their spiritual blindness, they have no idea that they are fighting against the very things that bring the blessings of God on a nation. Dupes may be attorneys, preachers, politicians, educators, abortionists, activist judges, entertainers, "rights" crusaders, or theologians who deny the divinity of Christ and the resurrection. Satan's minions lie in wait for the hapless dupe they can use to lead many astray.

Most dangerous of all are those from either group who get elevated to positions of enormous influence where they can ruin lives on a massive scale. If Satan could be said to have apostles, they might be such people as Hitler, Lenin, Marx, Hefner, and top leaders of various false religions.

You and your children have rights – not given you by the government, but given to you by Almighty God and supposedly guaranteed by government. But be aware – there are people trying to take those rights away from you, and, in many cases, succeeding. But even though Christians still have many rights in the public arena, if we're made to believe we don't have them, we might as well not have them. It's the same principle as terrorism: you don't need a bomb to terrorise people, all you need is a telephone. You can divert flights and shut down airports just by claiming there's a bomb on an airplane. Likewise, threats or misinformation can frighten school governors or employers into forbidding the children or workers to exercise their freedom of religious expression.

So now that we know about the danger to our way of life posed by these organisations, what can we do about it? We can know our rights, and know where to go for help if we're ever challenged. Where can we find out about our rights?

Often all it takes is a little legal information to help a confused school authority or city council decide to do the right thing. Most school governors are not wicked people. Many of them simply don't understand the legal rights of believers and have been intimidated by false information. In many cases, when these rights are explained to them by Christian legal societies or attorneys, cases are resolved without lawsuits and the students' rights are restored.

Those who try to corrupt our society, especially our children, need our prayers too. Because Jesus especially cherishes children, he said, *"Whoever causes one of these little ones who believe in me to sin, it would be better for him if a millstone were hung around his neck, and he were drowned in the depth of the sea"* Matthew 18:6 NKJV. We all must some day give account of ourselves, and *"it is a fearful thing to fall into the hands of the Living God"* Hebrews 10:31 NKJV. Now we need to follow the commandment of Jesus, who has his arms open wide: *"Pray for those who spitefully use you and persecute you"* Matthew 5:44 NKJV. Pray first that God will defeat their efforts, and second that he will reveal Jesus to them, save their souls and help them use their legal skills in righteous causes.

Plan 7: Speaking Out

Express your opinion to your elected officials, who work for you, the people. It's your right to petition those who serve you in high places, and several organisations make it easy to do.

Don't limit your vigilance to national governmental activities. Much mischief (and much good) is done at local levels. When thousands of citizens let officials know what they think, it does make a difference. Take the time to write a courteous, well-reasoned letter. Government representatives get so few of these that they pay more attention to them than you might think.

You can also express your opinions to companies that do things that offend you. Let us give you some home-grown examples:

Since 2005, both in the UK and in the US, in an effort to be 'politically correct', many major department store chains outlawed "Merry Christmas." "Happy Holidays" or "Wintermas" was fine. Reindeer and Santa were sanctioned, but no crèches, no carols that mentioned Jesus. He was effectively ousted from his own birthday party. In the US some even chased away the Salvation Army bell ringers who were collecting money in front of the stores, breaking years of tradition and depriving many poor people of aid at Christmas time.

A hue and cry went up. Besides the influence of personal letters, phone calls and television talk shows, more than 400,000 people signed an email of protest sponsored by the American Family Association. By just filling in a few lines and clicking on a submit button you could add your voice to a politely worded but firm letter to the heads of all offending companies, telling them that there were other places you could shop.

Every one of the US companies backed down and promised to do better next year. And they did. One even gave a million dollars to the Salvation Army and another set up a way for people to give to the Sally Ann's through the company's website. Even the US House of Representatives jumped into the fray with the bipartisan "Resolution to Protect Christmas

Symbols and Traditions." It actually had no power as law but merely expressed the sense of the House on the issue. But few congressmen interested in getting re-elected would want to be caught not signing such a resolution.

We've also seen a number of obscene and irreverent television shows lose their sponsorship because of an overwhelming outcry from decent citizens. In January 2006, the National Broadcasting Company (NBC) introduced a new TV series called "The Book of Daniel," which made a mockery of Christians. American Family Association gathered an e-mail petition and sent it to NBC and participating sponsors. Nearly 700,000 people signed the petition and thousands called and e-mailed local affiliates. NBC caved in and the show was cancelled immediately. By October NBC was at it again. They announced they were going to show a Madonna special, in which she sings from a mirrored cross, wearing a crown of thorns. In spite of mounting protests they kept insisting adamantly that this time they would not back down, until their local affiliates again began to bail out under the pressure of 750,000 e-mails and many phone calls. NBC, facing the potential loss of 25 million dollars, cut the scene from the show.

And the list goes on. It would be naïve to believe these companies had strictly charitable motives for their change of attitude. Nevertheless, they did listen, and that's the good news.

Of course, the battle continues. Some networks are still defying the rules and stretching the envelope, and some are even suing the Federal Communications Commission for their "right" to show anything they want.

Plan 8: Cleaning Up Our Culture

We said earlier that any society has a responsibility to protect the moral environment for its children. Few would dispute the finding that the most influential forces in moulding the lives of most young people today are no longer the family or the school or the church; they are our television sets, movie theatres, music, and the worldwide web. These entertainments establish the norms our society lives by. They implant gradually and subtly, by their dramas, images, language and costumes (or the lack thereof) the viewpoints of those who determine their content.

The people who decide what they want us to see, how they want us to feel about it – and what they don't want us to know – have an inordinate amount of power. They can promote or marginalise any viewpoint they want to. Those who control the news can even help rig elections by puffing their favourite candidates while showing others in a bad light.

Much of that content is determined by economics. If sex sells, make it sexier; make the violence more violent; the irreverence more irreverent – and the ratings will rise and the box office swell. Ergo: the public, especially the young and impressionable, are pleasurably having their moral values shaped and reshaped without even realizing what's happening to them, just like a frog in a pot of water that's gradually being brought to a boil. But in this case the one who is bringing the pot to a boil is none other than *"the prince of the power of the air,"* as the Bible calls Satan see Ephesians 2:2.

At a time when sexual immorality is rampant, with all its destructive consequences, television and films are demonstrating to a generation of young people, through beautiful and glamorous role models, that casual, unmarried sex is a perfectly normal, acceptable and exciting way of life. And the networks are rapidly filling with shows that defiantly glorify the homosexual life style. Girls, especially, may be wildly influenced by what they see in television, films and glossy magazines that celebrate the lifestyles of beautiful and glamorous role models – "stars" with the morals of alley cats. Do you see that girl, the one with the loose mouth and the loooow neckline? Isn't she beautiful! So enticing, seductive, tantalizing... King Solomon had an apt term for her – he compared her to a fine gold ring: *"A beautiful woman lacking discretion and modesty is like a fine gold ring... in a pig's snout!"* Proverbs 11:22 TLB, emphasis ours.

Despite the fact that family-acceptable films make, on average, eleven times as much money as indecent ones, there are those who pride themselves on making smutty films for the principle of it. They call it *"adult* subject matter," but it's really more reminiscent of naughty little kids trying to outdo each other with newly learned vulgarities. It may be one of those "but everybody says that; it's the way my generation talks" things. But Jesus said, *"Out of the overflow of the heart the mouth speaks"* Matthew 12:34b NIV. What we *speak,* or in this case *produce,* is an expression of what we cherish in our hearts, so raunchy producers had rather give vent to their crudity than produce uplifting entertainment that's foreign to their values.

Although some fine films are being made, much of the film industry is not only fouling its own nest but polluting the rest of the world as well. Because of much of the movie and TV entertainment that is exported around the globe, Western culture seems to people of the Muslim world to consist of materialism, vulgarity, and promiscuity. And because many Western countries are seen as "Christian nations," Christianity is seen as materialistic, vulgar, and promiscuous. The Wrecking Crew strikes again.

People who crave crude entertainment say to us who don't, "If you don't like it, just don't watch it, but don't try to influence what we watch." But it isn't as simple as that. A part of any society's responsibility is to provide a safe and wholesome environment for its young generation. Teenage boys, in particular, need to be protected from powerful images that inflame their raging hormones and rushing adrenalin, and seduce them into destructive activities, then destroy them with guilt. One music network in America, watched by three quarters of our boys and girls, averages 13 sexual scenes per hour.[37] Some others are just as bad. Marinating young minds in such a miasma is a recipe for ruined lives. Sexual addiction is as addictive as narcotics.

Titillating entertainment creates a lust for pornography, and pornography may lead to sex crimes. Dr Mary Anne Layden of the University of Pennsylvania Health System said, "I have not treated a single case of sexual violence that did not involve pornography".[38]

The Church has more than enough economic clout to bring a lot of this to a screeching halt, if only Christians would stop patronizing offensive entertainment and let its producers and sponsors know why. Could it be that the reason this problem is not being dealt with is that many Christians are themselves being seduced by that same spirit? Have we become so captivated by entertainment that we've lost our sensitivity to what offends the Holy Spirit within us?

Some people, even Christians say, "I don't believe in censorship." But any civilized society has censorship. There are certain acts and states of undress that can't be shown on the public airwaves during certain hours, and some not at all. The question is where are the lines drawn, and can't those lines be moved up a bit to afford more protection to society? And how about requiring parental warnings on video games, magazines and CDs?

In the USA the First Amendment protecting freedom of speech has been twisted to provide a safe haven for all but the very worst pornographers to spew their filth into society with impunity, so long as they observe certain rules of distribution. But with the newfound clout afforded by millions of decent people finding avenues to express their united opinions[39] there is hope that some of this coarsening of our culture can be cleaned up.

The battle for decency gets more intense. FCC Chairman Kevin J Martin has said, "We used to receive indecency complaints by the hundreds; now they come in by the hundreds of thousands. Clearly, consumers – and particularly parents – are concerned and increasingly frustrated."

What can you do about it? First, arm yourself with information. Register your opinions with the appropriate government agencies and TV sponsors. Together you *can* help to clean up television and defend the children of your nation.

This problem can be attacked from two directions: In addition to not patronising immoral entertainment and letting its producers know why, we can support, pray for and encourage those who are working to produce uplifting entertainment. Pray also that our leaders will figure out how to better regulate the Internet.

On the bright side, there is already a growing dichotomy in the entertainment industry: while the dark side gets darker, there are signs that the light side is getting brighter. Since the remarkable success of several biblical or Christian-themed films, a few producers have realised there's an audience out there that they've missed, and a few studios are beginning to produce more of them. It's a start. Our prayers are being answered.

Plan 9: Sharing the Gospel

It's so obvious it almost goes without saying: It's why God put us here and why he leaves us here. It's why he didn't take us to heaven the moment we were saved. It's the Great Commission.

Jesus said, *"You shall receive power when the Holy Ghost has come upon you and you shall be witnesses to me"* Acts 1:8. *"Go into all the world and preach the gospel to every creature"* Mark 16:15 NKJV. Everything else we do as the Church is incidental to that.

The soul of our nation will be changed only as individual souls are changed. Only changed lives can change a nation. And only the gospel can change a life.

In our efforts to reach the world with the good news, some are called to go; all are called to give. As we support our local churches and give to missions, evangelistic efforts, and mercy ministries, the gospel will spread. As we share our faith and our testimony with others, the Body will grow.

We must be careful not to judge who might receive the gospel and who might not. Sometimes the one with the hardest shell is closest to the Kingdom. We're told not to judge those who are outside the Church. God himself will judge them see 1 Corinthians 5:12. If God gives us an opportunity to share our faith with someone and we say to ourselves, "He's too hard; he won't believe," and we don't tell him, what we're doing is making his decision for him. It might be kinder of us to think of him as a pre-Christian, and help him on his way if we can. Sharing our faith is actually a step of faith for us: we're saying to ourselves, "I can't convince this person, but the Holy Spirit can, if I do my part and tell him. He did it for me, he has done it for millions, and he can do it for this person." Not everyone will believe, but we're not responsible for that.

When Jimmy was a young aircraft carrier sailor, he was assigned to a division of forty-nine men, and set out to win them to the Lord. Jimmy tells the story: "My section leader, Dave, was the meanest, toughest brawler of them all, and he tried to make life tough on me because my witness was bugging him. One night Dave snapped. He grabbed me and shoved me backwards all the way across the compartment, with wild eyes blazing into mine. I thought, 'Lord, am I about to become the first martyr from the USS Boxer?' Then Dave blurted frantically, 'Pray for me! I need to be saved!'

"Dave's violent conversion turned the division on its ear, and nine more guys received the Lord. Crewmembers in other divisions throughout the ship heard about it and revival spread. Thirty more Christians joined the fellowship, and in time thirty more men accepted Christ. When Dave got out of the navy he went home, sparked a revival in his family's church, went to seminary and became a pastor. I later had the satisfaction of preaching in his church."

Jesus compared believers to *leaven*, or yeast, added to dough, that causes the whole loaf of bread to rise. He called us the *light of the world* that dispels darkness.

He also called us the *salt of the earth*. Salt has many uses: it flavours, preserves, deodorises, polishes, cleans, removes stains and repels garden pests, to name a few. It also creates thirst and has healing qualities.

In the spiritual realm, does any of that sound like the job of the Church?

Plan 10: Saving a Generation

EMERGENCY! EMERGENCY! EMERGENCY!

Please forgive us if we seem to lose our cool about this. If we seem strident and urgent, it's because we are. Some things are inappropriate in soft tones. Urge your church to instigate a crash programme to win and disciple teens and pre-teens. Traditional churches are losing this generation in droves. The old business-as-usual church activities don't attract

These kids communicate in radically different ways than their predecessors did, and make little attempt to understand them.

This generation, more than any before it, is being inundated with life-ruining sex, violence, and anti-God indoctrination. This is no less than a satanically inspired blitzkrieg, orchestrated from the pit of hell. Ninety percent of teens say porn pops up on their computers while they're doing homework, and many of those addicted to porn say that's the way they first encountered it. Kids can even pick up Internet pornography on their cell phones, and parents may have no way of knowing about it. Music videos and video games are more violent and sexual than ever. Over 1,000 studies show that the more sex and violence you see the more sexually active and violent you become.

"Most people who come to Christ do it before they are twenty. After that age it's very difficult to win them. Many of them have a real hunger for truth, but churches today invest very little in reaching and discipling them".[40] Ask the Lord what you, as an individual, can do about this tragedy. *What's needed is not just more "isn't it nice what they're doing to entertain our kids" activities, but Holy Spirit-empowered, prayer-drenched ministry to meet their deepest felt needs, get them saved, and make them ministers to their generation.*

So here's the good news! Today there are plenty of potential young intercessors and witnesses just waiting for encouragement and leadership. Each September, at "See You at the Pole," millions of high school and college students gather around their school's flagpole early in the morning to pray for their parents, their teachers, and their nation. Spiritual awakening is happening on many college campuses. Directors of mission agencies today are impressed with the new passion and dedication in the young generation who know Christ. Christian missions conferences are growing rapidly and new recruits for missions often want to go to the hardest and most dangerous places where the gospel has not been preached.[41]

At first glance, the zeal among young believers is a reminder of the sixties generation – radical, wound-up, and energised by rock music; but instead of drugs and sex, they are into righteousness and renewal. There is a growing political awareness among them as well, which will soon become apparent and alarming to those who would destroy our foundations.

So, there it is: if we care about the soul of our nation and the souls in our nation; if we want to keep the freedoms we've enjoyed for so many years, then we have to understand the problems, recognise the dangers, and become part of the solution.

And let us not be weary in doing good, for in due season we shall reap if we do not lose heart
Galatians 6:9.

---

[37] Gary D Foster Consulting. www.GaryDFoster.com
[38] FRC Washington Update.
[39] American Family Association, for one, has 3,000,000 supporters and growing.
[40] Ron Luce, President, Teen Mania Ministries.
[41] Breaking Christian News, December 7, 2005.

Talk About This:

1. Has the book given you any new or surprising information about anti-Christian organisations in Britain? Could you explain those things to someone who might not yet be aware of them?

2. Is it important for believers to really understand their rights? Can an informed Church make a difference in our society? p164-5

3. How can you influence your parliamentary representatives who are voting on issues important to you? Will you make your voice heard? p165

4. Can Christians influence businesses that take anti-Christian positions? How? Are you willing to try? p166

5. What can you do to help clean up our culture before God takes drastic action? p166-7

6. What is our most powerful means of influence in our society? p168-169

7. Who are the most important people in our society? How should the Church be helping them? p170

Pray About This:

a   Take a quiet moment to do the **Getting Ready** points on page 172. If you have trouble with any of this, ask for help from your fellowship leader.

b   Select prayer subjects from the **Prayer List for National Intercession** on pages 172-174. You don't have to start at the beginning; Start by looking over the list and praying whatever seems most important or urgent. You can take another session to finish the complete list.

c   This is just a beginning. Although the class may move on to other subjects, consider taking time to pray for the nation in each session, and practise to make national intercession an ongoing part of your life!

EPILOGUE

Points for Prayer

What's the best way to put all this together and make it work in your prayer life?

Let's recap some personal guidelines to begin with, and then move right on to some specific prayer work.

Getting Ready

1. Humble yourself before God. Do a quick pride check.

2. Confess and repent of any known sin.

3. Take care of any unforgiveness you need to release or restitution you need to make.

4. Reckon yourself dead to sin and alive to God through Jesus Christ your Lord see Romans 6:8

5. Put on the whole armour of God see Ephesians 6:10-20.

6. Build your faith through thanksgiving for God's personal blessings to you.

7. Spend time in praise and worship and thus invoke the presence of God.

8. Submit your thoughts, opinions and desires to God.

9. Resist the enemy; forbid him to speak to you see James 4:7.

10. Listen!

Now Let's Pray!

Throughout the book we've given you sample prayers. Some short ones are integrated into the text; the longer ones at the end of certain chapters can be prayed a section at a time, incorporating your own words with ours to get you started.

In addition you can:

- Pray the daily news
- Make daily declaration and invocation
- Wait on God
- Use the following prayer list
- Try covering only a few points in each session, giving time for each.

A Prayer List for National Intercession

1. **Sins of the Nation:** Confess national sins. Ask God for mercy and forgiveness.

2. **Government officials from national to local levels:** Pray for blessing and guidance for the godly; salvation – or removal and replacement – for the corrupt.

3. **Your city:** Pray for its leaders and all aspects of its life. If Christians around the nation simply intercede for their own cities, we will saturate the entire country with prayer.

4. **The Law Courts:** Pray for justice for everyone. Ask for judges who will make decisions in line with God's will.

5. **Anti-God organisations.** Pray against the work of those that seek to destroy the nation's foundations, inhibit Christian expression, and promote forbidden practices.

6. **The Military:** Pray for wise leadership, strong Christian influence throughout the ranks, blessing and protection in battle.

7   **Law enforcement agencies:** Pray for salvation, wisdom, compassion, and protection for law officers.

8. **Abortion:** Repent about our legalised "shedding of innocent blood," which is one of the seven things the Scripture says specifically that God hates Proverbs 6:16-19. Ask for legislators who will fight to protect the unborn. Pray for compassionate, Christ-like hearts: wisdom, strategy, and blessing from God for those who take public action in this arena.

9. **Immorality:** Oppose the legalisation of immorality. Ask God to pull down legislators who support sin and to raise up those who will support godly principles.

10. **Violence:** Resist the violent spirits that stir up terrorists, anarchists and street criminals in our city and nation. Pray that God will continually protect us from the weapons of our enemies.

11. **The media:** Ask for people of integrity and truth in reporting. Pray for the removal of pornography in all phases of media. Pray for the salvation and transformation of the people who pour this stuff into our society.

12. **Arts and entertainment:** Pray against immoral, blasphemous and occult influences that permeate these powerful forces in our society. Pray for those righteous producers and entertainers who are trying to clean up their field, that God will use them mightily.

13. **The economy:** Pray for business leaders, national and international banking concerns, and for trade unions. Ask for righteous and wise leaders; bring them under the influence of the Kingdom of God in prayer.

14. **Schools:** Pray for Christian teachers and officials in our school systems and ask God to raise up more of them. Speak in prayer and in public against moral corruption and occult influences in our schools; pray for higher academic achievement by our students.

15. **Families:** Intercede for your own, your neighbours', and those in your church. Pray for healed relationships; academic, spiritual, and moral motivation for children; and for the salvation of the lost.

16. **Your church:** Pray for your fellow Christians and their needs. Pray for your pastor and staff; they need your prayer support!

17. **Christians in other nations:** Pray for strength and deliverance for those under governments that deny them their religious, civil and human rights. Pray especially for those persecuted for their faith.

18. **Areas of special need in other nations:** Pray about world economy and food shortages, wars and human rights violations, using newscasts and newspapers as guidelines. Pray for international outreaches that are combating disease, hunger, poverty and ignorance – and thus spreading the compassion and saving power of Jesus throughout the world.

19. **The Middle East:** God has specific end-time prophetic plans concerning his chosen people Israel. Pray for wisdom for our national leaders, that we as a nation will not find ourselves on the wrong side of God's plans.

20. **The poor and hungry:** Pray as you would for yourself (fasting will help you identify with their hunger); give mercy ministries and inner city missions at least the money you would have spent on food on the days you fast.

21. **Revival:** Pray for a great restoration of vision and dedication to God within the Church. (We see God at work in these areas already. We need more!)

22. **Principalities and powers:** Resist ungodly ruling spirits in your city and nation through intercession, spiritual warfare, and invocational declaration.

23 **Intercessors:** Ask God to raise up an army of intercessors nationwide.

24. **Souls.** Pray for national and world evangelisation: for labourers for the harvest, a great ingathering of the lost, and the completion of the Great Commission.

25. **Ears to hear:** Ask the Holy Spirit to pray through you, and let him use you as his vessel for intercession:

We don't even know what we should pray for, or how we should pray. But the Holy Spirit prays for us with groanings that cannot be expressed in words. And the Father who knows all hearts knows what the Spirit is saying, for the Spirit pleads for us in harmony with God's own will. Romans 8:26-27 NLT

Spread the Word!

If any or all of these intercessory efforts strike fire with you, please spread the message. Tell every Christian you know. Tell them about praying and fasting on Third Thursdays, or First Fridays, if that's what is happening in your area. Tell them about daily invocations, praying the news, and helping mercy ministries. Urge them to exercise their civic responsibilities, to learn their rights and stand up for them. Most of all, tell people about the saving, transforming power of Jesus. Promote and support evangelism, especially of the young. And tell your pastor about this book. Better yet, lend it or give it to him! See how you can assist your pastor in any plans he may have to practise ongoing intercession for the nation in your church.

"But," some Christians may say, "Isn't Jesus coming back soon to take us all away? So why bother with intercession?" Yes, Jesus is coming back. One day we will stand on the earth with him in immortal bodies, and ultimately all enemies, including death, will be destroyed. see 1 Corinthians chapter 15.

But Jesus didn't say, "Sit and wait;" he said, *"Occupy till I come"* Luke 19:13 KJV.

The Church is still an occupation army, and the devil is still at large. There are still souls to save, hurting people to heal, children to protect, and societies to reclaim for the Kingdom of God.

When is Christ coming? We don't know. But Jesus said to read the signs and be ready to meet him. We're to live as though he might come back at any moment but work as though he might not come back in our lifetime.

When Jesus comes on the clouds of heaven in power and great glory, with ten thousands of his saints, to execute judgment on all, *"every eye will see him." Every knee shall bow, and every tongue shall confess that Jesus Christ is Lord, to the glory of God the Father." "And he shall reign forever and ever"* see Matthew 24:27-31, Jude 14, Philippians 2:10-11, Revelation 1:7; 11:15b.

"Even so, come, Lord Jesus!" Revelation 22:20 NKJV.

APPENDIX A

The Intercession Group

What an opportunity you have! The dynamism of intercessory prayer and action isn't just theory; it is truly a pivotal, world-transforming realm. You and your group are on to something powerful here, something blowing in the spiritual winds across the nations. It is a call for informed, dedicated people who are willing to sacrifice some time and effort to become co-workers with God. We want this prayer/study guide to help you come to a new level of understanding, authority and faith in unlimited possibilities. Together, you will be practicing in a kind of *intercession laboratory* - an experiment in prayer and lifestyle that can impact you, your family, your nation, and the world.

Instructions for the Leader

Almost anyone can moderate the group. The teaching and appropriate page references are built into the discussion questions in the book; just follow those and you'll be guided step by step through the sessions. We consider it a great honour to help you do it.

First, your group should decide how many sessions you want to give to this study. There are eighteen chapters/sessions. If you can't give that much time you could cover two chapters per session. If so, you'll need to decide whether to do two discussion times and two prayer times per session, or combine both chapters into a single discussion/prayer time at the end of each session. You might try it both ways and see which is better for you.

Here are some further simple suggestions to help things go smoothly:

1. If your group is large, you may want to break into small groups of five or six people so everyone has a chance to pray.

2. Suggest people keep prayers short, a dozen sentences or so at a time, and then wait for others to pray. They can always pray more than once: Don't be intimidated by short silences.

3. Suggest that prayers remain at a conversational level: shouting distracts others and destroys their focus on God; mumbling keeps them from hearing and agreeing with your prayers.

4. Stress that agreeing in prayer is extremely important: people should not be too inhibited to say "amen" or "yes" when someone else is praying. Let God and the group know they are in agreement.

5. Offer prayer subjects from the list in the book. Try covering a few in each session instead of doing the whole list at once. People may take turns, praying the written prayers aloud, a paragraph each. As the group gains confidence, encourage

people to pray their own prayers. They can be simple, two or three sentences at first, but you can pray them with faith because you're praying in obedience to God and with excitement because of what God is going to do through you!

6. As time goes by, the intercessory tank may need "refuelling." Find some dynamic teaching, books or CDs, to keep the group motivated. This will help you see what God is doing nationally and internationally through his intercessors, giving you the "big picture."

As you listen patiently together for the Holy Spirit to bring his thoughts into your hearts, you'll grow sensitive to his voice. Then you will find him leading you into the highest level of intercession—intercession that is born in the heart of God.

A Word to Pastors and Leaders

As an incentive to cooperation among Church leadership, we'd like to suggest the practice that's being used with great success in many places: a multi-racial, multi-ethnic, *monthly* gathering of local church leaders. These visionary men and women are bringing about racial, cultural and denominational unity in their communities. There are three main objectives to these fellowships:

1. To give pastors and leaders a place to bond with their peers. This may bring some reconciliation and understanding among themselves, which would be a good model for their people.
2. To monitor the needs of the community and strategise as to how the united Church can minister to them.
3. To have this become a unified pastoral intercessory prayer force for the community and the nation. Together they can then lead their churches into ongoing intercessory prayer.

We suggest that on say the first Friday of each month pastors hold a combined area-wide prayer meeting, led together by various pastors, encouraging the observance of prayer and fasting for the nation.

These pastors' meetings may mean the sacrifice of some time and some pride and prejudice. This may require vulnerability and lowered defences.

We saw this happen in a remarkable way at the Summit Conference of Church Leaders in America, which we described in Chapter 17. The leaders were from all across the denominational spectrum – mainline churches, conservative evangelicals, Pentecostals and Catholics. The diversity of doctrinal positions and worship practices represented was enormous. In addition, some of these leaders had been feuding for years.

We wondered how we were ever going to attain the unity we needed for effective strategy-and-intercession meetings. Obviously, we needed someone special to open things up and break the ice. The person we had planned on cancelled at the last minute. The only substitute available was not one we would have chosen. Although we liked him a lot, we feared he was too famous, charming, learned and glamorous to bring a sense of humility into this crowd of "Very Important People."

Well, our substitute got up looking every inch the most successful of pastors. He walked to the podium, smiled a wavering, fast-fading smile, and then lowered his head. "Brothers and sisters," he said softly, "If I don't have a new touch from God, I can't go on. Please pray for me." He then began openly to share his journey into desperation.

There was a moment of shocked silence. Then these men and women of God began to pray for a new touch from heaven – not only for him, but also for one another. They put their arms around one another's shoulders and prayed for forgiveness and reconciliation.

God's first requirement had been met – *"If my people will humble themselve... "* From that point on, God's agenda was met as he gave us strategy for calling the Church to intercessory prayer nationwide.

It was a miracle. And we almost missed it!

It happened because of one man's true humility and desperate hunger for God. God can move just as powerfully in local communities if the leadership is as wise, humble and open as this. As long as the basic tenets of the gospel are not violated, the Church should be able to operate in cooperation and love. As leaders listen to each other with understanding instead of attempting to reinforce pet doctrines, not only might they actually learn something from one another, but they will also set the perfect example for their congregations.

Although we see a wonderful rising tide of ministry networks and citywide pastor's coalitions forming across the country, united churches and ministries are still in the minority. Too often, "successful" ministries, which should be leading the way, become tunnel-visioned by an entrepreneurial mindset. They fail to recognise that there are some things – such as the evangelisation of the world – better done together than alone, no matter how big they may be or how far they've reached. Unity – oneness of purpose – gives the Church her credibility with the world.

Our commission is to call people to be reconciled to God. But how can we call people to be reconciled to God when we aren't reconciled to each other? Without cooperation and networking, we are like an army broken into independent camps, each with its own leader and battle plan, firing at random at the enemy and taking occasional pot-shots at one another.

When we consider Jesus' prayer, *"that they may all be one, as you, Father, are in me, and I in you; that they may be also one in us, that the world may believe that you sent me"* John 17:21 NKJV the implication is: why should the world believe when we who call ourselves by his name can't work together in unity?

It will take all of us acting together in love and agreement to help solve the problems of racial prejudice, injustice and poverty rampant in our society. These problems are the Church's opportunities for reconciliation, justice, mercy and evangelism. We won't win our nation without addressing them, and according to Isaiah 58, neither will our prayers for the healing of our land be heard, no matter how much we pray and fast.

Satan has only to divide us to defeat us. He knows that *"every kingdom divided against itself will be ruined, and every city or household divided against itself will not stand"* Matthew 12:25.

He knows that united churches, moving in grace and love, generate a force – through agreeing prayer, spiritual warfare, and joint outreach – that even the gates of hell can't withstand.

Derek Prince said it well: "When we think about a big city – like Miami, for instance – we would say there are many different churches in Miami. But I don't think that is how God sees it. After all, the Book of Revelation tells us Jesus is going to marry the Church – his Bride – and I do not believe Jesus is a bigamist. He's only going to marry one Church. So we can think about many churches, but God sees only one Church. When Paul wrote his epistles, he didn't write to the Baptist Church in Corinth, or to the Church of the Open Bible in Rome, or to the Evangelical Church in Ephesus. He always wrote to the Church in the city. We are a long way from that reality today, but I don't believe God has ever changed his mind.

"Therefore, I believe it important that the leaders of congregations within a city or region know how to relate to one another. It's very easy to become self-centred – to think about "my church" or "our church" and to focus on that alone. But that is not a scriptural attitude. I believe we as leaders should see ourselves as co-elders in the same church."[42]

As leaders come together in humility, eager to bless and serve one another, they will find that much of their distrust and many of their differences were groundless, generated by Satan, who fears a loving, united Church more than anything. If we stand together, we will be stronger than the forces of darkness. United leadership builds the Church that wins the world.

We know you're busy. We can just hear you saying that with all your other responsibilities, you don't have time for such meetings. We'd like to suggest that you think over some priorities. No matter how large and busy your church is, its individual programme isn't as important as the work of the Body of Christ as a whole. Until each pastor's vision is enlarged to move with the Body rather than as an independent unit, the Church will remain weak and divided. Unity must begin with you, the pastors and leaders.

"But," you say, "there aren't any such meetings in my community. Who will start them?" How about you?

We urge pastors and worship leaders to implement the plans proposed in this book. As you teach them to your people, there will be intercessors all over our cities lifting their voices together from their homes, schools and workplaces. Together we will make a powerful difference in our world as we literally shape the destiny of cities and nations through concerted intercession.

Remember, this is an ongoing war. When things look discouraging, don't stop praying. There should never be a time again when churches fail to make intercession for the nation a priority. We also pray it will never become only a ritual but always be ministered with understanding and fervour.

Making Sure of Your Salvation

For many, this will be elementary teaching, but for some it could be a revelation, or perhaps a final resolution of your relationship with God. It's worth a page or two of spiritual review to make your foundation sure.

God's plan for your salvation springs from his undeserved but overflowing love. It's simple enough for a child to understand: we all have earned an eternal death penalty through our disobedience and sin. God's law requires the payment of the penalty; God's love paid it.

For the wages of sin is death, but the gift of God is eternal life through Jesus Christ our Lord. Romans 6:23 KJV

Jesus Christ, God's Son was born for this purpose: In his mercy, God has revealed himself to us in a form we can comprehend, and in a body suitable for sacrifice. He became a man so he could die and thus pay the penalty for your sins.

For God took the sinless Christ and poured into him our sins. Then, in exchange, he poured God's goodness into us. 2 Corinthians 5:21 TLB

Through his sacrifice, you are offered forgiveness and eternal life. But you, like all of us, must personally receive this sacrifice – this Saviour and his gift of life. When you do, you become a child of God.

To all who believed him and accepted him, he gave the right to become children of God. They are reborn! John 1:12,13a NLT

Your part in this transaction is to turn away from your sins, confess your need of forgiveness and ask the Lord to save you. Your prayer can be simple, but it is a kind of weighty, eternal wedding vow. Perhaps something like this:

Lord Jesus, I'm truly sorry for all my sins and I ask you to forgive me. Thank you for taking my punishment by dying in my place. I thankfully receive you as my Saviour. Make my soul clean now by your divine power. I pledge my heart, my allegiance and my obedience to you all the days of my life. Amen.

Then confirm your salvation by confessing Jesus publicly:

> *If you confess with your mouth, "Jesus is Lord," and believe in your heart that God raised him from the dead, you will be saved. For it is with your heart that you believe and are justified, and with your mouth that you confess and are saved.* Romans 10: 9-10 NIV.

In a way, it's like getting married: you take your vows "before God and this company." You make your commitment to God and he makes his commitment to you. You have entered into an eternal covenant with him and he with you. Here is Jesus' vow:

> All whom my Father gives to me will come to me, and him who comes to me I will most
> certainly not cast out – I will never, no never reject one of them who comes to me.
> John 6:37 AB

Once this covenant commitment is made, the Holy Spirit will begin to change you from the
heart outward. You'll find yourself becoming a new person inside:

> Therefore, if anyone is in Christ, he is a new creation; old things have passed away;
> behold, all things have become new. 2 Corinthians 5:17 NKJV

Being born again is as real and life changing as being born the first time. Once you've done it,
nothing will ever be the same. A new life, eternal life, begins:

> Jesus said:"Most assuredly I say to you, he who hears my word and believes in him
> who sent me has everlasting life, and shall not come into judgment, but has passed
> from death into life." John 5:24 NKJV

And now that you've done it, ask God to lead you to a church where you can grow and serve.
They will teach you, provide the sacraments, and give you counsel, prayer, fellowship and love.

Welcome to the family.

---

[42] Derek Prince, *The Ethics of Ministry* www.dpm.org

POSTSCRIPT

Jimmy and Carol's book of Prayer Strategies forms an essential resource for the musical presentation of **HEAL OUR LAND**. Few people in any Western nation would dispute the fact that their nation is sick today. The financial crisis of 2008 and the following economic recession highlighted the moral and spiritual problems that had been developing for three or four decades.

Throughout the past generation of rapid and radical social revolution that has swept across the Western world church attendance has been in decline and many Christians have felt discouraged, prayer life has been weakened and evangelistic outreach has been at an all-time low. Many Christians have found it difficult to stand firm against the tide of immorality and foul language that has dominated the entertainment industry, which has even produced blasphemous representations of Jesus. Christian witness in this maelstrom of social change has been weakened by disunity among mainline churches and fragmentation in newer church networks.

It is against this social background that the musical, **HEAL OUR LAND** is being presented in towns and cities across Britain. Its appearance comes in the perfect timing of the Lord when many people throughout the United Kingdom are depressed through the impact of unemployment and hardship; they were shocked at the revelations of greed and corruption among trusted bankers; and they were disillusioned with their political leaders following the revelations about expenses and allowances in 2009. The British public are going through a period of re-evaluation of their personal and social values which is producing a new openness to the gospel. There is a hunger for truth that is not being satisfied by the media or by national leaders and least of all by the shallow lives of celebrities.

It is into this window of opportunity that **HEAL OUR LAND** comes with its message primarily directed towards Christians - both committed and nominal. The musical appeals especially to young people, although its message is directed to all ages. It challenges us to recognise the extent to which the whole of our Western civilisation is under attack and that if we remain in apathetic indifference, all our freedoms will be swept away and we will find ourselves in new forms of bondage. The proud boast that we sing on the last night of the Proms, "Britain never, never, never, shall be slaves" already has a hollow ring.

The musical also leads us to confess our need of God and to seek his help as we recognise the strength of the forces that are seeking to undermine the whole of our Judaeo-Christian heritage and our personal and social values. **HEAL OUR LAND** gives an opportunity for Christians to come together and allow God to re-envision and equip his people for the task that lies ahead. When God gives us a task he not only equips but he also empowers his people.

Ideally churches in an area will already have been praying and planning for this musical to be effective. In each city where it is held the week preceeding the presentation will be filled withprayer meetings and sessions. The musical itself having stirred christians into action and commitment leads naturally onto at time of outreach.

The outcome we can expect to see from the **HEAL OUR LAND** presentation is:-

1. A fresh emphasis upon mission

2. Greater Christian unity

3. Many people becoming believers in Jesus

4. A greater inter-ethnic harmony

5. An army of prayer warriors

6. Christians obeying the commandment of Jesus to love and care for each other

7. Believers praying for their city/town/community

8. Christians interceding for the nation and praying for leaders

9. A greater involvement of Christians in public life

10. Christians showing a special concern for the young, the powerless and the needy.

Make your plans and act now...

- Contact us
- Sign up to be an intercessor
- Join a choir in your area
- Join an evangelistic team
- Receive regular prayer/news

A project of the Centre for Contemporary Ministry
Visit our website for event information **www.healourlanduk.com**

The Centre for Contemporary Ministry (CCM)

The Centre for Contemporary Ministry (CCM) has been in the forefront of community transformation in the UK since the 1980s. Founded in London as a Christian education charity it moved to Moggerhanger in Bedfordshire in 1996.

CCM's base at Moggerhanger Park was owned in the 18th century by the Thornton family, cousins of William Wilberforce. The family had linked to the Clapham Group of Christians who were active campaigners for the abolition of the slave trade and for social justice. CCM's ethos is very much in harmony with these principles.

CCM is active in finding and encouraging new forms of evangelistic outreach. Following extensive research CCM initiated the 'Sharing Show' at the Christian Resources Exhibition in 2006 which has now become an annual event. This led to the development of new initiatives in evangelism starting with 'Love Cornwall' which was followed by 'Jesus loves Leicester', 'Love Ashford' and a number of similar events. Understanding community and culture interaction is one of CCM's major objectives and is one of the outcomes sought in all CCM's community projects. A good example is Park Farm which used to be 'Home Farm' and part of Moggerhanger Park estate which is being developed into a youth and family centre with a strong emphasis upon interactive learning.

In 2007 CCM leased an 18th-century square rigger re-fitted it as a slave ship, sailed up the Thames into the pool of London, moored it alongside Tower Pier and opened it to the public. This was part of the national commemorations of the 200th anniversary of the abolition of the slave trade which not only gave a graphic presentation of a period of history but also was a landmark in seeking reconciliation and improving community relations.

All the ministries at Moggerhanger Park have a strong emphasis upon prayer. CCM has been active in sponsoring prayer days for the nation some of which are regularly held at Moggerhanger. Dr Clifford Hill records of regular bimonthly Update Message on CD and audiotape on the 'State of the Nation' (available on subscription).

For further information please visit our website **www.contemporaryministry.com**

Contact: CCM, Moggerhanger Park, Bedford, MK 44 3RW
Telephone: 01767 641005

YOUR NOTES